Outstanding Dissertations in
LINGUISTICS

edited by
LAURENCE HORN
YALE UNIVERSITY

AUTOSEGMENTAL REPRESENTATION IN A DECLARATIVE CONSTRAINT-BASED FRAMEWORK

JAMES M. SCOBBIE

NEW YORK AND LONDON

First published 1997 by Garland Publishing, Inc.

This edition published 2013 by Routledge
711 Third Avenue, New York, NY 10017
2 Park Square, Milton Park, Abingdon, Oxfordshire OX14 4RN

First issued in paperback 2016

Routledge is an imprint of the Taylor & Francis Group, an informa business

Copyright © 1997 James M. Scobbie
All rights reserved

Library of Congress Cataloging-in-Publication Data

Scobbie, James M.
 Autosegmental representation in a declarative constraint-based framework / James M. Scobbie.
    p.   cm. — (Outstanding dissertations in linguistics)
 Revision of the author's thesis (Ph.D.—University of Edinburgh, 1991)
 Includes bibliographical references and index.
 ISBN 0-8153-2949-0 (alk. paper)
   1. Grammar, Comparative and general—Phonology.
2. Autosegmental theory (Linguistics)   I. Title. II. Series.
P217.S298 1997
415—dc21
                                                         97-17752

ISBN 13: 978-1-138-96423-5 (pbk)
ISBN 13: 978-0-8153-2949-7 (hbk)

For Kirsty

Contents

Preface   xiii

Acknowledgments   xix

1 Introduction   3
  1.1 Overview 3
  1.2 Towards a declarative phonology 7
      1.2.1 Procedural and declarative aspects of phonological theory 7
      1.2.2 Developments in monostratal syntactic theory and their potential influence on phonology 10
      1.2.3 Monostratal precursors to AVP 13
          • Natural Generative Phonology. . . . 14
          • Prosodic Analysis. 15
      1.2.4 Summary 15
  1.3 Phonological representations and their relationship to phonetics 16
      1.3.1 Constraining phonological representations . . 16
      1.3.2 Phonetics is not phonological detail 17
      1.3.3 The 'concreteness problem' 19
      1.3.4 Summary 23
  1.4 An introduction to attribute-value structures 23
      1.4.1 Background 23
      1.4.2 Monotonicity and declarativity 24
      1.4.3 Attribute-value structures 25

viii   *Autosegmental Representation in a Declarative Framework*

      1.4.4   Unification   28
      1.4.5   Type and token identity   33
      1.4.6   The sign   34
  Notes.   35

2 Attribute Value Phonology   39
  2.1 Hierarchy   39
      2.1.1   Feature hierarchies   39
      2.1.2   The root matrix   42
      2.1.3   Syllable structure   43
  2.2 Sequence   48
      2.2.1   The essential sequence: the skeleton   48
      2.2.2   Tiers: sequences of paths   51
  2.3 Association: a symmetric relation between features?   55
      2.3.1   The anchoring of autosegments   55
      2.3.2   Association as simultaneity   57
      2.3.3   Association as overlap   58
              Sagey (1988)   58
              Bird & Klein (1990)   59
              Hayes (1990)   60
  2.4 Association as dominance   63
      2.4.1   The problem of symmetry   63
      2.4.2   An asymmetric, transitive association   64
      2.4.3   Hammond (1988)   66
  2.5 Localising association   66
      2.5.1   What must association be able to do?   66
      2.5.2   Asymmetry as the source of local association   68
      2.5.3   Feature co-occurrence   70
  2.6 Rules   72
      2.6.1   Assimilation   73
      2.6.2   Feature filling rules   75
  2.7 Summary: structures and gestures   77
  Notes.   79

3 Localising Multiple Association   83
  3.1 Introduction   83
      3.1.1   The nature of the problem   83
      3.1.2   Overview   84
  3.2 Two constraints   85

Contents ix

       3.2.1 The No Crossing Constraint 85
              The NCC in its natural habitat 85
              Why the NCC is unsuitable for AVP 88
              Crossing paths in AVP 89
       3.2.2 The Sharing Constraint 91
       3.2.3 AP's need to replace or supplement the NCC 93
       3.2.4 Summary 98
  3.3 Uses of multiple association in Autosegmental Phonology 99
       3.3.1 The representation of length 99
       3.3.2 Assimilation 101
       3.3.3 Harmony systems 102
       3.3.4 Nonconcatenative morphology 103
       3.3.5 Tone 104
  3.4 Structure sharing in AVP 104
       3.4.1 Geminates 105
       3.4.2 Assimilated sequences 105
       3.4.3 Syllable structure 106
  3.5 Properties of locally shared structure 109
  Notes 111

4 The Integrity of Shared Structure   **114**
  4.1 Formal integrity and the prosodic causes of epenthesis 114
       4.1.1 Formal requirements 114
       4.1.2 The prosodic causes of epenthesis 116
  4.2 An AVP account of formal integrity 121
       4.2.1 The role of the Sharing Constraint 121
       4.2.2 The OCP and degemination 123
       4.2.3 The OCP: gemination and dissimilation . . . 125
       4.2.4 Summary 126
  4.3 Formal integrity and the No Crossing Constraint . . 127
       4.3.1 Deriving integrity from crossing associations . 127
       4.3.2 Problems with the NCC approach 129
  4.4 Summary 135
  Notes 136

x Autosegmental Representation in a Declarative Framework

5 Inalterability and Licensing 139
- 5.1 Introduction: different conceptions of the problem . 140
  - 5.1.1 Blocking 140
    - • Inalterability. 140
    - • Geminate phonotactics. 141
  - 5.1.2 Licensing 142
- 5.2 Data 143
  - 5.2.1 Cautionary remarks 143
  - 5.2.2 Examples of inalterability 144
    - *Latin lateral allophony* 144
    - *Semitic spirantisation* 146
      - 1. Tigrinya. 146
      - 2. Tiberian Hebrew. 146
    - *Coda weakening* 148
      - 1. Hausa. 148
      - 2. Axininca Campa. 148
    - *Glide/vowel alternations* 149
  - 5.2.3 Summary: inalterability as a unified phenomenon 149
- 5.3 Standard rule-blocking approaches to inalterability . 151
  - 5.3.1 The Linking Constraint 151
  - 5.3.2 The Uniform Applicability Condition 154
  - 5.3.3 Apparent differences between the Linking Constraint and the UAC 156
    - *Menomini lowering* 156
    - *The diacritic use of strong satisfaction* 158
  - 5.3.4 The application of strong satisfaction to phonotactics 160
  - 5.3.5 Demanding non-geminate input is a redundant way of avoiding inherently ill-formed output 163
- 5.4 A constraint-based approach to inalterability 166
  - 5.4.1 Introduction: the explanatory power of constraints 166
    - *Why phonotactic constraints are essential* . . 167
    - *Rule/constraint interaction* 169
  - 5.4.2 Inalterability rules as defaults 170
  - 5.4.3 Excursus: default and conditional constraints in AVP 173

Contents   xi

    5.4.4   AVP analyses 177
              The distribution of Tigrinya [x] 177
              Tiberian Spirantisation 181
              The distribution of allophones of Latin /l/ .. 181
              Alterable geminates 182
              1. Lithuanian Backing. 183
              2. West Greenlandic Lowering. 183
              3. West Greenlandic Palatalisation. . 183
              4. Luganda Palatalisation. 183
    5.4.5   Summary 183
  5.5   A constraint-based approach to coda weakening ... 184
    5.5.1   Analysing defective distributions 185
              Inadequacies of the blocking approach 185
              Licensing in Autosegmental Phonology 185
    5.5.2   AVP's constraint-based approach 187
    5.5.3   Linking coda weakening and inalterability .. 188
    5.5.4   Summary 190
Notes................................ 191

6   **Long Distance Dependencies**   **195**
  6.1   The spreading and sharing of phonological information 195
  6.2   Nonconcatenative morphology and multiplanar phonology........................... 197
    6.2.1   Discontinuous geminates 197
    6.2.2   How to test for a multiplanar phonology ... 199
    6.2.3   Are discontinuous geminates fake geminates? 200
    6.2.4   Plane conflation 201
  6.3   Chaha 203
    6.3.1   Background description 203
    6.3.2   Nonlocal inalterability in geminate devoicing 205
    6.3.3   A problem: the case of /b/ 206
    6.3.4   An alternative analysis of devoicing 209
  6.4   Side-effects 210
    6.4.1   Javanese..................... 211
    6.4.2   Against Javanese side-effects 213
    6.4.3   The status of the Javanese data........ 215
              The motivation for planes in Javanese 216
    6.4.4   Secondary lowering in Yokuts 217

xii *Autosegmental Representation in a Declarative Framework*

    6.5   Harmony 218
    6.6   Long distance dependencies in AVP 221
          6.6.1   Phonetic factors 221
          6.6.2   Structure spreading in harmony 223
          6.6.3   Spreading in nonconcatenative morphology . 224
    Notes............................ 226

7 Conclusion   229
    Notes............................ 231

References   233

Index   245

Preface

Enormous changes in phonology have occurred since the original appearance of this thesis. The phrase 'constraint-based phonology' has almost universal coverage now, it would seem. I'm pleased that, despite all this change, there's an important place for this work, and that of *declarative* constraint-based phonology generally. But this thesis is not solely about constraint-based phonology, as the title of the book indicates. The investigation of autosegmental representation is central too. Thus the specific proposals about local and long-distance dependencies and other aspects of theory familiar from Autosegmental Phonology are crucial to the worth of this book. I address both issues together, because it is simply not possible to develop 'rules' and 'representations' in isolation. We need to consider how the representational content of lexical entries is moulded by grammatical rules. In this thesis, this is seen as an issue of constraint interaction: the pool of more general rule-like constraints and the more specific representation-like constraints combine monotonically. This simple model of constraint interaction continues to be worthy of close examination.

It would be nice to draw some comparisons between declarative and non-declarative models of constraint satisfaction and interaction. It's not possible to do that here. In any case, other publications are available which, to some extent, address this issue. Nor do I think it appropriate to list references on this topic. If one thing dates quicker than phonological theories, it is lists of phonological theories. Nor do I want to take this dissertation out of context by giving it an updated frame of reference. These are tasks the reader is best placed to perform. It does seem appropriate, however, to take the opportunity to expand on remarks in the original acknowledgments (which follow), and to enlarge on the context in which this work was carried out, and to give an idea of the subsequent context of research, since I think they form a coherent programme.

As an undergraduate in the Department of Linguistics in Edinburgh, I was lucky to attend classes in Syntactic Models, run by Ronnie Cann. Three things became clear, I thought: nontransformational syntax was hugely superior to its rivals; nontransformational phonology didn't exist; syntactic data derived from the vagaries of introspection was bogus. It seemed obvious to me that it would be valuable to approach phonology in a similar way to Gazdar, Klein, Pullum and Sag. With Ewan Klein in a neighbouring department, Cognitive Science, in which I had attended exhilarating classes as part of my undergraduate degree (in Linguistics with Artificial Intelligence), I had a goal.

A Masters year (1986-87) began in hopes of either producing an HPSG phonology out of a hat and analysing chunks of data, or of investigating the syntax-phonology interface in a similarly unification-based way. The original idea was to look at productive external sandhi, using unification (structure sharing) to deal with the word-edge overlap of information. At this stage, the work was morpheme-based: phonology was just a part of the sign, and phonological information would be unified just like morphosyntax. What I learnt during 1987 was that while it would be possible to formalise bits of phonology in categorial grammar or HPSG, this ignored the complexities of phonological representations themselves. The appropriate course of action would have to involve a much more fundamental look at the nature of phonological rules and representations. In addition, it was apparent that 'constraints on representations' were seen as a significant step forward in nonlinear phonology, and since there is a natural intuitive cross-over from the phonological constraint to the constraints so common in unification-based syntax, I found myself trying to regularise this movement towards constraints by investigating declarative phonology more closely.

Early on, in 1987, I had come to a decision about the things that I regarded as flaws in nonlinear phonology. For example, I made the major decision to ditch ordered tiers (Scobbie 1988). Most of the ordering information on tiers is redundant, and with the appearance of Sagey (1988), I was sure that the way to approach constraint-based phonology was to take the clear viewpoint offered by declarative systems and poke the current theories when they paid lip-service (as I saw it) to constraints on representations without going all the way. In a progress report at the time, I wrote "the major people I want to criticise/emulate are Steriade, Archangeli and Pulleyblank, Clements and Goldsmith." Aim high!

An extremely important event was the 1989 Lingusitic Society of America Summer Institute in Tucson. This had one negative effect: I missed the Conference on Laboratory Phonology in Edinburgh organised by Gerry Docherty and Bob Ladd (my Linguistics supervisor). Given that he always interested me when he brought Labphon issues to my attention, and given that I am now fully committed to this methodology, the fact that I wasn't in Edinburgh (but was touring California, New Mexico and Arizona on the way to Tucson) makes we wonder how my dissertation would have turned out if I'd been there — especially since the Institute pulled me in another direction.

There were three of us from Edinburgh: me, Steven Bird and Mike Broe. I don't recall a fervent of collaboration between us — but we were at many of the same classes, and the shared assumptions we possessed, together with the brass-neck to ask questions in otherwise quite well-behaved classrooms, boosts my retrospective feelings of shared purpose. In the classes we quickly met Mark Ellison and Kevin Russell, and I am pleased to acknowledge my debts to them all, since the discussions and interaction we had were so instrumental in forming this work, and in helping me understand the potential of constraint-based frameworks. In fact, this formal potential is better fulfilled in their work than in mine. During the Institute I found myself being drawn more and more towards the concerns of current phonologising, as expressed in these classes, and the benefits that constraint-based conceptualisation could bring.

The theoretical classes I attended were given by Diana Archangeli and Doug Pulleyblank on phonology (especially harmony), Bill Poser on the phonetics/phonology interface, and Alan Prince on prosodic morphology. These classes fizzed with amazing scholarship and the lecturers displayed remarkable dedication to the students attending them. They also confirmed my hopes that we might, in exploring declarative frameworks for phonology, be genuinely able to offer something useful to the field.

The assessment paper I wrote for Archangeli and Pulleyblank's class was about declarative interpretation of autosegmental spreading parameters. They'd been arguing for parameters such as 'left-to-right' and 'iterative' on harmony rules, rather than supposing that spread is a universal principle. This fitted well with the constraint-based perspective, which saw a continuum of generalisation. These specific statements of spreading make good constraints. Moreover, the lexical entries, with floating features and exceptional links, are well stated as constraints also. I thought that Archangeli and Pulleyblank's rules has residues of procedural rule application. I saw the parameters used to spread a feature F rightwards such as 'Direction: left-to-right' as implicitly procedural: *start* on the left and *then* associate property F to the next-rightwards target... and so on. I suggested reinterpreting the parameters in terms of declarative edge-of-domain alignment constraints (the leftmost target has some property F) and adjacency constraints (if a target is F and there is a target immediately to the right of F, the latter target must also be F). I mention this because this material was not destined to appear in the thesis. For practical reasons, I restricted myself to arguing that local and long distance dependencies are distinct without devising a long distance model. I came back from the Institute greatly motivated, and this thesis is the result — which brings me to certain practicalities.

My thesis, titled "Attribute Value Phonology" (January 1991) was originally available in a reduced size photocopy from the Centre for Cognitive Science, Edinburgh as part of the Thesis Series. My revised single-spaced formating was not great, some typos sneaked through, and the quality of some of the phonetic characters was poor. I hope to have corrected those errors in this version. One particular typo I should point out is that the attribute CONS appeared in a number of diagrams rather than ONS (for onset), for example in Figure 3.1 and (3.27). A few minor changes have been introduced where formating dictated.

At the Linguistics Institute, I was lucky to make a number of extremely clever and charming friends who have completely transformed my life and my wife's, by motivating and enabling an extended period of work and play at Stanford University, and shorter periods at Leiden University. These experiences have greatly influ-

Preface

enced the course of my work. One aspect of working in the USA in 1991 and 1992 is that I could see where mainstream North American phonological theorising was heading. So I knew the time had come to broaden my work greatly, and to hold back on further phonological theorising without either undertaking extensive work on a particular language, or on a particular phenomenon from a partially phonetic perspective. I looked for work in Scotland, and the serendipity of the job market dictated that I would follow the latter research path.

In the last few years, I have been working in an independent institution in Edinburgh, namely Queen Margaret College, in the Department of Speech and Language Sciences. This has given me great scope to learn about acoustic and articulatory phonetics, language acquisition and developmental phonological disorder. Since completing the thesis, I've become convinced that an even greater reassessment of the basics is required. Phonological data is often shuffled around, like a strange game of Chinese whispers. It seemed perfectly respectable to produce a phonological dissertation, like this one, where real speech data is absent and where no checking of the analysis against a corpus is performed. This now seems merely expedient. If we seek to understand phonological systems, we need to clarify and ground the data, formalise our grammars, and be scientific in our approach. Flaws in formal argumentation in this thesis I can live with: false predictions I can live with. Both have value in moving the field forward. In retrospect the only aspect of this work I would seek to change is the way in which I simply accepted the canon of published data. I would like to go back and supplement the theory with a little rigour in my assessment of the data. We all owe it to ourselves as phonologists to be a little more scrupulous about our raw materials.

Acknowledgments

Having studied at Edinburgh University for eight years in the departments of Linguistics and Artificial Intelligence, the Centre for Speech Technology Research and the Centre for Cognitive Science, I have too many debts to acknowledge them all individually. Edinburgh is the most exciting place to study linguistics, and I could have wished no better experience. For everything, thanks. I would like, however, to pick out for special mention Kirsty, my wife, who tempted me to Edinburgh, and Roger Lass, who kindled in me a real interest in linguistics. I doubt Roger even remembers me, but he is in no small way responsible for what I've been up to.

As for the period 1987–1990, I would especially like to thank my supervisors Ewan Klein (Cognitive Science) and Bob Ladd (Linguistics). The results of their close interest in my work is evident throughout this thesis, and their detailed comments on numerous versions of this thesis were incisive and motivational. Good advice is a rare commodity, so thank you both. Thanks also to Steve Bird for detailed comments on parts of an earlier draft, which were much appreciated. The reader has a *lot* to thank these three for! For many valuable discussions, thanks to Diana Archangeli, Steve Bird, Mike Broe, Alice Neundorf, Bill Poser, Alan Prince and Doug Pulleyblank. They have vastly improved this work. For further help of all kinds, thank you Patrick Blackburn, Jo Calder, John Coleman, John Local, Mike Reape, Pete Whitelock, Linguistics Association of Great Britain audiences, the Edinburgh phonology workshop and everyone at the Linguistic Society of America Institute in Tucson (1989) especially Gillian Ramchand, Jennifer Cole and the Navajo class. Let me not forget all the Sun Loungers for keeping me sane and last but far from least, Betty Hughes.

Financial support was from the *Carnegie Trust for the Universities of Scotland.* I am honoured that they felt I deserved their support. Thanks also to the LSA.

My parents have always given me the freedom and trust I needed, and always been there. I see much of them in me, for which I can only be profoundly grateful.

Finally I record my greatest debt, to my wife Kirsty. Without her I would never have gone to Edinburgh in the first place, 8 years ago, never started into linguistics and never have kept going. I dedicate this work to her.

James M. Scobbie, January 31st, 1991

I would like to take this chance to express my deep thanks to my examiners, Harry van der Hulst (Leiden) and Richard Shillcock (Edinburgh).

James M. Scobbie, April, 1991

I'd like to add my acknowledgments for help and support during the period leading up to this publication. Financial support for the formating and indexing was provided by the ESRC, as part of the project "The Scottish Vowel Length Rule: the Phonetics, Phonology and Acquisition of a Marginal Contrast" (R000 23 7135). Queen Margaret College, Edinburgh, has been an excellent environment in which to work, and I express my thanks to my colleagues. Special thanks are due to Janet Pierrehumbert, Jacques Durand, Bob Ladd, Bill Hardcastle and John Coleman for variously good thoughtful advice and valued support. Kristi Long at Garland has been benevolently on my shoulder, keeping me geed up. Cathy Sotillo was especially selfless at the last minute with formatting help. Again I need to express my thanks to Kirsty for putting up with my absence at home when I should have been there and my absent-mindedness when I was. For Struan and Rory: not words but kisses.

James M. Scobbie, October 9th, 1997

Even jist sitn doonin writn. A ey useti think, whenever a felt like writn sumhm, that that wiz awright, aw yi hud to say wuz, ach well, a think ahl sit doonin write sumhm, nyi jiss sat doonin wrote it. But no noo, naw. A canny even day that for five minutes, but ahl sitnlookit thi thing, nthink, here, sumdayz wrote that afore. Then ahl go, hawlin aw thi books ootma cupboard, trynti find out hooit wuz. Nwither a find out or no, it takes me that long luknfurit, a canny be bothird writn any mair, wance av stoapt. An anyway, a tend ti think if it's wan a they thingz that might uv been writn before, there's no much point in writn it again, even if naibdy actually huz, is there?

Taken from *Honest*, by Tom Leonard (1989), which appears in *The Devil and the Giro: Two Centuries of Scottish Stories* (edited by Carl MacDougal) and is reproduced with kind permission of Canongate Books Ltd, 14 High St, Edinburgh, Scotland, EH1 1TE.

Roughly speaking: *Even just sitting down and writing. I aye used to think, whenever I felt like writing something, that that was alright, all you had to say was, oh well, I think I'll sit down and write something, and you just sat down and wrote it. But not now, no. I can't even do that for five minutes, but I'll sit and look at the thing, and think, here, sombody's written that before. Then I'll go, hauling all the books out my cupboard, trying to find out who it was. And whether I find out or not, it takes me that long looking for it, I can't be bothered writing any more, once I've stopped. And anyway, I tend to think if it's one of those things that might have been written before, there's not much point in writing it again, even if nobody actually has, is there?*
Transliteration — J.M.S.

Autosegmental Representation in a Declarative Constraint-Based Framework

Chapter 1

Introduction

1.1 Overview

This thesis presents ATTRIBUTE VALUE PHONOLOGY, a monostratal, constraint-based and declarative approach to phonological competence. AVP is a development of Autosegmental Phonology (Goldsmith 1976; 1990), reconstructed partly on the basis of ideas from various declarative approaches to syntax and semantics termed Unification-Based Grammar (*cf* Shieber 1986). It thus constitutes a general framework for the analysis of phonological phenomena and makes specific theoretical proposals.

The motivations for such work are threefold:

Explanation. Since there is an accelerating tendency in phonology away from procedural analyses, it makes sense to investigate an entirely nonprocedural phonology. This is a practical possibility in the light of the formal developments which have been made in the study of complex feature structures, underspecification, unification, and other areas. In a declarative framework the non-procedural aspects of current phonological theory would be obligatory; and thus independently motivated. Furthermore there are problematic aspects of Autosegmental Phonology ('AP') which AVP is intended to solve.

Cross-fertilisation. The success of declarative theories in the study of syntax and semantics is in marked contrast to the negligible systemisation of such ideas in phonology. Syntacticians have not attempted to test the techniques they deem important on phonological phenomena, and, moreover, phonologists have been slow to exploit the developments which such monostratal frameworks have made. Unless we are prepared to let research in the various disciplines become out of step, the development of a phonology tailored for a Unification-Based Grammar ('UBG') is a major priority. Such a phonological theory would enhance our understanding of both areas of study.

Formalisation. Autosegmental Phonology, in common with most phonology since Chomsky & Halle (1968), is not sufficiently formalised. It neither defines nor is based on any formal meta-language, and so the workings of the theory cannot be precisely determined. The consequences of any extensions to, or modifications of, the 'formal framework' are therefore difficult to determine. To adopt a well-understood formalism as a basis for phonological investigation increases the value of the investigation.

Viewed as a framework within which phonological theories can be constructed, AVP owes a great deal to Unification-Based Grammar, in particular its DECLARATIVE, or CONSTRAINT-BASED, architecture, and its use of attribute-value structures themselves as the fundamental representational structures. Given simple augmentation of such structures with an index (described in detail below) to make them suitable for phonological use, this framework allows the construction of a set of diverse theories all of which inherit certain desirable characteristics.

Briefly, DECLARATIVE theories can have no extrinsic rule ordering. In other words the order in which constraints on well-formedness (rules, roughly) are brought to bear is irrelevant. There are therefore no intermediate stages of structures which are not surface-true. Instead of ordered rules, Unification-Based Grammars require that a form must satisfy CONSTRAINTS, each of which equally defines any given representation (hence the term 'Constraint-Based').[1] UBG's are also MONOTONIC, in that any given representation is defined by the cumulative definitions of its con-

Introduction 5

stituent parts. Constraints only define *well*-formed structures (of varying specificity) and the deletion of constraints is impossible. Consequently UBG's require underspecification to capture alternations.

I have fleshed out this general framework by making certain specific theoretical decisions. While AVP has some characteristics familiar from the phonological literature — it is prosodic, monostratal, autosegmental, and makes use of complex feature hierarchies — it is *not* a formalisation of Autosegmental Phonology. It is in some ways a radical departure from AP. Many of these differences are not necessarily dependent on the choice of a declarative framework and are proposed solely in the search for a more restrictive theory. Some specific changes AP are:

- Sequence is encoded only by a single skeleton consisting of ordered indices assigned to structures' roots.

- Association is defined as the converse of the dominance relation defining attribute-value structures, not as simultaneity or overlap.

- The No Crossing Constraint is not used.

- The Sharing Constraint forces all structures to be CONVEX: multiple association is possible only between skeletally adjacent slots.

- There is a fundamental representational difference between local and long distance dependencies.

- Multiplanar phonological representations are ruled out.

Acting together, the theoretical proposals and the formal framework account for certain characteristic behaviours. AVP posits a skeletal sequence of hierarchical attribute-value structures, and has a single account of the INTEGRITY and 'INALTERABILITY' of their component substructures, irrespective of whether they form part of a simple segment of a geminate. Whether a structure is shared by two skeletal slots is formally irrelevant to its behaviour.[2]

AP, on the other hand, assumes that configurations involving multiple association are a natural class, distinct from configurations of single association, and uses multiple association to account for integrity and inalterability. As we will see, this causes many problems, since the phenomena only hold of multiple associations made between adjacent features. AP attempts to ameliorate these problems, but in the process totally undermines its account of the phenomena it sets out to explain. In AVP the Sharing Constraint ensures that association itself is banned between nonadjacent items. The declarative nature of the framework then explains why geminate associations may not be broken (integrity) and why the shared substructure in a geminate must, like any other (sub)structure, be well-formed (inalterability).

The remainder of this chapter puts AVP (as one particular conception of declarative phonology) in perspective, addresses the relationship of phonetics to phonology in AVP, and finally gives an introduction to the attribute-value structures which AVP uses.

Chapter 2 presents the central ideas of Attribute Value Phonology and compares and contrasts AVP with Autosegmental Phonology (particularly as characterised by Goldsmith 1990). Chapter 3 adds an important principle to AVP to tackle the problem of associative locality — the No Crossing Constraint of Goldsmith (1976) is replaced by the SHARING CONSTRAINT, which forces all structure to be CONVEX, *i.e.* to hold only for contiguous stretches of the skeleton.

I next show how the system as set up so far accounts for geminate integrity (Chapter 4) and inalterability (Chapter 5). I also show how AVP's constraint-based treatment of inalterability deals with the awkward distribution of geminates in languages with weak codas by the means of LICENSING (Goldsmith 1990), formalised using conditional constraints.

Chapter 6 demonstrates that AVP is justified in requiring all phonological structure to be monoplanar. Nonconcatenative morphology does *not* motivate the use of multiplanar phonological representations. The use of multiple association in harmony is similarly unmotivated, and I tentatively propose that a harmony involves the specification of a single type of structure for a domain in which there are individual tokens of that structure.

1.2 Towards a declarative phonology

The definition of DECLARATIVE theories of grammar given by Pollard & Sag (1987:7, 8) is that, in contradistinction to PROCEDURAL theories, they "characterise *what* constraints are brought to bear during language use independently of *what order* the constraints are applied in" (original emphasis). This procedural neutrality makes declarative theories ideally suited to the characterisation of such linguistic competence as is common to both the interpretation and production of language.

It should be clear that a theory cannot be both declarative and nondeclarative. There is no hybrid theory: a declarative theory embellished with a minimal amount of extrinsic rule ordering is, simply, no longer declarative. In this section I will investigate how this issue relates to the architecture of various phonological theories.

1.2.1 Procedural and declarative aspects of phonological theory

Insofar as it is possible to tell, phonological theories are almost invariably procedural.[3] In the generative paradigm, phonological rules proper have acted as procedural devices, for they modify an underlying form by applying *in a specific order*, till at the end of the derivation a surface representation is reached. Such REWRITE RULES are intended to describe alternations. A phonology can make use of other devices, however, intended to capture other generalisations, in particular the *non*-alternating generalisations about distribution and segment types which make up a large proportion of any language's phonology.[4] Such PHONOTACTIC RULES are intuitively nonprocedural, since they pertain to the well-formedness of various representations regardless of quite *how* they could be derived. Whether they are indeed nonderivational depends on the particular formal theory in which they are used, but this intuitive relationship between phonotactics and a declarative architecture is strong, partly because a nonprocedural treatment of such constraints is very simple. There is potentially, then, a close link between extrinsically ordered rewrite rules and derivational (procedural) theories on the one hand, and phonotactic constraints and declarative theories on the other.

Though formally the addition of rule ordering to a grammar makes the entire grammar procedural, it is generally believed that it may be worthwhile to partition a theory into compartments of rewrite and phonotactic rules. But, assuming the relationship above between phonotactic rules and declarative theories, to add some phonotactic rules to a phonology in no way alters its procedural status. If, moreover, two types of rules *are* held to be necessary, some account must be given of how they interact, irrespective of the formal considerations just mentioned. If no such account is forthcoming, perhaps one of the classes of rules can be eliminated altogether, and the problem of their interaction solved that way.

For example, the types of phonotactic rules used in Chomsky & Halle (1968) ('SPE') and later generative phonology were redundancy rules and morpheme structure rules ('MSRs'). Both were seen to be problematic components of a rule-based procedural phonology (see Stanley 1967 for example). Chomsky & Halle (1968) formalised phonological rules and the ordering relations among them, but they did not provide more than a preliminary account of phonotactics. No formalisation of these constraints was proposed that was anything but "alternative and equivalent" (SPE:387) to the rewrite rules. SPE therefore did not properly address the problem of how to integrate nonderivational constraints on well-formed structure and derivational rules with arbitrary power to alter such structure.

This is not to say that SPE did without phonotactic rules, for to prevent any unwanted interactions, they were forced to precede the derivational rewrite rules as a group (though this resulted in the replication of generalisations), and were therefore still differentiated from the rewrite rules. MSRs and redundancy rules were effectively nonderivational constraints on *underlying* representations, forcing them to abide to certain sequential or configurational norms. The ban on the English syllable onset [fn] would be expressed at this stage. Of course [fn] is not a possible onset at any stage of the phonology but there were no constraints on surface structure to express this. Such facts were merely an epiphenomenal combination of underlying constraints and the body of rewrite rules.

Introduction 9

This treatment of rewrite rules and constraints is unsatisfactory, however, for these epiphenomena actually constitute valid facts of the language, not fortuitous accidents. Kisseberth (1970) pointed out that an SPE-style analysis of Yawelmani would use MSRs to ban (amongst other things) sequences of more than two consonants. A bank of rules (two consonant reduction, one vowel insertion and three vowel deletion) which bear no formal similarity to each other 'conspire' together to maintain this phonotactic generalisation, because such sequences are impossible on the surface also. Since surface phonotactics were not part of that theory (only underlying morphotactics) this CONSPIRACY remains unexpressed by the grammar. If surface phonotactics *are* to be employed, then a new account must be found of how the phonotactic and procedural rules can be integrated.

One could imagine that either phonotactics prevent rewrite rules from creating ill-formed structures ('constraints-as-filters') or allow rules to apply but then (luckily!) are able to repair the offending structure ('constraints-as-triggers-of-repair-strategies'). This problem remains unsolved.[5]

If it is not possible to integrate procedural rules and surface-structure phonotactics, is it possible to do without either one of them? Sommerstein (1977:§8.1) discusses Postal's (1968:220ff) 'proof' that constraints on surface form are redundant, and therefore can be done away with. Postal's position demands that Morpheme Structure Conditions are used to define 'possible morphemes.' Rewrite rules then can derive all surface forms from these underlyers. The proof is invalid, however, since the assumption Postal makes that MSRs can define all possible morphemes is incorrect (Shibatani 1973; Singh 1987). It is undeniable, then, that 'tactics' of some form *are* required if we want to delimit 'possible words.' The crucial question, however, is whether they are *mor*photactics or *phono*tactics. Most phonologists now accept, partly due to Kisseberth's work, that distributions are defined phonotactically, not morphotactically. The realisation that tactics very often must refer to syllable structure played a large part in this. Postal's demonstration is therefore invalid, and Sommerstein concludes that in fact it is the MSRs which are redundant.

How phonotactics and rewrite rules interact is therefore still a pressing problem. Nonprocedural solutions to problems are in-

10   Autosegmental Representation in a Declarative Framework

creasingly common, most clearly in the form of conditions on well-formedness like the Obligatory Contour Principle (see below). Since phonotactics are essential, some theories of phonology (see below) reject the existence of rewrite rules altogether, opting for a *monostratal* architecture in which derivations play no particular part. This has the consequence of allowing the phonology to be declarative, and is the position taken here.[6]

1.2.2 Developments in monostratal syntactic theory and their potential influence on phonology

In the study of syntax and semantics a range of grammars based upon complex feature structures have been proposed which have been very successful in the analysis of a large range of phenomena. A range of properties characterise these grammar formalisms, especially their declarative monostratal nature and their formal precision. A representative selection of these so-called 'Unification-Based Grammars' (Sag *et al* 1986; Shieber 1986; Johnson 1988) would include: Functional Unification Grammar ('FUG') (Kay 1979); Lexical Functional Grammar ('LFG') (Bresnan 1982); Generalised Phrase Structure Grammar ('GPSG') (Gazdar 1982; Gazdar, Klein, Pullum & Sag 1985); Head-Driven Phrase Structure Grammar ('HPSG') (Pollard & Sag 1987); Unification Categorial Grammar ('UCG') (Calder, Klein & Zeevat 1988).[7]

Linguists developing these declarative approaches to syntax have been slow to investigate the possibilities for a declarative phonology, probably because no major phonological theory is at first glance compatible with such frameworks. Phonologists for their part have generally failed to take advantage of the advances in feature theory and elucidation of non-transformational rules which have been made in Unification-Based Grammar — let alone investigate the nature of the phonological component of HPSG or UCG say. Against this background of parallel development it is hardly surprising that no realistic declarative approach to phonology has been advanced.[8]

Generative phonologists have been disinclined to embed their theories in a framework which denies them certain traditional techniques: rule-ordering; deletion; feature changing rules; multistratal

Introduction 11

derivations. Ironically these techniques can now be perceived as expedients rather than the bedrock of a phonological theory, judging both by the methods used and the topics addressed in the recent literature. Moreover appeals to fundamentally declarative techniques appear to an extent which suggests we may be witnessing a gradual evolution towards declarative phonology.[9] Since procedural aspects are still important in all phonological theories this agglomeration of the nonprocedural demands that we either develop an appropriate theory of their interaction or reject one set of techniques.

Characteristics of the declarative style are:

Structured hierarchies of features. The development of grammars based on complex feature structures has been paralleled by a developing hierarchical view of subsegmental features in Lass (1976); Mohanan (1983); Mascaró (1984); Clements (1985); Sagey (1986); Steriade (1987a); Browman & Goldstein (1989) and many others.

Feature percolation. Ensuring that a given feature appears on certain structurally related nodes as a means of capturing generalisations is recognised as necessary by Clements (1985); Waksler (1990). This does not mean that phonological percolation conventions have necessarily been nonprocedural; for instance see Hayes (1990).

Underspecification. This is common as a basic way to capture alternations rather than using banks of rules. The arguments in favour of underspecification in phonology are based on reducing redundancy and abstractness, see Kiparsky (1982; 1985); Pulleyblank (1983); Archangeli (1984; 1988); Archangeli & Pulleyblank (1986); Steriade (1987b).

Non-procedural rule application. A reduced reliance on extrinsic rule ordering was originally discussed by Koutsoudas, Sanders & Noll (1974) as a means to reduce abstraction. See also Venneman (1972b); Hooper (1976). Rule-ordering has recently been seen as an unexplanatory means to account for data: Hayes (1986a) rejects a counter-feeding analysis in favour of enriched representations, and Goldsmith (1990:353) comments:

12   *Autosegmental Representation in a Declarative Framework*

> this is an excellent example of the more general proposition that geometrized autosegmental and metrical analyses tend to require far less extrinsic ordering, all other things being equal, than purely segmental analyses.

Itô (1989) rejects the ordering of onset creation rules before coda creation rules as an explanation of universal tendency for intervocalic consonants to be onsets.

Templates. Templates are proposed as constraints on syllable structure by Selkirk (1982). See also Itô (1986) who argues strongly against the use of rewrite rules for this purpose. Templates are basically nonderivational constraints on possible structures.

Conditions on well-formedness. Conditions such as the Obligatory Contour Principle (Leben 1973; McCarthy 1986a; Odden 1988; Yip 1988; Paradis & Prunet 1990) are of central importance as (universal) triggers of phonological alternations. Locality Principles such as the No Crossing Constraint (Goldsmith 1976), and the requirement for full syllabification (Selkirk 1982; Itô 1989) are further examples of nonderivational requirements, compliance with which forces alternations. Government-Charm is an approach to phonology (the consideration of which would take us well beyond the remit of this work) which makes central the use of conditions of well-formedness, though *not* to the exclusion of procedural mechanisms (see Kaye *et al* 1985). Feature Co-occurrence Restrictions (Archangeli & Pulleyblank 1989; Kiparsky 1985; Archangeli 1988) are a good example of language specific constraints. See also Kiparsky (1982; 1985) and Borowsky (1989) on Structure Preservation.

Surface phonotactics. Cairns (1988); Itô (1986; 1989) and Goldsmith (1990) are part of the trend towards studying the aspects of universal grammar responsible for surface distribution.

Of course not all of these developments are compatible: Goldsmith (1990:295) comments that the degree of underspecification is inversely proportional to the need for highly articulated featural organisation. Furthermore the authors cited would not necessarily accept a nonprocedural interpretation of their work. Nevertheless, these concepts, which have been proposed on purely phonological grounds, are either required by, or are compatible with, the requirements of a declarative formalism.

As noted above, declarative theories (by definition) involve no extrinsic rule ordering so alternations cannot be analysed in this way. Instead the partial specification of lexical entries is the means by which alternations are captured. Such partial descriptions are part of the 'pool of constraints' on the (surface) well-formedness of representations. They combine with the more general constraints supplied by the grammar. All such constraints apply equally, and in any order, and are similar to the phonotactic templates outlined above. Indeed a constraint-based phonology could equally well be called 'template-based.'[10] A final similarity is that declarative formalisms have employed hierarchical representations constrained by feature percolation as a central part of their formal vocabulary.

If, therefore, a reconstructed autosegmental theory were designed as a constituent part of a Unification-Based Grammar then the declarative nature of the formalism itself could provide an explanation for why the theoretical developments outlined above are declarative in character. And, since these developments have been widely accepted as necessary for a proper understanding of phonological systems, we might be able to get much closer to accounting for why a phonological system is as it is. It is therefore reasonable to suppose that investigating phonology in the light of the results of UBG is worthwhile.

1.2.3 Monostratal precursors to AVP

It is not only in autosegmental frameworks that we can find nonprocedural ideas playing an important part, and two theories require special mention. Natural Generative Phonology ('NGP') and Firthian Prosodic Analysis share common concerns with declarative phonology and due to certain similarities in approach there is a good prospect that future research will benefit from a closer investigation of these theories.[11]

Natural Generative Phonology. NGP is associated most directly with Venneman and Hooper (see for example Venneman 1972ab, 1974ab; Hooper 1976) and was one attempt to reduce the potential abstractness of phonological analyses during the 'abstractness controversy' of the 1970's (Kiparsky 1973; also Hyman 1975 for discussion). Despite being an attempt to revise post-SPE phonology from within, NGP was still radical in its adoption of the True Generalisation Condition:

> A very strong constraint on rules would be one that does not allow abstract rules at all. It would require that all rules express transparent surface generalisations, generalisations that are true for all surface forms and that, furthermore, express the relation between surface forms in the most direct manner possible. We will call this condition the True Generalisation Condition. The True Generalisation Condition claims that the rules speakers formulate are based directly on surface forms and that these rules relate one surface form to another, rather than relating underlying to surface form.
>
> Hooper (1976:16)

This monostratal position means that NGP does without extrinsic rule-ordering, destructive operations and abstract underlyers — the similarity with declarative phonology is quite striking.

Anderson (1985:341) summarises the criticisms of NGP (see particularly Gussman 1980) by suggesting that, in limiting phonology to the study of surface-true generalisations, it "throws the baby out with the bath water." This point of view seems analogous to the dismissive attitude of syntacticians towards phrase structure grammars prior to the seminal work of Gazdar (1981; 1982), which showed the superfluity of deletions and transformations. This and subsequent work has shown that it is quite possible to keep tight hold of the baby in monostratal syntax. There is no reason to assume that the same is not true for monostratal phonology. We would be wrong, therefore, to assume (as Anderson does) that the declarative approach places any *a priori* limit on what is considered data. Apparent cases of absolute neutralisation and analyses apparently demanding feature-changing analyses (such as Navajo

Introduction 15

sibilant harmony, Poser *p.c.*) need not be hastily written off either as nonphonological or nondeclarative. They simply require a more sophisticated declarative analysis.

Prosodic Analysis. It is impossible to consider Firth's Prosodic Analysis (Firth 1948: see also Robins 1957; Palmer 1970; Bazell *et al* 1966) in any detail here, but there are one or two important points that should be noted. Anderson's appraisal of Firth's writings "on phonology in particular" as being "nearly Delphic in character" (1985:179) is an interesting one, and may well be due to the declarative nature of Prosodic Analysis (see Broe 1988). Prosodies are ambiguously interpretable as rules *or* representations, a distinction central to most generative frameworks (and most certainly to Anderson's book).

A PROSODY is a paradigmatic choice of phonological property applying to some structure or position. For example an initial stop might be aspirated or nonaspirated. The stopness is a defining characteristic of the particular PHONEMATIC UNIT selected for the position. The prosody of aspiration is a independent property of the position itself. The prosody resembles both an initial aspiration rule and a distinctive feature.

The formal equivalence of rule and representation is a familiar aspect of Unification-Based Grammar. In UBG lexical entries are partial descriptions of a certain specificity, while rules are just *more* general — they describe those parts of a representation which are predictable and can be abstracted out from lexical entries. Both types of partial description are constraints on well-formed representations. If prosodies *were* to be taken to be rules, then they would be rules which were not subject to extrinsic ordering. Both this declarativeness and the collapse of the rule-representation distinction are common features of AVP and Prosodic Analysis.

1.2.4 Summary

Kisseberth (1970) effectively raised the problem of the integration of nonprocedural phonotactics and procedural rules in a single theory. This problem is more acute than ever because of the importance of nonprocedural solutions in phonology. Various attempts have been made to solve this problem, but none has been successful.

My position is that because declarative constraints are essential, procedural rules must be dispensed with. An entirely declarative phonology, a constraint-based phonology, is the result.

1.3 Phonological representations and their relationship to phonetics

1.3.1 Constraining phonological representations

A central tenet of generative phonology is that representations are formally distinct from the rules that manipulate them. Basically a string of symbols is modified by string rewriting operations, the initial representation being the lexical entry and the final representation being the interface with phonetics. In Unification-Based Grammars, 'rules' and 'representations' are the *same* formal stuff. A UBG makes use of CONSTRAINTS, and whether they originate in the lexicon or grammar is irrelevant. In AVP, a phonological representation (being a sequence of attribute-value structures, as we will see) is partially described by the lexical entries which make it up, by universal aspects of phonology, and by language-particular factors. In other words the form of the representation being constructed is constrained to be of a certain sort by these pieces of information. Since constraints are used to express both rule-like and non-rule-like aspects of the phonology, the rule/representation dichotomy is not applicable in a UBG.

A simple lexical entry might consist of sequence of attribute-value structures including one, S, for a high back vowel, say. The body of nonlexical constraints might include an implication that $S \to S'$, with the intended effect that all high back vowels are also round. The second constraint is not an operation rewriting S as S' — it is merely a *conditional* description. It describes all attribute-value structures *except* those which are high, back and *un*rounded (because a logical implication $p \to q$ is exactly equivalent to $\neg(p \wedge \neg q)$). The constraints define well-formed phonological representations.[12]

1.3.2 Phonetics is not phonological detail

The phonological representation described by the grammar and a group of lexical entries must correspond in some manner to phonetic entities. A model theoretic approach to the phonology-phonetics interface pairs each *syntactically* well-formed representation with its *semantic* interpretation. A simple interpretation of an attribute-value structure would be a set of phonetic events which are considered possible realisations of that representation. The conventional restrictions on this relationship constitute the rules of PHONETIC IMPLEMENTATION.

Phonetic implementation ensures that a given piece of phonological structure corresponds in a predictable way to a given type of articulatory (and acoustic) entity. This does not mean that a phonological representation is merely a phonetic representation with most of the predictable details missed out. An attribute-value structure is not gradually modified into, say, an articulatory score — these are different things altogether, and there is no expectation that the formal language which is used to represent phonological relationships is capable of forming the core of a more expressive phonetic language. Nevertheless, *some* aspects of the phonology are transparently related to phonetics, in particular the fact that they both consist of a *sequence*, and it is to this relationship that I now turn.

AVP is intended as a component of a *sign-based* grammatical architecture, where the SIGN is the high level structure containing information about syntax, semantics and phonology (at least). It is an interface between these modules, and every morpheme and morpheme-combination is a sign. The value of the PHONOLOGY attribute in a sign is special, and quite unlike any other structure, simply because it alone describes temporally realised physical linguistic objects: *phonetic* objects.[13]

The phonological representation (and it alone) is sequential — but not so that it can gradually undergo modification into a phonetic representation. It is just that a phonological description must be able to characterise phonetic temporal order in *some* way. The principal advantage of distinguishing the sequence of phonological structures from the corresponding temporal phonetic sequence is that we can state the ill-formedness of a given phonological structure independent of the well-formedness or otherwise of some phonetic configuration which could be an exponent of that structure.

The purpose of phonological representations is to convey syntactic and lexical distinctions. Each such representation is realisable by a class of phonetic events. Phonological constraints limit the form of possible structures and the possible sequences of structures, but these well-formed representations correspond only indirectly to the temporal phonetic configurations which express them. No phonological constraint directly concerns phonetics. Consequently, if some structure typically realised as a mid vowel sound is unable in some language to be phonologically nasal, this does *not* imply mid vowels in this language are never phonetically nasalised. Phonology defines the space within which contrastive words can be constructed, and such constraints do not apply directly to phonetics.

This is not to say that phonological structure and phonetic exponents are arbitrarily related. The way in which the sequence of phonological attribute-value structures and the phonetic continuum are related is quite predictable. Given two structures, one of which precedes the other, then their exponents must be similarly sequenced temporally. If the structures are of the same sort this will be absolute — the velum cannot be both raised and lowered at the same time! If they are of a *different* sort the phonetic story is more complex though the details of phonological precedence are identical. While the voiceless exponent of /p/ precedes the voiced exponent of /l/ in *play* (because the vocal cords cannot be simultaneously vibrating and still), the voicelessness of the stop *overlaps* the lateral's oral cavity articulations.[14] We would not wish the phonology to describe this interval of voiceless lateral articulation (symbolised [l̥]), however, since this would indicate the configuration was part of the *phonology* of English. *Other* languages (*e.g.* Welsh) may make use of it but there is no well-formed structure in English describing it. It is not a phonological *segment* of English comparable to /p/ and /l/.

Just because there is no /l̥/ phoneme does not mean that a *phonetic* 'segment' [l̥] cannot exist. That [l̥] exists is a fact of English phonetic implementation, not of the phonological level itself. The phonetics-phonology relationship does not demand that every gesture realising /p/ must occur *en masse* before every gesture realising /l/. Instead I suggest that it makes the less severe requirement that all exponents of a structure must *overlap* at some point in time. This point in turn has to precede the analogous point for the exponents of the subsequent structure. This allows the temporal extent of gestures to vary and to overlap adjacent gestures. The voicelessness of /p/, for example, outlasts its labial articulation so it overlaps the lateral articulation which follows. This means that gestures corresponding to adjacent structures can be partly synchronous, however.[15] 'There is a voiceless lateral' is not a statement of the phonology.

An attribute-value structure, then, is a phonological unit which is part of a sequence. The exponents of each aspect of the structure overlap at some point in time. This precedes the corresponding point of the subsequent structure, but the duration of the individual gestures is not represented phonologically. There is no sense in which a structure 'takes up' a given amount of time. Phonological length does not necessarily result in phonetic length. The exact temporal extent of a gesture will differ according to universal, language specific, idiosyncratic, contextual and no doubt yet other factors.

1.3.3 The 'concreteness problem'

The view of phonetics assumed here is influenced by Browman & Goldstein's (1986; 1989) 'gestural score' approach. Their GES-TURES are patterns of actual actions in the vocal tract, and AVP views gestures as the classes of phonetic objects which a phonological feature describes. Gestures are phonetic, but for Browman & Goldstein (1989:201) they are also *phonological* units inasmuch as

> phonological structures are stable 'constellations' (or 'molecules,' to avoid mixing metaphors) assembled out of these gestural atoms.

In their view a phonological system of contrasts is defined on gestural scores, but they do not show how the system of contrasts is actually organised, concentrating instead on showing how phonological contrasts are neutralised by the increasing overlap of gestures.[16] The overlap of gestures may well be able to account for all assimilatory fast speech phenomena, but it is still necessary to construct a contrastive system using structures which encode phonological well-formedness, as opposed to characterising a phonetic snapshot at some slice in time. This observation is echoed by Huffman (1990:102) who notes:

> The problems with the theory as presented [in B& G (1986)] is that it gives no indication of what might limit the combinatorial possibilities of gestures, and their phasing relations.

Browman & Goldstein treat phonetics and phonology as stages on a continuum of detail. The most explicit statement of phonetics would be stated in the same meta-language as the quite different statements of phonology, with the consequence that we would be faced with a 'concreteness controversy.' While the 'abstractness controversy' of the 1970's (see above) was concerned with the ability of phonological formalisms to express arbitrary amounts of non-phonetic phonological information (generally recapitulating historical developments), the problem of concreteness facing modern phonology is its capacity to express arbitrary amounts of non-phonological phonetic material.

For B&G, the alignment of gestures serves to express aspiration, in particular the phonetic voiceless lateral of English. Since the 'stable' alignment of gestures constitutes phonological status, how can we make phonological generalisations such as 'there is no voiceless lateral in English'? Is the aspiration of [p] not stable? This is not to deny that the fact that English has aspiration is clearly phonological. The issue is how the fact is expressed.[17]

A similar criticism can be made of Autosegmental Phonology since it is capable of expressing arbitrary amounts of phonetic detail. Goldsmith (1976:16) proposes AP as "a hypothesis about the geometry of phonetic — and ultimately phonological — representations." And, "phonological rules ... relate phonological and phonetic levels" (p5) rather than being used to define the phonological level itself. It would seem that again the difference between phonetics and phonology is one of degree, where the detail that differentiates the levels is governed by phonological rules which add ever increasing amounts of detail.

Introduction

Goldsmith's stated motivation for the autosegmental approach is the inadequacy of the Absolute Slicing Hypothesis (Goldsmith 1976:17):

(1.1) *Absolute Slicing Hypothesis*
The normal assumption about phonological representations implies that in processing a signal, we learn to shift [the 'horizontal' co-temporal alignment of the phonetic score] around slightly... — we 'justify' it — and patch it up so that it may be sliced up vertically into the phonologically, and hence psychologically, real segments.

In other words a messy *phonetic* score (presumably a description of the signal) is modified and tidied to produce a neat phonetic score, at which point vertical cuts can be made to produce segments, where the segments are *phonological*. Goldsmith correctly discounts this hypothesis, but does so on the grounds that certain prosodic aspects of the signal (such as intonation) are not part of any particular segmentable section of the signal more than they would be part of any other segmentable section, in which case Absolute Slicing must perforce segment these features incorrectly. Goldsmith's position hinges on the assumption in (1.1) that phonology is merely a tidied-up, segmentalised phonetics, and his solution to the problem is to relax the amount of segmentalisation required. Absolute slicing is abandoned in favour of autosegmental slicing.

The impossibility of Absolute Slicing could, however, be due to the impossibility of slicing altogether. It may be phonology simply is not chopped up phonetics, whichever way the cuts are made. If, however, phonology is a partial description of phonetics, then however detailed we allow the description to be, it is still a description. Consequently, though there are patently no *phonetic* segments, this does *not* mean that a phonological description consisting of a discrete sequence of structures is incoherent, so long as they appropriately describe the signal.[18] It does *not* follow that there are no phonological segments simply because it is impossible to define phonetic segments.

Of course the phonological descriptions Goldsmith was criticising were also inadequate, and it is indeed the case that some phonological features are the property of several different segments, but this is a different problem. AVP's phonological segments SHARE structure in order to deal with this, which overcomes many criticisms leveled at SPE's matrix sequence.

More recently Goldsmith (1990:277) has criticised attempts to see association between autosegments as a phonetic relationship:

> autosegmental phonology does not derive its multi-tiered structure from a decision as to how best to translate a fine-grained description of an articulatory event into one consisting of the discrete units called segments, autosegments or components.

Goldsmith (1990:10) dismisses Sagey (1988) as

> a model of autosegmental phonetics ... [because Sagey characterises association temporally. It may well be that] ... from a purely phonetic point of view the association lines represent simultaneity in time [but Goldsmith's point of view] ... is not to be a purely phonetic ... [one].

He seems to reject the continuum of phonetic-phonological representation,[19] but the difference between the earlier and later views has not been accompanied by any re-evaluation of the basis for the multi-tiered structure which was the basic proposal of Goldsmith (1976).

If AP is phonological, and not merely a less detailed autosegmental phonetics, then it still suffers from the ability of its multi-tier representations to encode detail which we might expect to be addressed by phonetics. For instance it is able to represent instrusive stops in English simply by adding more association lines (see Clements 1987). In addition to encoding the necessary overlap of articulations to do this, the analysis is claimed to capture timing facts about the duration of these stops. Questions have to be asked about the limits of such concreteness. Such expressive power in phonology constitutes a serious problem which has not been addressed. How much detail can AP express, and how much should it express?

1.3.4 Summary

I believe the problems above are due to a pervasive ambiguity about phonological representations. They are seen as tidied-up phonetics, so any fact of phonetics can, if it is so desired, be tackled phonologically. When the phonological level is viewed as comprising of unified partial descriptions of a gestural phonetics then phonological statements cannot be seen as the 'same' as phonetic ones. The amount of detail such a phonology should encompass is an empirical issue, but the idea of phonology being constructed from phonetic 'atoms' is, I suggest, misguided. It makes us forget the prerogatives of each domain.

In AVP the well-formed phonological structures of a language are qualitatively distinct from the objects they describe. Aspects of phonetics which no phonological structure describes (such as [l̩] in the case of English) do not require us to modify the definition of acceptable phonological configurations because they simply are different from such configurations.[20] The patterns of phonological dominance (association) and precedence are constrained by the grammar and lexical entries. The temporal precedence and overlap of the exponents of such representations are only indirectly subject to these constraints.

1.4 An introduction to attribute-value structures

1.4.1 Background

In this section I will give a general introduction to aspects of the attribute-value formalism on which AVP is based. I will assume for the purposes of this paper attribute-value structures (AVSs) as described in Pollard & Sag (1987), who base their discussion on the finite state automata approach of Kasper & Rounds (1986). See also Pollard (1989) for a discussion of sorted AVSs. AVS formalisms are also defined in terms of an attribute-value logic (Johnson 1988) or directed acyclic graphs (Shieber 1986). The discussion will remain relatively informal and necessarily brief, and further details should be sought from Pollard & Sag (1987) or Shieber (1986), which constitutes an ideal introduction to the subject.

1.4.2 Monotonicity and declarativity

An AVS description of a linguistic object (whether it be a sentence or syllable) is an attribute-value structure. The particular form of the structure (and by extension the object being described) is constrained by a variety of sources, such as language specific rules, universal grammar, particular lexical entries and the context. Unification-based grammars are MONOTONIC because this pool of constraints is never subject to destructive operations deleting or changing constraints. Consequently every constraint in the pool must be compatible with every other — one way to ensure this is to demand that they all UNIFY (see below).

Unification grammars are DECLARATIVE. It does not matter *how* it comes to be that constraints are pooled, only that they *are*. A particular performance task may specify an order in which constraints are brought to bear, depending perhaps on whether it is generational or interpretative, but this is not part of the grammar itself. Because such ordering is not part of the grammar, it is impossible for any ill-formed structure to later be made *well*-formed by the application of a rule. Such an alteration of status requires destructive operations. An ill-formed structure cannot be defined by a consistent set of constraints and so some would need to be altered or deleted. An inconsistent set of constraints cannot be made consistent by the addition of further constraints.

In AVP phonological information from different sources all contributes *equally* to defining well-formed structures, and such information can be contributed in any order. Deletion rules, feature changing rules and patch-up filters which rectify ill-formedness by triggering one of these destructive operations cannot be used. The MONOSTRATAL architecture means a structure either *is* or *is not* well-formed. In a MULTISTRATAL approach some structure can be well-formed at one level (underlying representation) even though it would be ill-formed at another (the surface), thereby requiring destructive transitional operations. Allowing such multistratal derivations is a very powerful facility. The order in which rules apply to forms and indeed the entire derivation itself becomes a central part of the phonology. AVP does not embody a procedural derivation as part of the grammar itself.

Introduction

In sum, AVP is based on a formalism which permits no extrinsic rule ordering, requires partial specification to analyse alternations, and which provides a well-defined and logically consistent formalism for expressing hierarchical structure.

1.4.3 Attribute-value structures

An attribute-value structure is well-formed if it consists of a SORT (also 'type') and possibly a number of well-formed attribute-value pairs. An ATTRIBUTE is one of a set {HIGH, PLACE, SUBJECT, ONSET...}; a VALUE is an AVS. The lowest ('terminal') value in this recursive hierarchy is an ATOMIC VALUE, a member of the set of sorts: {*boolean*, +, -, *place, lateral, melody*...}. For example the atomic values *boolean*, *gen* and *plu* would be assigned to attributes like HIGH, CASE or NUMBER.

AVSs are recursively defined, and so are ideal for encoding hierarchical structure. For an example of a complex AVS see (1.2), which might be part of the representation of a vowel. It is represented in the form of an attribute-value MATRIX.[21]

(1.2)   Matrix representation of an AVS

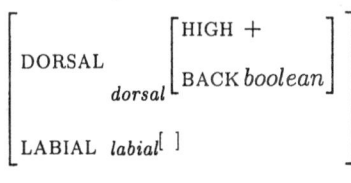

place

The structure (1.2) is the value of the attribute PLACE. It is a structure of sort *place*. The atomic values '+' and '*boolean*' are just sorts of null structures.[22] Such null structures are not drawn. The complex value of LABIAL is a structure about which no other information is known than its sort, *labial*. Its value is unspecified. (In fact we know some things about $_{labial}[\ ]$, see below.)

Sorts are organised into a SUBSUMPTION LATTICE (see Pollard 1989) which expresses whether an object of one sort is necessarily of a second sort. Any object of the sort '+' is necessarily of the more general sort '*boolean*' and we say that the latter sort SUBSUMES the first. Such facts are represented by imposing a partial ordering of subsumption on sorts, which forms a LATTICE:

(1.3)   Part of the subsumption lattice of sorts

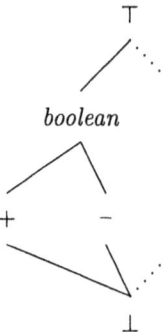

The sort *boolean* subsumes + and − because it is the JOIN (the disjunction) of the sorts which PARTITION it.[23] A conjunction of sorts is their MEET. The meet of + and − is ⊥ ('bottom'), an AVS which has no consistent semantic interpretation.[24] The 'top' of the lattice ⊤ subsumes all the other sorts: it is the maximally general structure.[25] Attributes like HIGH have the atomic value *boolean*, and such a value can be further specified as one of the two sorts which partition it. This specification might be due to a rule or be expressed in an underlying form. An atomic value cannot, by definition, be more than a sort, but generally a sort labels some structure of attribute-value pairs. If a structure is specified as bearing the maximally general sort ⊤ then it is effectively a VARIABLE ranging over all structures.

The value of DORSAL in (1.2) has two attributes: HIGH and BACK. HIGH has the atomic value '+.' It cannot also have the value '−'; the sorts + and − are incompatible. Their unification is ⊥, indicating inconsistency (the meet in (1.3)). Another attribute, LOW, could be added to the value of DORSAL without inconsistency since only one structure is involved, namely $_{dorsal}$[ ]. In this way the AVS expresses naturally the impossibility of a structure being both [HIGH+] and [HIGH−], while allowing the possibility of the value of DORSAL comprising both [HIGH⊤] and [BACK⊤].

Because of the hierarchical nature of AVSs it is useful to be able to refer to a PATH of attributes. This is just a finite sequence of attributes such as [ ], [PLACE] or [PLACE[DORSAL]], no-

Introduction   27

tated [A1|A2|A3]. We now can now talk of paths and their values as a generalisation of attributes and values.[26]

The definition of AVSs used here corresponds to a directed acyclic graph, or DAG. AVSs are 'acyclic' since they exclude self-referential cyclic structures in which an attribute's value contains the selfsame attribute. Two attributes are able to SHARE the same value, however, making AVSs a more general graph than the familiar tree. Though trees are also acyclic, their arcs do not possess the ability to share values. As we will see, such RE-ENTRANCY is required by phonology (as well as in syntactic and semantic descriptions) to analyse situations where some piece of sub-structure is a component of more than one root matrix; in assimilation for example. An AVS is 'directed' because paths and values have an asymmetric relationship: paths IMMEDIATELY DOMINATE their values.

In addition to matrix diagrams, *graphical* representations of AVSs are fairly common. They use directed arcs to indicate immediate dominance. Attributes label the arcs. Arcs link vertices, and the vertex to which an arc points is the value of the arcs's attribute. This vertex may be labelled with a sort, and the value's internal structure consists of the subgraph rooted at this vertex. See (1.4) for an example, the structure represented being the value of PLACE shown in (1.2) above.[27]

(1.4)   *dag* version of structure in (1.2)

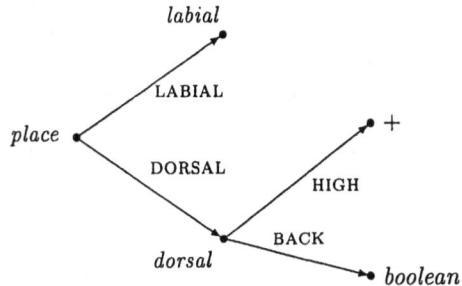

1.4.4 Unification

Firstly it is necessary to discuss subsumption in relation to AVSs, having already introduced it in the discussion of sorts above, before moving on to unification. Given two AVSs S_1 and S_2, S_1 SUBSUMES S_2 ('$S_1 \succeq S_2$') if it is more general than S_2.[28] We could also say that S_1 expresses less information than S_2, or that S_2 is more specific and therefore picks out fewer entities in the world. (1.5a) subsumes (1.5b) since (1.5a) contains no more attributes than (1.5b) and (for the attribute they have in common) the sort *boolean* subsumes the sort +. Similarly (1.5b) subsumes (1.5c) since (1.5b) has fewer attributes and (for the attribute they have in common), + subsumes +. So we see that structures are related by subsumption just as sorts are.

(1.5)   Patterns of subsumption

a. $[\text{NASAL } boolean]$

b. $[\text{NASAL } +]$

c. $\begin{bmatrix} \text{NASAL} & + \\ \text{CORONAL} & \top \end{bmatrix}$

(1.5a) can describe both nasals and non-nasals, but only those structures capable of bearing some value at all for a nasal attribute. (1.5b) characterises all nasals and (1.5c) all coronal nasals.

The UNIFICATION $S_1 \sqcap S_2$ of two structures S_1, S_2 is basically their *union*, with the proviso that the result is itself a well-formed structure. In a subsumption lattice of structures, the meet of two structures is their unification. This lattice is based on the sort lattice in the obvious way, so the meet of two AVSs such as [NASAL +] and [NASAL −] is ⊥ because the unification of + and − in (1.3) is ⊥. Unification can be interpreted as an operation which takes features structures as input and returns a feature structure containing all and only the information of the inputs, unless the output is ⊥, in which case unification fails. But this is a procedural interpretation of a relation expressed declaratively in the lattice. The unification of two AVSs S_1 and S_2 is merely another AVS S_3 — see (1.6) — the most general AVS which is subsumed by both S_1 and S_2.

Introduction

Notationally, $S_3 = S_1 \sqcap S_2$ if and only if S_3 is the most general structure such that $S_1 \succeq S_3$ and $S_2 \succeq S_3$.

(1.6) Generalised subsumption lattice of structures

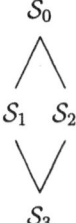

The following biconditionals express the standard relationship between $\succeq$, $\sqcap$, $\sqcup$.

$S_i \succeq S_j \text{ iff } S_i \sqcup S_j = S_i$

$S_i \succeq S_j \text{ iff } S_i \sqcap S_j = S_j$

In (1.6), $S_0 \succeq S_1$, $S_0 \succeq S_2$, $S_1 \succeq S_3$, $S_2 \succeq S_3$.

(1.7) Possible values for (1.6)

a. $S_1 = \begin{bmatrix} \text{HIGH} + \end{bmatrix}$

b. $S_2 = \begin{bmatrix} \text{LOW} - \end{bmatrix}$

c. $S_3 = \begin{bmatrix} \text{HIGH} + \\ \text{LOW} - \end{bmatrix}$

d. $S_0 = [\,]$

If it is said that the unification of (1.7a) and (1.7b) is (1.7c), it must be remembered that this does not indicate a process whereby (1.7a) and (1.7b) combine to give (1.7c) but is a simple statement of truth (or falsity). The constraint that all linguistic objects describable by (1.7a) must also be describable by (1.7c) does not necessitate a rule adding (1.7b), though it often convenient to talk of two structures 'unifying.'

It is informative to look at the unification of two structures which are the values of different paths within the same feature structure. When the values of two paths are unified, the paths share a value which corresponds to the most general structure to subsume both the 'inputs.' For a highly simplified example, suppose we constrain feature structures so that in every case their melody must unify with their syllable's nucleus if the melody is /a/ (a low vowel). It so happens that our structure's syllable's nucleus is specified as /H/ (high tone). Each structure in (1.8a) contributes some information, and thanks to our constraint this information is unified in (1.8b).[29]

(1.8)   a. $\begin{bmatrix} \text{MELODY} & [/a/] \\ \text{SYLLABLE} & [\text{NUCLEUS } [/H/]] \end{bmatrix}$

   b. $\begin{bmatrix} \text{MELODY } \boxed{1} & \begin{bmatrix} /H/ \\ /a/ \end{bmatrix} \\ \text{SYLLABLE} & [\text{NUCLEUS}\boxed{1}] \end{bmatrix}$

In effect (1.8b) indicates that /a/ is given a high tone if it is syllabified into a nucleus where the nucleus is itself high tone. Note that using unification to express this relationship between vowel quality, syllabification and tone ensures the information can only be combined if it is compatible. A low toned /a/ cannot be syllabified into a high tone nucleus. This exemplifies a basic reason for adopting unification as the prime operation on phonological structures — preserving information consistently like this is a basic requirement of any phonological theory.

The syllabification rule might be a simple constraint or TEMPLATE like (1.9). As discussed in the text, it merely states that a melody and a nucleus's melody share the same value. Though not shown, unification demands that the shared structure must have a unifyable sort, in this case *melody*. Using *boolean-high* and *boolean-round etc* means that the values of attributes like HIGH and

Introduction

ROUND are unable to unify. (1.9) is a highly simplified example (it describes a language in which each melody constitutes a syllable!) but it should give the basis of an understanding of the possibilities of unification.

(1.9) $\begin{bmatrix} \text{MELODY} & \boxed{1} \\ \text{SYLLABLE} & \begin{bmatrix} \text{NUCLEUS}\boxed{1} \end{bmatrix} \end{bmatrix}$

The constraint in (1.9) is represented in the same form as I represent feature structures, rather than using a description language particular to partial descriptions of feature structures, and indeed it is quite possible to treat (1.9) as an AVS. All such templates in the grammar must unify (together with material from the lexicon) to produce well-formed representations. Templates like this are less common than conditional negative or disjunctive constraints, however, and these are more easily interpreted as partial descriptions of the final representation than as representations themselves which all unify in a specified manner.[30] Templates are then also interpreted in this manner.

Generalisations are often conditional in form:

- If a structure is a low vowel, then it *must* be the nucleus of its syllable and not a glide.

In this case a conditional constraint is used. The notation for this is shown in (1.10).[31]

(1.10) $\begin{bmatrix} \text{MELODY}|\text{PLACE}|\text{DORSAL}|\text{LOW}+ \end{bmatrix} \longrightarrow$

$\begin{bmatrix} \text{MELODY} & \boxed{1} \\ \text{SYLLABLE}|\text{NUCLEUS}\boxed{1} \end{bmatrix}$

The most important distinction between (1.10) and the analogous rule in AP is that the 'rule' of (1.10) is indistinguishable from (1.9). Either both are interpreted as representations or as descriptions of representations. If the former, the propositional connectives form part of the formal syntax of attribute value structures, and (1.10) constitutes a complex sort of structure. It unifies with another structure S in a special way. If the antecedent of (1.10) does not subsume S then the unification is just S. If the antecedent *does* subsume S, then the unification of (1.10) and S is equal to the unification of the consequent of (1.10) and S. (1.10) and (1.9) are equivalent because of the interdefinability of the propositional connectives — (1.9) can be rewritten as the conditional (1.11) because ⊤ unifies with every structure. The antecedent is vacuous.

(1.11) $\quad \top \rightarrow \begin{bmatrix} \text{MELODY} & \boxed{1} \\ \text{SYLLABLE} & \begin{bmatrix} \text{NUCLEUS}\boxed{1} \end{bmatrix} \end{bmatrix}$

Another common form of constraint is the negative constraint or FEATURE CO-OCCURRENCE RESTRICTION ('FCR'). $\neg S$ is true if S is false, so a constraint $\neg S$ unifies with all structures whose unification with S is ⊥. If there is a constraint that no structure be high *and* low, then the restriction (1.12) is part of the pool of constraints. The pool remains consistent so long as every structure lacks the combination of [HIGH +] and [LOW +].

(1.12) $\quad \neg \begin{bmatrix} \text{HIGH} + \\ \text{LOW} + \end{bmatrix}$

Despite the term FCR, there is no real distinction between 'negative' and 'positive' constraints. FCRs, templates and conditional constraints are all interdefined and often interchangeable. For a second example of this, consider the conditional generalisation

- If a melody structure is a midvowel, it must be non-nasal.

This can be expressed by a conditional constraint.[32]

$$\begin{pmatrix} [\text{LOW}-] \\ [\text{HIGH}-] \end{pmatrix} \longrightarrow ([\text{NASAL}-])$$

Because of the logical nature of the system the generalisation above is equivalent to

Introduction

- No melody structure can be a midvowel and nasal.

which is the natural interpretation of the FCR

$$\neg \begin{pmatrix} [\text{LOW}-] \\ [\text{HIGH}-] \\ [\text{NASAL}+] \end{pmatrix}$$

In fact, parallel to the equivalence of S and $\top \to S$, $\neg S$ is equivalent to the implication $S \to \bot$.

For a final example of a complex constraint consider a disjunction: $S_1 \vee S_2$. This is interpretable either as a partial description of two structures or as a disjunctive structure itself. (The atomic structure *boolean* is similarly no more than a shorthand for the disjunction $(+ \vee -)$, but one provided for in the sort lattice.) See the sources given at the beginning of the section for further discussion.

1.4.5 Type and token identity

If an attribute is defined but has no specific value, this is symbolised with $\top$, the maximally general structure. It is important to note that two attributes with some value $\top$ do not necessarily indicate the *same* maximally underspecified structure. If we add specifications to one, this does not necessarily indicate that the other is similarly specified. We have to be careful when taking of the 'same' structure. We need to distinguish between TOKEN IDENTICAL structures and merely TYPE IDENTICAL ones.

When the values of two paths are unified the paths necessarily share token identical values. (See also (1.8b) above.) In (1.13) the index variable $\boxed{1}$ shows that the two different matrices have a token identical value for the A paths, in other words that their values are unified. The values for the B paths are merely type identical.

(1.13) $\begin{bmatrix} \text{A}\boxed{1} \\ \text{B}+ \end{bmatrix} \begin{bmatrix} \text{A}\boxed{1} \\ \text{B}+ \end{bmatrix}$

It is instructive to use a graphical notation at this point: we can see token identity is revealed as RE-ENTRANCY (1.14a), where

34 Autosegmental Representation in a Declarative Framework

two arcs (corresponding to two paths) point to the same value. (A value is the material located at a vertex.) Type identity involves no such sharing of structure (1.14b).

(1.14)   a.   b.

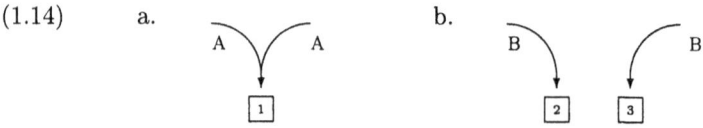

If in (1.14a) we unify + and [1] (*i.e.* specify [1] to be +) then both paths terminating in [1] have that one value. If we unify [2] and [3] in (1.14b) then the values of the path do not change (both are maximally underspecified) but we now know that they represent necessarily the *same* object, even though it is maximally underspecified. AVP allows structure to be shared, no matter how underspecified it may be. Two segments may each have a maximally general value for their PLACE attributes, but nevertheless the value can be constrained to be the *same* for each segment.

This sharing of structure is directly comparable to the many-to-one associations in autosegmental diagrams. In fact AVP uses re-entrancy to reconstruct multiple association, and the distinction between tokens and types will be of great importance.

1.4.6 The sign

Before moving on to a discussion of AVP itself I will introduce Pollard & Sag's conception of the relationship between the major linguistic levels, which AVP adopts. The approach is a development of the rule-to-rule hypothesis of Bach (1976) (and claims the ancestry of Saussure 1915). In sign-based grammar, every constituent, whether it be a morpheme or sentence, is described by a special sort of attribute-value structure which serves to relate the various linguistic levels, the SIGN:

$$(1.15) \quad sign\begin{bmatrix} \text{PHON} & \top \\ \text{CAT} & \top \\ \text{SEM} & \top \end{bmatrix}$$

A sign partitions a grammatical unit into (at least) phonological, categorial (syntactic) and semantic components. Signs

Introduction   35

can describe words, sentences, and principles of grammar. The principles (they could be called rules) are, therefore, highly underspecified representations, although they have a different use: a sign for a rule must unify with the sign expressing the lexical content of, say, a phrase, imposing dependencies within that sign as well as perhaps adding content. I have little to add about the relationship of phonology to the other modules of grammar other than note that a sign-based grammatical architecture offers opportunities for a re-evaluation of the traditional views of the syntax-phonology interface. Interesting results have come from the parallel re-evaluation of the syntax-semantics interface in HPSG and UCG.

Notes

[1] The meaning of term 'constraint' in declarative approaches can differ from its meaning elsewhere. All phonological statements, indeed all grammatical statements, limit the universe of linguistic objects being described. A lexical entry is a partial description of a linguistic object — it imposes constraints on what that object may be. So does the context of utterance, universal aspects of syntactic organisation and language specific phonological factors. All add to the pool of constraints.

[2] In fact I reject the current conception of geminate inalterability altogether, hence the quote marks in the text. This rejection amounts to treating geminates and nongeminates alike.

[3] The more informal a theory is, the fewer grounds there are for making the distinction. Even the status of generative theories can be unclear.

[4] Such statements capture facts such as the impossibility of an English syllable beginning [fn]. This is a *phonological* constraint — there is no bar on the phonetic realisation of a word like *phonetic* being something like [fnetik].

[5] There are sporadic proposals. For example, Calabrese (1987):

> my idea is that when the metaphony rule applies to lax mid vowels, it creates a lax high vowel. This lax high vowel is disallowed in Salentino and therefore it must be cleaned up. In order to treat these facts...I will use filters that block configurations of phonological features. In order to prevent configurations that violate

these filters, clean up rules change these configurations into allowed ones...
A feature filling rule ... is blocked by a filter. A feature changing rule ... is instead allowed to apply even if the feature configuration that it produces is blocked by a filter — the clean up rules will fix it later.

[6] Singh (1987:273) also concludes that "the appropriate response to Postal's redundancy objection is to eliminate phonological rules." Singh, like Calabrese, permits representations to be created by the phonology which are ill-formed, and then uses repair strategies to "fix or alleviate their violations as and when they arise." He also allows phonotactics to act as filters, however, and so must deal with the problem of the the interaction of filters and repair-strategy-triggers. If 'repair strategies' are nonmonotonic then obviously Singh's approach is incompatible with that presented here, but it could be that all such 'repair strategies' merely *add* information, in which case they are exactly like the conditional constraints presented below. 'Ill-formed' would mean 'not certain to be well-formed' in such an instance.

[7] I should also mention the programming environment in which many of the above can be expressed: PATR-II (Shieber *et al* 1983).

[8] Some advances in *computational* phonology have been made, but such work is often concerned with practical issues such as speech synthesis and speech input. The impact of current phonological theories on such work is negligible compared to the place of syntactic theories in relation to parsing. See for example the computationally sophisticated but essentially linear and morphophonological Kimmo (Koskenniemi 1983). An exception is the work on intonation and tone by Pierrehumbert & Beckman (1988). In addition to this thesis, Bird (1990a;1990b); Bird & Klein (1990); Broe (*in preparation*); Waksler (1990) and Klein & Calder (1987) investigate aspects of declarative phonology. See also Wheeler (1988).

[9] Of course movement towards a target does not imply the target will be reached.

[10] Conditional templates would be required which, if their antecedent matched some portion of the skeleton, would require that their consequent did too. As far as I am aware, templates are not currently permitted to be conditional.

Introduction 37

[11] See Broe (1988) for a very interesting account of the historical development *from* Firth's British School *to* Unification-Based Grammar.

[12] Although I am drawing the distinction between a constraint (stated in a description language) and the structure indicated by the pool of constraints, this is not a necessary step. A simple constraint such as the structure S 'describes' itself. Constraints are said to partially describe an AVS in order to avoid the formal complexities that result from viewing conditional or negative constraints as being AVSs themselves.

[13] I will assume that the phonetic objects described by phonology are scores for articulatory planning and the parsing of psychoacoustic input rather than actual acoustic signals, but nothing crucial depends on this assumption.

[14] The same story could be told for the acoustic correlates of this articulatory description.

[15] That we would want to call such vertical slices through time 'segments' is quite another matter.

[16] I accept their arguments that a wide range of so-called phonological alternations are best described by invoking gestural overlap. I do not accept the conclusion that phonology is therefore gestural — instead I take their arguments as evidence that the alternations in question are not phonological.

[17] I would opt for English-specific voice onset statements as part of the panoply of phonetic implementation statements rather than B&G's sophisticated yet still segmental phonetic [l̥].

[18] Of course this begs the question of exactly *how* phonological structures describe the phonetic gestural score, whether they be phonemes, morae or syllables. The details of phonetic implementation are as yet little understood, but basically this is an empirical, not a theoretical problem. It is important that these two aspects of research proceed contemporaneously, however.

[19] The reason for the disclaimer is that "while phonetic reality may motivate a phonological representation, it neither justifies nor ultimately explains it" (Goldsmith 1990:10). This of course is correct, but it does not follow that association lines cannot mean simultaneity phonologically.

[20] Of course the language learner may restructure the underlying system in the acquisition process because this is the simplest way to replicate observed phonetic behaviour.

[21] The matrix has no theoretical significance — it is merely a com-

mon way of *drawing* structures. Drawings are difficult to formalise directly.

[22] For reasons given below, the sort *boolean* in (1.2) is shorthand for *boolean-back* and + is shorthand for *+high*.

[23] Recall that *boolean* is shorthand for *boolean-high, boolean-low* etc.

[24] There is no object which it describes, by definition.

[25] It partially describes every object since it gives no information.

[26] Kasper & Rounds (1986) define an AVS as a conjunction of atomically-valued paths, a definition equivalent to one based on attributes and their AVS values. They are not concerned with the use of AVSs in phonology, however, and I suggest an amendment to their definition below to make it suitable for AVP.

[27] The orientation of (1.4) is irrelevant and it could as easily be drawn with the root to the top or bottom as is common in phonological representations. Moreover the use of straight lines has no significance. Finally note that the status of the *labial* vertex differs from that of the *boolean* and + vertices since the latter two are atomic structures. How we know that the value of LABIAL can have a ROUND attribute but that the value of HIGH cannot is dealt with by the definition of AVSs, as we see below.

[28] Actually, S_1 must be at least as general as S_2 in order that a structure subsumes itself. (Subsumption is reflexive in addition to being transitive and asymmetric.) I generally ignore this in the text to aid readability.

[29] Note that in (1.8) the index $\boxed{1}$ shows the two paths share a single value. The choice of the location(s) at which $\boxed{1}$ is expanded is not significant. The semantic interpretation of an AVS is sensitive only to indices and their content, not *where* an index is expanded. This avoids the problems Itô observes in Hayes's diagramatic use of matrices (Hayes 1990:62–64).

[30] A structure ¬S would unify with all structures which do not unify with S, with result S.

[31] Recall that I have used a common abbreviatory convention in (1.10) to avoid a great deal of nested brackets: [DORSAL|HIGH +] is merely a shorthand for $\left[\text{DORSAL}\left[\text{HIGH}+\right]\right]$.

[32] Much structure is elided to save space. The round brackets indicate that the enclosed substructures form part of the one structure. A unique path which begins [MELODY] dominates each substructure and so their position in the hierarchy is predictable. The same structure is described in either side of the implication arrow. See below.

Chapter 2

Attribute Value Phonology

2.1 Hierarchy

2.1.1 Feature hierarchies

In the phonological literature the idea of a hierarchy of features is proposed to capture the range of possible feature interactions (see, for example, Clements 1985). For instance the features *high*, *back*, *low* characterising positions of the dorsal section of the tongue often pattern together, in that phonological generalisations require reference to the '*dorsal* features'.[1] Clements captures these patterns by making features such as *back* leaves of a feature tree, and making them daughters of a *class* (nonterminal) node labelled *dorsal*. Rules can then refer to the class node rather than a conjunction of its daughters.

(2.1)

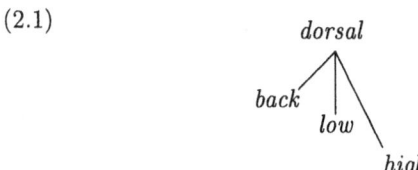

Autosegmental Representation in a Declarative Framework

Sort	Attribute	Value's sort
root:	MELODY	melody
	SYLLABLE	syllable
melody:	PLACE	place
	LARYNGEAL	laryngeal
	NASAL	boolean
	CONT	boolean
	STOP	boolean
	SONORANT	boolean
place:	CORONAL	coronal
	DORSAL	dorsal
	LABIAL	labial
	TONGUE-ROOT	tongue-root
dorsal:	HIGH	boolean
	LOW	boolean
	BACK	boolean
coronal:	STRIDENT	boolean
	ANTERIOR	boolean
	DISTRIBUTED	boolean
labial:	ROUND	boolean
tongue-root:	ATR	boolean

Table 2.1: Partial Sort Assignment

Although there remains controversy over the substantive content of the feature hierarchy, the point to note is that attribute-value structures are highly suitable for the representation of hierarchy. All that is needed to model (2.1) is to assign the structure (2.2a) as the value to a class attribute DORSAL as in (2.2b).

(2.2) a. $\begin{bmatrix} \text{HIGH} & \top \\ \text{BACK} & \top \\ \text{LOW} & \top \end{bmatrix}$ b. $\begin{bmatrix} \text{DORSAL} & \begin{bmatrix} \text{HIGH} & \top \\ \text{BACK} & \top \\ \text{LOW} & \top \end{bmatrix} \end{bmatrix}$

To do this, and to ensure that no attributes other than HIGH, BACK and LOW can be specified as part of the value of DORSAL, a 'sort assignment' (Table 2.1) is used.

Attribute Value Phonology   41

Such an assignment defines the feature hierarchy, and imposes a sort (not shown in (2.2)) on each structure.² I do not intend to defend a particular hierarchy, and give Table 2.1 as a partial example only. Various proposals about syllable structure are made in the course of the text.

The sort *melody* is PARTITIONED into the subsorts *cons* and *vowel*, which can be expressed in this way:

melody → *cons* ∨ *vowel*
¬(*cons* ∧ *vowel*)

I used a sort lattice above to express such facts above, and (2.3) expresses this.

(2.3)   Part of the subsumption lattice of sorts

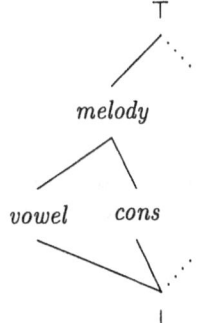

The choice of these subsorts determines the melodic content of the structure and its syllabification possibilities. (2.3) can encode a three-way distinction between the nonalternating *vowel* /a/, the nonalternating *cons*-onant /t/ and the underspecified *melody* /u~w/. Such glide~vowel alternations are discussed briefly below.

If an attribute-value pair is of the form [ATTR *boolean-attr*], *i.e.*, the sort of the value is that given in the sort assignment, which is the most general it can be, then the value of ATTR is UNSPECIFIED. By extension a class node is unspecified if each of its daughters is unspecified. The difference between LABIAL being unspecified for ROUND is quite different from it not being specifiable for VOICE. The latter option is not permitted by sort assignment, while the former case simply means that there is no evidence to posit any value more specific than *boolean* as the value of ROUND.

Diagrams can be used to express such partial specifications, and so $_{labial}[\ ]$, or [LABIAL⊤] act as shorthand for

$$_{labial}[\text{ROUND } boolean\text{-}round]$$

2.1.2 The root matrix

In AVP a phonological description is a sequence of (well-formed) attribute-value structures. More precisely, the value of the phonology attribute PHON consists of a set of unordered $\langle index, \text{AVS}\rangle$ pairs. The sequential nature of the phonological representation is captured by imposing an ordering on the indices.[3] In turn, this enables us to discuss the ordering of two AVSs S, S' themselves, given the conventions that S precedes S' if and only if $\langle i, S\rangle$ precedes $\langle j, S'\rangle$, and that $\langle i, S\rangle$ precedes $\langle j, S'\rangle$ if and only if i precedes j. An important aspect of the sequence of matrices is that two structures with the same index are equivalent to a single complex structure which is the unification of the two.[4]

(2.4) shows a schematic set of $\langle index, \text{AVS}\rangle$ pairs, together with the ordering of the indices expressing their sequencing.

(2.4) $\{\langle i, S\rangle, \langle j, S'\rangle \ldots\}$

$i \prec j \ldots$

Each structure in (2.4) has the sort *root*. The attribute-value matrix (AVM) is the main notational form I will use to represent structures, and so I will call each of these indexed structures a ROOT MATRIX.[5] In AVP every phonological representation consists of a weakly ordered set of root matrices. The sort *root* can be partitioned into *vowel* and *cons*, so by extension it is possible to refer to the sequence of vowel roots *etc.*

Since every phonological representation consists of a sequence of root matrices, it is convenient to think of the root matrix as being rather like a segment. The partial specification of an attribute-value structure may be extreme, and in fact a structure might consist of only a single path. In such a case, the nonbranching root structure (path) corresponds as much to the traditional feature as

Attribute Value Phonology 43

it does to the highly underspecified segments of AP (see Goldsmith 1985). A sequence of root matrices can even be seen as a sequence of syllables. The root matrix is the primitive formal phonological unit to undergo sequencing and thus constitutes a basic phonological unit, whatever use it is put to.

(2.5) shows the notation I will use for the root sequence as an alternative to the set notation of (2.4). No explicit indication of the index or sort is required, and linear order suffices to indicate precedence in most cases, *i.e.* when the indices are linearly ordered themselves. When the looseness of ordering given by the weak ordering is required, the set notation can be re-introduced.

(2.5)
$$_{sign}\left[\text{PHON}\langle [\ ], [\ ], \ldots [\ ]\rangle\right]$$

AVP provides a framework in which the Root matrix 'segment' is uniquely privileged relative to other *unindexed* attribute-value structures. In this way it is more similar to Chomsky & Halle (1968) than Goldsmith (1976), yet, thanks to the ability of root matrices to *share* substructure, strict segmentation is not forced on the formalism (see below).

2.1.3 Syllable structure

The word *Andy* is typically seen as a sequence of four segments and two syllables. (2.6) shows a schematic AP-style syllabification with one subsegmental tier, the *place* tier, included. Sometimes it is stated that the lines indicating syllable membership (linking the formally different from the association lines linking root and *place* tiers.[6]

(2.6)   AP syllabification of *Andy*

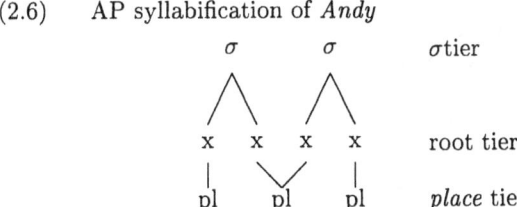

However, the inference that the differences between segment and syllable require the formal characteristics of the 'lines' to differ is not a necessary one. In HPSG both syntactic constituent structure and category structure are represented formally by dominance in an attribute-value structure. AVP adopts a similar approach for prosodic constituency and sub-segmental structure (see §3.4).

In AVP each root matrix has two attributes, MELODY and SYLLABLE, which express melodic structure and syllabification respectively. MELODY and SYLLABLE are sister attributes, so are equally basic components of the root matrix. Generally syllable structure is regarded as a framework built over an underlying sequence of segments, but there is no reason for such directionality to be followed in AVP. The attribute-value representations represent both subsegmental and prosodic structure in the same way. The framework requires a constraint-based approach to syllabification which does not rely on a bank of ordered rules, but instead uses phonotactic co-occurrence statements to express dependencies between particular syllabic functions and particular melodies.[7]

To exemplify the framework I will present a schematic account of syllable structure based loosely on the moraic/demisyllable aspects of Goldsmith (1990). I propose that the value of SYLLABLE is a structure with sort *syllable*, partitioned into two subsorts, *light-σ* and *heavy-σ*.

syllable → *heavy-σ* ∨ *light-σ*

¬(*heavy-σ* ∧ *light-σ*)

Since the *light-σ* and *heavy-σ* subsorts inherit the attributes assigned to the more general *syllable* but not *vice versa*, we can specify in the syllable structure sort assignment, Table 2.2, that an attribute ε-SYLL (with value of sort *mora2*) is applicable only in the case of heavy syllables.

Thus the value of SYLL has two attributes if its sort is *light-σ* and three attributes if and only if it is *heavy-σ*. If it is merely *syll* it has two attributes but is compatible with having ε-SYLL, the third, if and only if the appropriate subsort is selected. This assignment effectively divides the syllable into two parts; an obligatory CV mora and an optional mora *mora2* This second mora is a reversed

Attribute Value Phonology

Sort	ATTRIBUTE	Value's sort
syllable:	ONSET	*melody*
	NUCLEUS	*melody*
heavy-σ:	ε-SYLL	*mora2*
mora2:	NUCLEUS	*melody*
	CODA	*melody*

Table 2.2: Partial Sort Assignment

and weakened echo of the first; hence 'ε-SYLL'. This assignment incorporates four syllabic functions: onset, nucleus, off-glide and coda consonant.

Re-entrancy is central to the representation of prosodic constituency in AVP, for tautosyllabic roots are those which share a value of SYLLABLE. Recall that re-entrancy is indicated by a boxed index in the matrix-style diagram (not to be confused with the sequencing index paired with $_{root}[\ ]$). Syllabification rules express relations like; 'if a *cons* precedes a *vowel* then they share the value of SYLL in which the former is the onset and the latter the nucleus'. Conditional constraints are used to express such phonotactics:

(2.7) Simple syllabification rule

$$\left\langle \left[\text{MELODY } _{cons}[\ ]\right], \left[\text{MELODY } _{vowel}[\ ]\right]\right\rangle \longrightarrow$$

$$\left\langle \begin{bmatrix} \text{MELODY} \boxed{1} \\ \text{SYLL} \quad \boxed{2} \end{bmatrix}, \begin{bmatrix} \text{MELODY} \boxed{3} \\ \text{SYLL} \boxed{2} \begin{bmatrix} \text{ONSET} \quad \boxed{1} \\ \text{NUCLEUS} \boxed{3} \end{bmatrix} \end{bmatrix} \right\rangle$$

For an example of how syllable structure is represented in this approach, consider again the word *Andy*. In AVP the sequence of structures corresponding to (2.6) is (2.8). In this sequence of roots each root's melody is different, although there is a shared place of articulation ($\boxed{4}$). While this sharing (of a $_{place}[\ ]$ structure) indicates a subsegmental dependency within the consonant cluster, the sharing of $_{syll}[\ ]$ indicates co-syllabicity. Note how a segment's

46   Autosegmental Representation in a Declarative Framework

Sort	Attribute	Value's sort
i-:	INITIAL	cons
-f:	APPENDIX	cons

Table 2.3: Partial Sort Assignment

syllable's nucleus can be identified, by following the appropriate path through the feature structures.

(2.8)   AVP syllabification of *Andy*

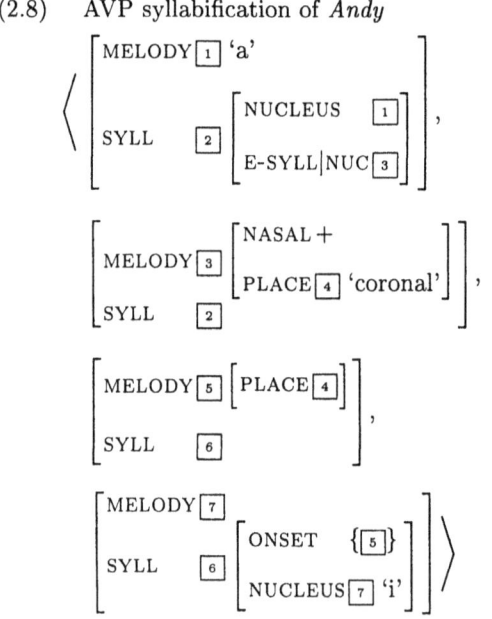

Before moving on I will consider a further example of the use of sorts. It is often observed that in English word margins permit a greater accumulation of consonants than is possible word internally. The functional reason for this is that consonant-only affixes have to accommodated. In addition to *heavy-σ* and *light-σ* we can recognise two word-boundary sorts, *i-* and *-f* — for word initial and word final 'extrametrical' clusters.

Attribute Value Phonology

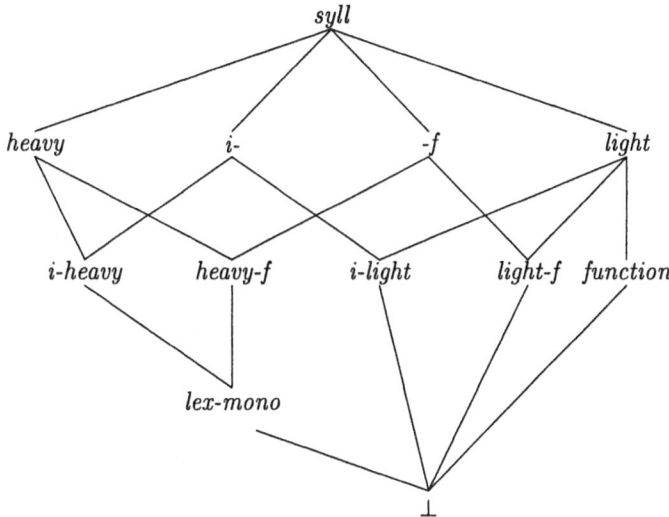

Figure 2.1: Partial Subsumption Lattice of Sorts

Table 2.3 shows that these subsorts add extra attributes to allow the syllable to encompass those consonants which do not occur word-medially, as found in past tense /t/, /d/ plural /s/, /z/ and so on.[8] A word-final syllable will have sort *-f* rather than *syll* and attributes ONSET, NUCLEUS, ε-SYLL and APPENDIX.

Figure 2.1 expresses the relationships between the various sorts mentioned above. For example, though a syllable cannot be both heavy and light, it is able to bear both initial and final extrametrical segments: this would be a monosyllabic word *lex-mono*. Word initial and word final syllables may be heavy or light, giving four possible interactions. In addition the sort *function* is assigned to a light syllable which is not a phonological word, one which does not bear stress or syllable appendix material. Function words such as *the*, *a*, *to* can be analysed as consisting of such a syllable. If a syllable is both initial and final in a *word* then it must be a lexical monosyllable *lex-mono*, capable of bearing stress and hence a subsort of *heavy*.

Pollard & Sag (1987) recognise a partition of *sign* into *phrasal sign* and *lexical sign*. One way on which this information could be used phonologically is to assign to the final syllable of every lexical sign the sort *-f* and *i-* to the initial one.

In order to be well-formed every melody in AVP must be dominated by the SYLLABLE attribute. Given the ability of Sort Assignment to assign extra attributes to subsorts, *the syllable itself* (in the form of one of its various subsorts) can act as the prosodic domain for word (and phrase) boundary distributions which would normally be classified as extrasyllabic. I think this is preferable to the alternatives: Clements & Keyser (1983) and many others who posit an appendix daughter to the syllable, but offer no account of what governs its appearance; Borowsky (1989), who postulates a derivational model in which a 'coda constraint' is 'switched off' allowing peripheral unsyllabifyable material to be incorporated; Goldsmith (1990), who proposes that the word-boundary clusters are not syllabified at all but attached directly to the (prosodic) word.

Even though the substantive details of Figure 2.1 are somewhat tentative, I feel confident of the ability of sort subsumption lattices to capture insightful subregularities, as they do in syntactic and semantic theories (Wedekind 1990). Sorts offer a suitable formalism in which to express the treatments suggested in the preceding paragraph.

2.2 Sequence

2.2.1 The essential sequence: the skeleton

Some characterisation of the sequence of phonological features is obviously an essential part of any phonological theory. As noted above, AVP adopts a sequence of root matrices: the value of PHON is a set of pairs $\langle i, _{root}[\ ]\rangle$, i an index. The indices are weakly ordered by the transitive, reflexive and antisymmetric relation of PRECEDENCE '$\prec^*$'. $\prec^*$ is the transitive closure of '$\prec$', the relation of IMMEDIATE PRECEDENCE. The weak ordering of indices (and hence roots) defines the SKELETON. The question arises as to whether substructures of the root should be sequenced, and if they are,

Attribute Value Phonology 49

what benefits and disadvantages arise. It is in this area that some of the greatest differences between AP and AVP exist.

In AVP there is no sequence other than the skeleton. In other words, indices are assigned to $_{sort}[\ ]$ if and only if *sort* = *root* (or one of its subsorts). This is quite different from Autosegmental Phonology. AP postulates subtiers such as the *place* tier, consisting of a sequence of *place* features, in which case AVP would require some kind of index percolation from one node to another (see Halle & Vergnaud 1980; Hayes 1990). Moreover in AP a sequence of *root* nodes can dominate a single *place* node, and conversely a single *root* node can dominate a sequence of features in a complex segment (2.9).[9] Allowing both types of multiple association demands tiers with intrinsic ordering — simple index percolation could not deal with this.

(2.9) One-many and many-one associations in AP

AVP uses SHARING to account for a single $_{place}[\ ]$ structure being dominated by a sequence of roots (*cf* (2.9b)), and this does not require any extra indices assigned to $_{place}[\ ]$ structures. But the corresponding situation (used in the analysis of contour segments such as affricates) — that some MELODY attribute could dominate the structures [NASAL +] *and* [NASAL -] — is *impossible*. This is because only one instance of any given attribute may be specified for a structure, or, equivalently, because the values of each instance of an attribute leaving a node must unify.[10]

The abandonment of sub-tier ordering does not result in the total loss of the expressive power of Autosegmental Phonology, because representations like that in (2.9b) are still possible. When a $_{place}[\ ]$ structure is shared by two roots, there is no need for an ordering index on $_{place}[\ ]$ (2.10).

(2.10) Re-entrancy to analyse multiple association in AVP

$$\left\{\langle i, \left[\text{MELODY}|\text{PLACE}\boxed{1}\right]\rangle, \langle j, \left[\text{MELODY}|\text{PLACE}\boxed{1}\right]\rangle\right\}$$
$$i \prec j$$

The paths dominating this structure have indices i and j. The $_{place}[\ ]$ structure $\boxed{1}$ is shared by paths emanating at i and j.[11]

The claim being made here is that it is not necessary for phonology to make use of autonomous subordered tiers. On the one hand, the sharing of structure (2.10) can capture one type of multiple association (2.9b). On the other, the very existence of ordered features within contour segments is empirically dubious in any case. We must doubt the necessity of a phonological sequence such as (2.9a), *e.g.* $[-cont][+cont]$, for two reasons.

- First of all, despite the claims of Sagey (1986), there are no phonological 'edge-effects' (in affricates at least, the most studied case). Lombardi (1990) shows that $[+cont]$, say, is equally accessible from left or right, and not rendered invisible by an intervening $[-cont]$.

- Secondly, the phonetic ordering of the exponents of the features seem always to be predictable: the order stop-fricative is always found in central and lateral affricates; nasal-stop segments are contextually predictable; pre-aspiration and post-aspiration are similarly predictable from the surrounding segments (see Kingston 1990; Clements 1990; Ohala 1990).

To ban subtier ordering as shown in (2.9a) is to make a strong predictive claim which at present appears to be substantiated.

In AP it is tacitly acknowledged that finding a definition of well-formed structures is problematic given the posited existence of contour segments. That is why the contradictory specifications are put onto an autonomously ordered subtier. Phonological sequence is involved (mirroring phonetic sequence) just so that AP can maintain that no single structure can be $[+F]$ and $[-F]$. AP allows itself the freedom for a class feature in the feature hierarchy to be able to dominate contradictory features, but does so if and only

Attribute Value Phonology

if the potential contradiction is somehow avoided by *sequencing* the features. Due to the lack of formalisation, it is unclear whether this ability of AP is a notational convention, a proper theoretical insight, or an *ad hoc* addition to the theory the consequences of which are not fully comprehended.[12]

2.2.2 Tiers: sequences of paths

Chomsky & Halle (1968) proposed a theory based on a sequence of matrices (2.11a), which were unable to capture nonlinear phonological information. Goldsmith (1976) advocated multiple tiers (2.11b) in order to solve this problem, but much of the motivation for (2.11b) depends on the unsuitability of the SPE approach. In the section above I presented AVP's approach, which sequences only the root of the feature hierarchy, but uses shared substructure to solve the representational inadequacies of SPE (2.11c). The value of A in (2.11c) is shared, like that in (2.11b), but without statements of precedence referring to A. Only the outermost root matrices are sequenced ($i \prec j$), parallel to (2.11a). Recall from §1.4 that '+' in (2.11c) is a single token, hence the boxed index, while the '+' values in (2.11a) are distinct tokens.

(2.11)   Sequences of identical structures in 3 theories

   a. (SPE) $[+A]_i[+A]_j$

   b. (AP)   i   j   root tier
                    \ /
                     +   A tier

   c. (AVP) $\left[A\boxed{1}+ \right]_i \left[A\boxed{1}+ \right]_j$

This does not mean, however, that the notion of 'tier' developed in AP is lost. Tiers can be addressed in AVP, but they are not the autonomous fundamental constituents of a theory of phonological sequence which Autosegmental Phonology makes them. This is because a submatrix like [HIGH +] does not enter directly into a phonological sequence. Only the *path* which terminates with HIGH is sequenced. It is as if [HIGH +] *inherits* ordering from the root, though no percolation convention is required (*cf* Scobbie 1988).

Paths bear an index because they all originate at an indexed root. Indeed paths are merely nonbranching root matrices. In AVP, if a structure [HIGH +] is to be part of any sequence, then it is part of the skeletal sequence, and an attempt to define the *high* tier must take this into account. Such a tier is *part* of the skeleton. In AP, features can be sequenced, so FEATURES must be defined in AVP to be paths, not submatrices like [HIGH +]. In AP a TIER is a sequence of features of the same type — the same definition can be used in AVP.

A feature is merely a highly underspecified segment — a segment whose only specified structure is [HIGH +]. While arbitrary attribute-value pairs are distinct from the segment-like sequence of roots, the feature/segment relationship is clearly one of degree in AVP. Each is a partial description. This can be seen in the graphical representation of two paths in (2.12b). Recall that in such graphs arcs are labelled with attributes and the vertices to which the arcs point are labelled with values. In matrix notation the paths

$$S_1, S_2 = [\text{MELODY}|\text{PLACE}|\text{DORSAL}|\text{HIGH}+]$$

are sequenced as the value of PHON (2.12a).

(2.12) A sequence of two paths

    a. [PHON $\langle S_1, S_2 \rangle$]

    b.

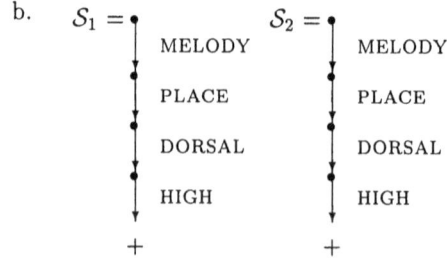

Attribute Value Phonology

The value of PHON can be likened to a bead curtain, consisting of strings of beads hanging vertically from a single rail. Each attribute is like a differently coloured bead and its value is the entire string below it. Since the hierarchical position of attributes is fixed, rows of a single colour are the analogue of a sequence of instances of some attribute. And just as we can describe the relative order of red beads in the red row, so we can refer to the sequence of PLACE attributes, say. But it is crucial to note that this is merely shorthand. If we think of the bead curtain we can see that to refer to the absolute locations of two red beads we must in fact refer to the locations of the strings of beads (the paths) leading down to them. In (2.13) this is made evident by some shared structure. The sequential position of [HIGH+] is determined only by the paths of which it is a value. It is *at i* and *j* on the skeleton.[13]

(2.13) Sequence of two paths
which share the dorsal features

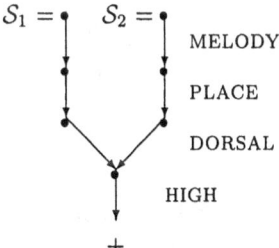

We know that if the curtain is sent swinging the beads do not change location, nor even if the strings are tied in knots — the true order of beads does not alter unless we cut the strings or detach them from the track, both of which are nonmonotonic operations. Though the arcs in the schematic sequence of melodies in (2.14) are straight, parallel and of equal length, this is of no import. The direction of the arc and the linear position on the page of the skeletal node are all that count. The point to remember is that asking for the whereabouts of some structure [HIGH+] is meaningless without referring to the path(s) for which it is a value.

54 *Autosegmental Representation in a Declarative Framework*

Such paths are autonomous segmental units.

(2.14) Melody tier

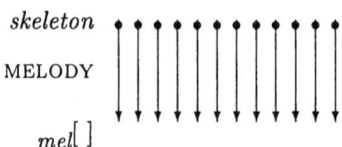

AVSs in graph notation resemble a bead curtain quite directly, but the notation resembles AP diagrams and so might cause confusion. For this reason I will generally use the matrix diagrams. In matrix notation the root of the graph of a path corresponds to the root matrix. Recall that a *high* feature in this notation is represented:

(2.15) $_{root}\left[\text{MELODY|PLACE|DORSAL|HIGH}+\right]$

Autosegmental tiers can be easily uncovered from the root sequence. The sequence of instances of the path in (2.15) is the *high* tier. Because of the nature of paths, the *high* tier consists in part of the *place tier*. This conception of the tier has some advantages over the autosegmental version.

1. A *high* feature in AVP carries with it its hierarchical structure, so has no operation to create the required structure. (See Archangeli & Pulleyblank's (1986) Node Activation Convention.) Rather, reference to the redundant information is omitted by convention.

2. No mention need be made of the class tiers unless they are directly involved in some phonological process. In AP the *place* tier has to form a bridge of associations linking the *high* tier to the skeleton. In AVP fixing the location of the path in (2.15) does this. Just because a *high* feature (2.15) is referred to does not mean a path [MELODY|PLACE] (on the *place* tier) needs to be.

3. There is no need for paths like [MELODY|PLACE] to have any phonetic realisation. The boolean valued paths have phonetic

relevance, and the *place* tier has a grouping function only. This distinction is unclear in AP where all tiers are equal autonomous sequences.

2.3 Association: a symmetric relation between features?

2.3.1 The anchoring of autosegments

In Autosegmental Phonology, each feature is an individual entity, an 'autonomous segment', in that it exists as part of a sequence of other features of the same type, a TIER. Indeed, multiple tiers are perhaps the most well-known characteristic of that theory. Perhaps the logically simplest statements of Autosegmental Phonology posits two tiers, which I will call 'tone' and 'melody' tiers (for the earliest exposition of AP see Goldsmith 1976; also Leben 1973).[14] These tiers have to be coordinated somehow, to derive a well-formed surface representation in which all features are mutually ordered. In the terms of the theory, autosegments are necessarily ASSOCIATED, though note that this need not obtain *during* a derivation. The first two aspects of the Well-Formedness Condition ensure this:

(2.16) *Well-Formedness Condition* Goldsmith (1976)

- Each tone is associated with at least one segment.

- Each segment is associated with at least one tone.

- Association lines do not cross.

Note that when such features are associated, a non-hierarchical pattern is produced (2.17). As Goldsmith (1990:11) notes,

> there is a natural tendency to think of tone as being a feature of a vowel... Nothing... in the autosegmental perspective... supports such a prejudice.

The tiers in (2.17) are equal, like the parallel rails of a railway.

56   Autosegmental Representation in a Declarative Framework

(2.17) Features on two tiers linked by noncrossing association lines

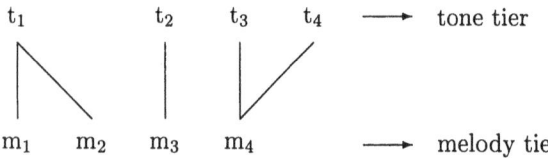

Autosegmental theory is a generalised version of the picture given so far; not just tone and vowel melodies have tiers, for any feature can be autosegmentalised. Each feature has its own tier. To be part of a valid surface form and be phonetically interpreted, autosegments must associated together, but to ensure that there will always *be* a tier to mediate the associations a specialised core tier is posited, called the SKELETON. In the simplest case this produces a 'paddle-wheel' representation of tiers radiating round from the skeleton, with a maximum radius of a single association. This also allows all tones and melodies to be associated to *something* — to be incorporated into the representation — without each being linked to each other in a factorial web of associations. This is an advantageous position since (2.16) is in fact too strong. Tones need *not* be associated to every segment (Halle & Vergnaud 1982; Pulleyblank 1986).

The paddle-wheel approach has not received much support and a further generalisation means that we find the current rich apparatus of class tiers which mediate between the skeleton and the feature tiers (Mohanan 1983; Clements 1985; Sagey 1986; Avery & Rice 1989; Iverson 1989; Yip 1989 *etc*). In this framework the *high*, *back* and *low* tiers must always be associated to a *dorsal* tier and no other. In turn *dorsal* is associated only to *place, etc*, and ultimately to the skeleton. Every autosegment must be ANCHORED in this way by ultimate association to the skeleton.

As indicated above, anchoring ensures that all features in an analysis can be interpreted phonetically. Features which are not underlyingly anchored at any particular position in the root sequence are called FLOATING features. Derivations including floating features are driven by the requirement to anchor them to the skeleton.[15] 'Prosodic licensing' (Itô 1986) and 'autosegmental licensing' (Goldsmith 1990) also depend on autosegments being appropriately anchored. Anchoring is thus an important theoretical notion.

A feature hierarchy complicates the notion of an autosegment being anchored. Consider a *high* feature. To be anchored, it must be associated to the skeleton. But thanks to the feature hierarchy this cannot be directly achieved, since the *high* tier can only be associated to the *dorsal* tier, not the skeleton. Similarly, *dorsal* must be anchored through *place* rather than to the skeleton directly.

To get around this problem, AP must allow a feature to be anchored without necessarily being associated directly to the skeleton. Anchoring must correspond to a *transitive* version of association. A very simple definition of anchoring is possible if we adopt a transitive association relation directly. Transitive association enables us to extrapolate from the facts that (1) f_1 and f_2 are associated, and (2) f_2 and f_3 are associated to the conclusion that (3) f_1 and f_3 are associated. Indeed, association has been implicitly transitive since the earliest days — at least it was interpreted phonetically as temporal simultaneity, which is a transitive relation.[16]

Given transitive association, *high* can be anchored if there is a path of associations leading to the skeleton:

(2.18) *Anchoring (with transitive association)*

A feature is anchored if and only if it is associated to the skeleton.

2.3.2 Association as simultaneity

Association has been interpreted as meaning SIMULTANEITY — two associated autosegments hold simultaneously (Goldsmith 1976:41–42; Clements 1985:228). Simultaneity is a *transitive, symmetric* relation, and was in fact the chosen interpretation before the feature hierarchy was conceived of. In (2.17), m_1 is associated to t_1, and *vice versa*. They therefore occupy simultaneous points in the sequence of features.

Note that t_1 and m_2 are also associated. If association is symmetric and transitive it follows that m_1 and m_2 are associated, and therefore simultaneous. Recent developments (Sagey 1988) point out the contradictions caused by this interpretation: m_1 and

m_2 being simultaneous is contradictory given the additional information in (2.17) that m_1 precedes m_2 on their tier. In other words, if association is defined as simultaneity — or indeed as *any* symmetric, transitive relation — then m_1 and m_2 are associated, which is not a result the theory is intended to produce.

Goldsmith (1990:352) rejects Sagey's criticisms on the metatheoretical grounds that association is phonological, while simultaneity is phonetic. Whatever validity these criticisms may have, they do not address the problem of how association as a relation is defined. Not all transitive symmetric relations are phonetic (for example 'supports the same rugby team as') and the problems Sagey brings up are directly due to the properties of the relation, not its interpretation. Arguing against the interpretation is therefore beside the point.

2.3.3 Association as overlap

Sagey (1988)

To obviate the contradictions observed in the association relation Sagey (1988) opts for a association relation which is symmetric but *intransitive*; one of OVERLAP IN TIME.[17] On this view features occupy *intervals* on their tiers rather than points. Two features are associated if and only if the intervals overlap, in which circumstances some point in each interval must be simultaneous.

As will become clear, an intransitive association is highly problematic when it comes to dealing with a hierarchised phonological structure.[18] In a situation where some autosegment h is associated to d, and that d is associated to p, the problem is that h is *not* associated to p. Consider (2.19), the lines in which link simultaneous parts of the intervals whereas association lines would relate autosegments, *i.e.* whole intervals.

In (2.19) p and d overlap because the first point of p is simultaneous with the last point in d. Similarly d and h overlap because the first point of d is simultaneous with the last point in h. But (assuming d is non-null) this entails that h wholly precedes p. This shows they do not overlap — that, given any such intransitive relation, h is not associated to p.

Attribute Value Phonology

(2.19) The intransitivity of overlap

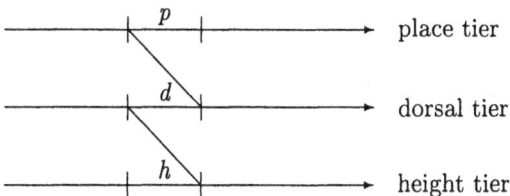

This is clearly unsatisfactory, but it also raises practical problems over determining whether autosegments are anchored. Suppose that we can somehow determine that p is anchored in (2.19). We know d is associated to p, and that h is associated to d. But because p and h are not associated, h is not anchored given the definition in (2.18). Given an intransitive association relation we must transitivise the definition of being anchored:

(2.20) *Anchoring (association is intransitive)*

- A feature is anchored if it is associated to the skeleton.
- A feature is anchored if it is associated to a feature which is anchored.

Unfortunately this approach requires two relations with distinct properties and purposes where surely only one is needed. Association indicates overlap of features while transitive association is used to compute whether a feature is anchored to a skeletal slot. The result is that a feature can be anchored to a slot without being associated to it.

Bird & Klein (1990)

This paper presents a partial formal framework for Autosegmental Phonology and adopts an essentially Sagean picture of association. They propose, however, an *event*-based approach to overlapping features rather than Sagey's point-based ontology.

60   *Autosegmental Representation in a Declarative Framework*

B&K employ an 'overlap' relation which is intransitive. Because they also adopt the autosegmental architecture, which uses multiple autonomous tiers, they require other transitive relations in order to express the full meaning of 'association'. This they acknowledge Bird & Klein (1990:40):

> Although we will be mainly concerned with exploring the interpretation of association as overlap, we expect that the interpretation of association as inclusion or as simultaneity will be useful on occasion, particularly in those cases where the transitivity property is required.

Bird & Klein (1990) is most unusual in that it is highly formal, resulting in admirable clarity, and so the implications of implementing Sagey's 'overlap' association are recognised.

Hayes (1990)

Hayes (1990) also adopts an intransitive association relation in order to analyse certain patterns of diphthongisation, but he does not claim that 'overlap' in particular is to be the interpretation of this relation. At the outset I should make clear that I am extremely doubtful that the motivating data requires phonological analysis in the way Hayes assumes: I do not accept that the numerous patterns of diphthongisation he cites are phonological alternations. The data bears all the hallmarks of phonetic processes, and I will assume that the data results from phonetic realisation, in some cases grammaticalised by diachronic reanalysis.[19] Since gestures are intrinsically movement-based, the existence of a diphthongal realisation of a long vowel does not imply phonological diphthongisation, merely a choice of a particular gesture. In time the more complex phonology/phonetic relations will naturally incur the reorganisation of underlying structure during acquisition. Whatever the status of the data which motivates Hayes's proposals, it is the latter with which I am concerned, and to these that I now turn.

Hayes's framework uses the following mechanisms:

Association, represented by co-indexing a feature and a slot in the skeleton.

Attribute Value Phonology

Tree-dominance, to define hierarchical feature structures.

A Percolation Convention, in order that a mother and daughter in some particular feature structure receive the same index,

Dominance, defined in terms of association and tree-dominance.

Hayes's definition of dominance can be defined (a simplification of his (60)) as:

(2.21) *Hayes's dominance (re-defined)*
A DOMINATES B iff A and B share an index and
A tree-dominates B.

Hayes argues for the first two relations on the grounds that association (simultaneity) and tree-dominance (category membership) are functionally different.[20] Features can be associated only to the skeleton, *i.e.* it is an intransitive association relation that is used, and an additional convention ensures that a mother and daughter in a particular feature structure bear the same index, in all but the diphthongisation cases, where the convention operates in a much more complex and inherently procedural manner. A *separate* definition of dominance is required in order that a structure like (2.22a) can be phonologically identical to (2.22b) in terms of this relation. Otherwise (an observation due to Itô), the fundamentally procedural nature of the approach would record in the difference between (2.22a) and (2.22b) the history of the derivation.

(2.22) An unwanted distinction

In order that the representations in (2.22) can be taken to be indistinguishable, Hayes defines 'dominance' (2.21), and indeed in both cases the 'dominance' relationships are the same: $F[i]$ and $F[j]$ both dominate $G[i,j]$.

Looking more closely, a problem emerges, however. G forms a subset node of F (F tree-dominates G) in (2.22) because G and F can only appear in this configuration. Every F tree-dominates every G. Using this relationship, $F[i]$ 'dominates' every $G[j]$ just in case $i = j$. In (2.22a) the tree-dominance of $G[i,j]$ by $F[i]$ together with the co-indexing indicates the dominance of (2.21). But in that case, what does the line in the diagram mean?

The line means neither association, dominance nor tree-dominance. It functions as a trans-derivational representation, showing that Itô's criticism has not been addressed. The line serves to tell us that (2.22a) arose from regressive association and (2.22b) from progressive assimilation, even though the new relation of 'dominance' provides a way to *ignore* this derivational history, if so desired.

We can picture these *five* relationships, as shown in (2.23). Every B is a subset node of every A, so A tree-dominates B (2.23a). A and C (no tree-dominance) are both indexed to the same skeletal slot in (2.23b), so though neither is associated to the other, they are co-associated to the skeleton. The 'line-relation' (the problematic case Hayes overlooks) in (2.23c) triggers co-indexation as shown in (2.23d) (not obligatory) thanks to the percolation convention. Finally (2.23e) is a case of dominance. It is the difference between (2.23d) and (2.23e) that Hayes attempts to remove, unsuccessfully.

(2.23) Five feature-to-feature relationships

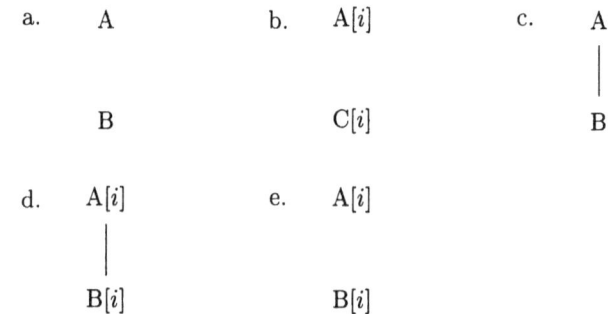

From what is clear in Hayes's approach, it has to be rejected on the grounds of over-complexity. Some points are worth restat-

Attribute Value Phonology

ing, and worth adopting, however. The difference between hierarchical dominance and temporal co-indexation is something that AVP takes as central. Such co-indexation is *not* interpreted as association in AVP, as we will see, but nevertheless Hayes's distinction is echoed by the indexation of the root matrix in AVP, and the quite separate definition of the feature hierarchy. The main reason Hayes needs to use so much extra machinery is that he supposes each subtier needs to be autonomous (an assumption I reject) and yet he uses an *intransitive* association relation. (See also Bird & Klein, above.)

2.4 Association as dominance

2.4.1 The problem of symmetry

The three examples given above — Sagey (1988), Bird & Klein (1990), and Hayes (1988; 1990) — are the only ones of which I am aware that propose an intransitive association relation. While this avoids the contradictions of representation that Sagey discusses, the consequence is that the necessary transitivity of association has been lost. While a symmetric transitive association relation is untenable, a symmetric intransitive conception of association is unwieldy at best, perhaps unworkable.

Is there no way in which a unitary notion of association can be sufficient? The contradictions discussed by Sagey (1988) were the result of a relation that is indeed transitive, *but is also symmetric*. Perhaps the problems of association lie in *this* assumption.

Consider a representation like that in (2.24), which display the Sagean problems for association. (2.24) shows the same contradictions as (2.17) when a transitive relation (simultaneity) is posited, for p_1 would be associated to (be simultaneous with) p_2 *and* precede it, a contradiction.

64   Autosegmental Representation in a Declarative Framework

(2.24)

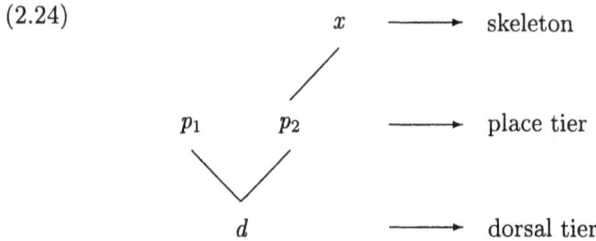

But if the symmetric and *in*transitive relation of overlap is used then there are still problems. Suppose d is anchored. Feature p_1 is associated to d, and *vice versa*, since association is symmetric. Since d is anchored and since p_1 and d are associated, p_1 appears to be anchored too. This is surely incorrect given the motivation behind anchoring.

2.4.2   An asymmetric, transitive association

My contention is that the problems being discussed are due to the assumption that association is *symmetric*. In (2.24) the correct result can be achieved if p_1 is not associated to d while d *is* associated to p_1 (and p_2). If d is anchored, p_1 is not, since it is not associated to d. This is the behaviour of an *asymmetric* association. IMMEDIATE DOMINANCE, the basic relation in the hierarchical attribute-value structure, is such an asymmetric relation. In AVP an attribute (or a path of attributes) immediately dominates its value, while in AP one feature immediately dominates another. In (2.24) p_1 immediately dominates d, but d does not immediately dominate p_1: indeed nothing does. This fact could be used directly to define p_1 as being unanchored. Under this view, being undominated equals being unanchored, with the exception of the skeleton, which dominates all features and is dominated by none. See (2.27) below for the proper definition of Anchoring.

One problem is that immediate dominance, being an intransitive relation, does not allow us to deduce from (2.24) that d is dominated by x. This is unsatisfactory since it is not enough that a feature is anchored: it is necessary sometimes to specify suitable anchors, either by content or skeletal position. In other words a *transitive* relation is essential in a hierarchical model. There is no need to be wary of this move: transitive dominance is not the same as simultaneity. Transitive dominance (in AVP) is defined in (2.25).[21]

(2.25) *Dominance*

Given an attribute (or path of attributes) $\mathcal{A}$ and a structure $\mathcal{S}$.

- $\mathcal{A}$ dominates $\mathcal{S}$ if $\mathcal{A}$ immediately dominates $\mathcal{S}$.

- $\mathcal{A}$ dominates $\mathcal{S}$ if $\mathcal{A}$ immediately dominates $\mathcal{S}'$, a structure with attribute $\mathcal{A}'$, and $\mathcal{A}'$ dominates $\mathcal{S}$.

It ought to be clear by now that the relation of dominance is to be identified with autosegmental association in AVP. In fact association is simply another name for (the converse of) dominance as defined in (2.26), a relation between values and attributes, but not *vice versa*. If A is associated to B, B is *not* associated to A.

(2.26) *Association*

$\mathcal{S}$ is associated to $\mathcal{A}$ if and only if $\mathcal{A}$ dominates $\mathcal{S}$.

We can now define anchoring using association (2.27). To be part of a phonological representation, a structure must be anchored to the skeleton. Phonological representations are thus *rooted* and *connected dags* (directed acyclic graphs).

(2.27) *Anchoring (final version)*

A structure is anchored iff it is associated to
$\langle i, \ _{root}[\text{MELODY}\ ]\ \rangle$

(2.27) is basically the same as (2.18) above, but since association is only to attributes, the MELODY path is named as the anchor for segmental melodies. The requirement for segmental anchoring is one plank of phonological representation. The other, that every melody structure is syllabified, means that each of the two sister attributes of the root matrix play a role in locating phonological information in its sequential, segmental and prosodic context.

2.4.3 Hammond (1988)

Before moving on I should point out that I am aware of one previous work in which an asymmetric association is proposed.[22] Hammond (1988) is a short note replying to Sagey (1988) which points out some problems in the adoption of an intransitive association relation. Hammond realises that if association is characterised as asymmetric, transitive (and irreflexive) then it avoids the contradictions Sagey discusses, and this is the form of association relation he proposes. His phonetic interpretation of association is that "association lines are ... interpreted as issuing an articulatory instruction to the slot" (1988:321). Apart from this phonetic characterisation, the main difference between the current view and Hammond's is his assumption — common to all AP — that multiple autonomous tiers are necessary. As a result of this assumption, he requires the Ordering Principle (§3.2.1).

2.5 Localising association

2.5.1 What must association be able to do?

Sagey (1986; 1988) introduces overlap because association interpreted as simultaneity is the cause of formal problems. We will see that the contradictions Sagey discusses for association do not arise if association is an asymmetric relation, as proposed here. Sagey considers four structures (2.28).

These configurations (2.28) are test configurations since they exemplify the degrees of freedom autosegmental diagrams require for the representation of multiple association. That is, AP wishes to use all these structures, bar the final one. The diagram with crossing lines (2.28d) is the one configuration which is banned, and this is summed up by the No Crossing Constraint (Goldsmith 1976). Sagey noticed that if association is interpreted as simultaneity (and the association relation has the same properties, as discussed above) (2.28a,b,c) are actually *ill-formed*. Sagey argues on the basis of this, quite correctly, that the association relation must be redefined. Her contention that overlap is the correct interpretation of association, as we have seen, has problems of its own. AVP's approach to these configurations differs from AP, because it

Attribute Value Phonology

does not *require* the same patterns to be well-formed. Two factors are important in this: AVP has sequence *only* in the skeleton; and association is the converse of dominance.

(2.28)   Test configurations

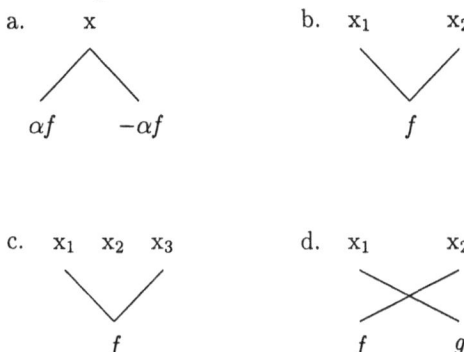

In AVP (2.28a) is ill-formed because a feature structure cannot contain two contradictory sub-structures. Indeed this is so in AP too, but [α f] and [$-\alpha$ f] are specially interpreted, by ordering them in time. In this case the lines in the diagram would not indicate association but some other quasi-temporal relation. So strictly (2.28a) stands out as quite different even in Autosegmental Phonology. As noted above such a configuration is the *only time* in AP that a node must dominate a sequence of features. The limited application of such structures does not merit the introduction of either ordered tiers other than the skeleton nor an extra type of association relation.

(2.28b) is well-formed in AVP because [f] is associated to x_1 and independently the same token [f] is associated to x_2. The point is that x_1 is not associated to x_2 because association is asymmetrically defined. (The same point holds for (2.28c).) We have now disposed of the set of Sagean contradictions because features are not associated unless they occur within a single structure. Association has been localised to the domain of the root matrix.

(2.28d) could be ruled out in AP if we imposed ordering on the [f]-[g] tier. But since this autonomous tier ordering is absent in AVP, not only is (2.28d) *well-*formed in AVP, *but there is no*

68   *Autosegmental Representation in a Declarative Framework*

reason why it should not be so. In fact it is topologically identical to (merely another way of drawing) (2.29), which has no crossed lines. In AVP features *f* and *g* are ordered by virtue of their association to the skeleton, not autonomously — recall the bead curtain. There are no indices specifying the order of [*f*] and [*g*] other than those of the skeleton.

(2.29)   Non-crossing version of (2.28d)

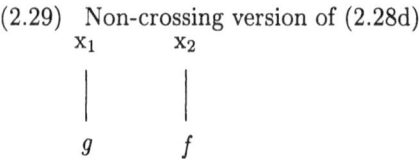

As things stand (2.28c) is well-formed, but in Chapter 3 I propose a locality principle which rules out a set of structures including (2.28c). This is because sharing cannot be allowed between any arbitrary structures. In other words the source of ill-formedness in complex representations must be reducible to (2.28c), not (2.28d). AVP differs from AP in the method it chooses to constrain sharing as a result of AVP's restriction of linear order to the skeleton. Many nonlocal associations which are banned in AP as 'line-crossing violations' will also be banned in AVP, but because they are reducible to (2.28c). Only multiple associations will be ill-formed with regards to locality.

In summary AVP uses (2.28d)/(2.29) and (2.28b) but not (2.28a,c). This greatly simplifies the range of phonological structures available. A structure can be associated to one or more attributes. Only *one* structure can be associated to any given attribute.[23]

2.5.2   Asymmetry as the source of local association

I believe that the best characterisation of the contradictory configurations outlined in Sagey (1988) is that they show the consequences of an over-extension of the use of association to relate *nonlocal* items. The contradictions in (2.17) and (2.24) arise because autosegments which ought *not* to be associated are said to be so. The problem with association-as-simultaneity is that it 'chains'

Attribute Value Phonology

over 'long distances'. It is possible to deduce, given a symmetric transitive association relation, that an autosegment is associated to any other along an arbitrary chain of associations, unless some restraint localising association is incorporated into the theory.

To handle this problem Sagey adopts an intransitive association relation. This removes such association-chains and therefore features cannot be associated if they have to be more than one association apart. A typical instance of this is features in a hierarchy between which there is a third node. Unfortunately some chaining of association *is* required, and will be adopted by the back door. Hierarchical structure is peripheralised in Sagey's account because hierarchy crucially requires the re-introduction of transitivity in one form or another.

AVP's solution to the problem of the chaining of association is to equate association with dominance, because of the importance of dominance in phonological structure. The feature bundle of Chomsky and Halle (1968) was a set of features, sequenced as a bundle. This strong vertical view of phonology gave way to a strong horizontal view — multiple tiers, again of equal import (2.11). The attempts to introduce a sequence of tree-like complexes defined on multiple tiers have been unsatisfactory because each node in the hierarchy has been part of a sequence. The problems of defining workable phonological structures in terms of this phonetic-like architecture have been discussed above. In order to solve these problems I have adopted as the basic phonological architecture a sequence of attribute-value structures.

(2.30) Schematic sequence of structures showing domain
of association

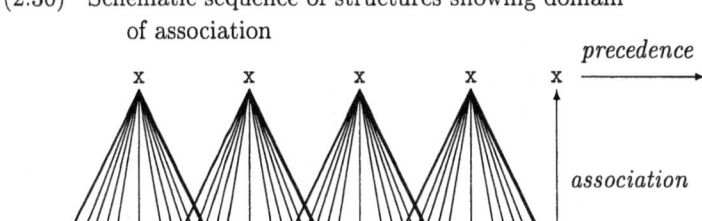

Dominance is a 'local' relation in that arbitrary nodes are not related: they must be part of the same structure. Because

70 *Autosegmental Representation in a Declarative Framework*

association is the inverse of dominance, the locality of association is guaranteed. The root matrix is a DOMAIN limiting association since the root x dominates all nodes associated to it. In (2.30) each domain is a drawn as a schematic triangular structure.

AVP is based squarely on the principle that hierarchical representations for subsegmental phonological entities should be used to their full potential. A sequence of structures each of which is an 'informational domain' is the basis of the theory. Each domain can be identified with its root, so we can even think of a phonological description being a linear sequence of roots. The *non*-linear aspect of phonology is modeled by material dominated by two or more roots (the double-hatched triangles in (2.30) which symbolise co-indexed values).

2.5.3 Feature co-occurrence

While the feature hierarchy determines which features are associated to which, all other things being equal, it does not play any role in controlling the co-occurrence of particular features and values. In AP *high* and *low* are both associated to *dorsal*, but this does not deal with the fact that [+*high*] and [+*low*] cannot co-occur. Unsurprisingly, an intransitive interpretation of association such as overlap makes the ruling out such feature co-occurrences become highly complex just in case the features involved are transitively associated.

For example, in Latin a velarised [ɫ] was not possible in an onset (Schein & Steriade 1986). To express this in AVP we might opt for a feature co-occurrence restriction (FCR) such as (2.31).[24]

$$(2.31) \quad \neg \left(\begin{array}{c} [\text{LATERAL}+] \\ [\text{HIGH}+] \\ [\text{BACK}+] \end{array} \right)_{\text{SYLLABLE}|\text{ONSET}}$$

This restriction is intended to ban these features from occurring in the same domain. In terms familiar from Autosegmental Phonology (though confusingly) the FCR is intended to prevent the features 'being associated'. AP would more usually represent the rule with a rewrite rule $F \rightarrow G$, but the FCR format is not significantly different with regards to the major point at issue: the FCR/rule deals with features which are not hierarchically adjacent.

There is some domain within which features must appear in order that a rule/FCR can apply to them. This is achieved in AVP because the FCR prevents the structures mentioned in the bracketed body of the rule from being associated to a common ONSET attribute. Since this would be possible only if the attribute dominated all the substructures, AVP, in effect, limits the FCR to the ready-defined domain of the root matrix. The FCR is merely a constraint on such matrices.

In a Sagean Autosegmental Phonology the domain must be separately defined. It does not correspond to 'associated features' or some such, since under her definition of association, the features are *not* associated. We can see this in (2.32), where [+*high*] is associated to *dorsal*, and *dorsal* to *place*, but [+*high*] is not associated to *place*.

(2.32)

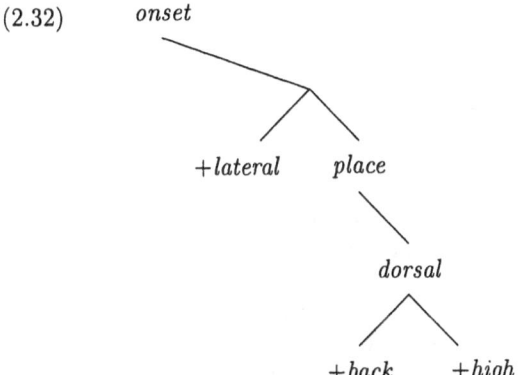

If association is interpreted phonologically as overlap then rules like (2.31) ought surely to be a statement that the features in question may not overlap. But (2.32) cannot be ruled out as phonologically ill-formed using overlap alone since there is no guarantee (since overlap is intransitive) that *onset*, [+*lateral*], [+*back*] and [+*high*] overlap at all. Some *other* mechanism is required.

As discussed, a *transitive* version of overlap (which is surely indistinguishable from simultaneity) requires some definition of the structural domain within which FCRs or rules would operate. The simplest case of two features being part of the same domain if one is associated to the other is of no use; see (2.24). Again, some

72   Autosegmental Representation in a Declarative Framework

other mechanism is required in order to prevent a word with, say, a lateral, a high vowel, a back fricative and an onset *somewhere* in it from triggering the rule.

Statements like (2.31) are intended to be restrictions on possible phonological structures, in order to rule out entire trees like (2.32) as ill-formed. Ensuring that a rule like (2.31) rules out a structure like (2.32) is relatively straightforward in AVP. (2.31) is of the form $\neg S$, and if (2.33)=S then (2.31) bans it. (Recall that (2.31) is logically equivalent to $S \rightarrow \bot$.)

(2.33)   An ill-formed structure

$$\begin{bmatrix} \text{SYLLABLE} & \begin{bmatrix} \text{ONSET}\boxed{1} \end{bmatrix} \\ \text{MELODY} \ \boxed{1} & \begin{bmatrix} \text{LATERAL} & + \\ \text{PLACE}|\text{DORSAL} & \begin{bmatrix} \text{BACK} + \\ \text{HIGH} \ + \end{bmatrix} \end{bmatrix} \end{bmatrix}$$

2.6   Rules

Rules in AP modify an underlying form, or add information to it, in order to arrive at the appropriate surface form. The detail in surface forms is not given lexically, in order to minimise redundancy. The rules therefore capture generalisations.

In AVP rules can be defined as non-lexical (conditional) constraints. While lexical entries constrain the final form of any representation to which they themselves contribute, the non-lexical 'rules of the phonology' constrain all representations — they therefore express generalisations. Redundant detail can be 'omitted' from lexical entries. The major difference between AP and AVP is that the rules of AVP may not alter the pool of constraints to which they are being added, and that such constraints are added in no given order. A procedural interpretation of AVP rules is possible, in which they always add information. But they could also be interpreted as *checking* fully specified underlying forms. Such issues of the procedural interpretation of rules are not to be confused with the declarative interpretation given here, however. This

Attribute Value Phonology 73

section offers some examples of the uses to which rules can be put, in addition to the discussion above of FCRs.

2.6.1 Assimilation

Take a sequence of matrices $\langle S_1, S_2, S_3 \rangle$ (2.34) where S_3 has a PLACE attribute with value $\mathcal{P} = \boxed{3}$. This amounts to saying that some structure $\boxed{3}$ on the *place* tier is associated to the third skeletal slot. The other structures have underspecified values for PLACE.[25] I have given these unspecified values different variable names to help identify them.

(2.34) Simplified sequence of matrices $< S_1, S_2, S_3 >$

$$\left\langle \begin{bmatrix} \text{MEL} & \begin{bmatrix} \text{PLACE} \boxed{1} \\ \text{VOICE} + \\ \text{NASAL} - \end{bmatrix} \end{bmatrix}, \right.$$

$$\begin{bmatrix} \text{MEL} & \begin{bmatrix} \text{PLACE} \boxed{2} \\ \text{VOICE} + \\ \text{NASAL} + \end{bmatrix} \end{bmatrix},$$

$$\left. \begin{bmatrix} \text{MEL} & \begin{bmatrix} \text{PLACE} \boxed{3} \mathcal{P} \\ \text{VOICE} + \\ \text{NASAL} - \end{bmatrix} \end{bmatrix} \right\rangle$$

Now, imagine a simple rule intended to ensure that all nasal-stop sequences are homorganic. This rule means that nasal-stop sequences need not be marked in the lexicon as homorganic. However, since AVP is declarative, such a rule does not allow any such sequence to be marked as non-homorganic lexically. The rule is not able to destroy such information so a failure to unify (contradiction) would result. (2.35) is a conditional constraint. Its antecedent is a pair of structures in the appropriate order. Its consequent says that the pair in the antecedent also share the value of their PLACE attributes.

74   *Autosegmental Representation in a Declarative Framework*

(2.35)   Homorganic nasal-stop sequence rule

$$\left\langle \left(\begin{matrix} [\text{CONT}-] \\ [\text{NASAL}+] \end{matrix} \right), \left(\begin{matrix} [\text{SON}-] \\ [\text{NASAL}-] \\ [\text{CONT}-] \end{matrix} \right) \right\rangle \longrightarrow$$

$$\left\langle ([\text{MELODY}|\text{PLACE}\boxed{4}]), ([\text{MELODY}|\text{PLACE}\boxed{4}]) \right\rangle$$

The antecedent of the rule, a sequence $\langle S_a, S_b \rangle$, subsumes a portion of (2.34), namely the sequence $\langle S_2, S_3 \rangle$, because $S_a \succeq S_2$, $S_b \succeq S_3$ and because the sequences are consistent. Thus the 'structural description' of the rule matches if $a = 1, b = 2$ and the result is no more specific than (2.34). The 'structural change' of the rule ensures that $\boxed{3}$ is associated to S_2's PLACE attribute. $\boxed{2}$ and $\boxed{3}$ are subsumed by $\boxed{4}$ so their unification is merely the more specific of the two, $\boxed{3}$.

The declarative meaning of such rules is familiar from logic. If the antecedent subsumes nothing the constraint is satisfied. If the antecedent subsumes anything, then the consequent must unify with it for the constraint to be satisfied. As a constraint on the well-formedness of phonological representations, the rule says that any representation such as (2.34) is ill-formed unless $\boxed{3}$ is the *same* as $\boxed{2}$. Consequently (2.34) is too general, since it does not represent whether or not $\boxed{2}=\boxed{3}$. It must in fact be replaced by the more specific (2.36) in order to properly describe valid phonetic objects.[26] Its specificness means that it does not describe the non-occurring structures which (2.34) on its own would be able to pick out.

(2.36)   Homorganic nasal and stop as part of $< S_1, S_2, S_3 >$

Note: M *stands for* MELODY

$$\left\langle \left[\text{M} \begin{bmatrix} \text{PLACE}\boxed{1} \\ \text{VOICE} + \\ \text{NASAL} - \end{bmatrix} \right] \left[\text{M} \begin{bmatrix} \text{PLACE}\boxed{2}\mathcal{P} \\ \text{VOICE} + \\ \text{NASAL} + \end{bmatrix} \right] \left[\text{M} \begin{bmatrix} \text{PLACE}\boxed{2} \\ \text{VOICE} + \\ \text{NASAL} - \end{bmatrix} \right] \right\rangle$$

Rules can be used to produce precise descriptions, so lexical representations need not be seen to do so. The rule and the lexical representation unify, they combine their information, and

Attribute Value Phonology

they each contribute some specificity to the phonological representations. Since they unify, they must both be the same sort of formal object. In a procedural interpretation, the rule has assimilated the (unspecified) place of a nasal to that of the item on its right. An analogous rule in AP would express this directionality. The nasal's matrix and following matrix now share some information (about a place of articulation) since an association has been made leftwards. But note that S_2 and S_3 have not moved, indeed no structure has changed position. It is merely that the values of two paths have been equated. 'After' the rule, S_2 and S_3 remain distinct, and the *place* paths remain distinct. Only the value of each path is affected, and now they have the identical value $\mathcal{P}$ (=$\boxed{2}$, =$\boxed{3}$). In these circumstances it might be more appropriate to think of all such assimilations as being *mutual* assimilations, except that S_2, being underspecified, contributes nothing to the result. Only if assimilation *replaced* structure would it make sense to think of directional assimilation with a source and a target. If unification is used on one specified and one unspecified structure then there will be an appearance of directional assimilation, but it is only an appearance.

2.6.2 Feature filling rules

Look now at another case of an association rule, a rule which states all high back segments are round.[27] Suppose the skeleton includes a structure (2.37). This is a partial description of a high back vowel, but the phonology of the language demands all such descriptions must actually pick out only high back *rounded* vowels.

$$(2.37) \quad \left[\text{MELODY}|\text{PLACE}|\text{DORSAL} \begin{bmatrix} \text{HIGH } + \\ \text{BACK } + \end{bmatrix} \right]$$

A rule is needed to force the inclusion of [ROUND +] in all such structures, *i.e.* to associate a substructure [ROUND+] to the matrix's *labial* attribute (2.38). The more specific representation (2.39) is the result.

$$(2.38) \left(\begin{bmatrix} \text{HIGH}+ \\ \text{BACK}+ \end{bmatrix} \right) \rightarrow [\text{ROUND}+]$$

76   Autosegmental Representation in a Declarative Framework

$$(2.39) \quad \left[\text{MELODY}|\text{PLACE} \left[\begin{array}{l} \text{LABIAL} \ [\text{ROUND}+] \\ \text{DORSAL} \ \left[\begin{array}{l} \text{BACK}+ \\ \text{HIGH}\ + \end{array} \right] \end{array} \right] \right]$$

At this point I should describe in more detail the notational convention for structures that I am using. In an implicational rule there is a set of structures in the antecedent and in the consequent. Each member of the set consists of a form $\mathcal{B}_{ss}$. $\mathcal{B}$ is the body of the rule, and consists of substructures grouped by round brackets. The subscript ss is an path, [MELODY] in the default case, with associated index. The structure in (2.39) can be given the shorthand representation (2.40).

$$(2.40) \quad \left(\begin{array}{l} [\text{ROUND}+] \\ [\text{BACK}+] \\ [\text{HIGH}+] \end{array} \right)$$

This information can be included on both sides of an implication, but if the same index and path are involved, as in (2.38), (2.41), they can be omitted as understood:

(2.41) $(\ place^{[\ ]}\ ) \to \text{SYLLABLE}|\text{ONSET}$

A rule like (2.41) indicates that for every index i at which there is some particular type of *place* structure (call it $\boxed{1}$) associated to MELODY, then $\boxed{1}$ must be associated to (dominated by) the onset path too, *i.e.* that there must be at i a structure:

$$\left[\begin{array}{l} \text{MELODY} \quad _{mel}\!\left[\text{PLACE}\boxed{1} \right] \\ \text{SYLLABLE}|\text{ONSET} \ _{mel}\!\left[\text{PLACE}\boxed{1} \right] \end{array} \right]_{root}$$

Such a rule prevents certain specifications of place of articulation from appearing in any ·syllabic role other than the onset (though they may be in in another role in addition to the onset; see Chapter 5).

Attribute Value Phonology

In sum, the rules of association in AP are not 'processes' of association in AVP, but constraints. They are stipulations that certain dependencies hold between paths of attributes; namely that their values are identical and thereby license a single phonetic gesture.

2.7 Summary: structures and gestures

Some major questions arise about the phonetic interpretation of association under the assumption that association is another name for (the inverse of) dominance. Some of these points were dealt with in Chapter 1 but some more detail is required now that the theory has been partly exemplified. In AVP, phonology is only concerned with dominance relationships within root matrices and the sequence of such matrices. Phonetic realisation assigns gestural interpretations to structures (see Browman & Goldstein 1989) ensuring thereby that phonological relationships of dominance and precedence are reflected in temporal coordination. These gestures (sets of particular phonetic exponents) correspond to structure tokens in a one-to-one manner. Given two structures associated to co-indexed paths, the exponents of the structures must temporally overlap.

Think back to the rule of nasal assimilation.[28] AVP posits two adjacent hierarchical structures containing paths which, it so happens, co-dominate (share) a single phonological entity, namely a complex piece of information. This information is simply the value of two paths and does not itself overlap anything.

Such re-entrancy does describe phonetic overlap, however. If each structure corresponds to a gesture on a one-to-one basis, then the gesture is fixed in the temporal score by reference to the indices on the paths which dominate the structure. Other co-indexed paths have structures as values, and the structures also describe gestures. Since the paths are co-indexed, the gestures must overlap. A structure which is shared is the value of two paths, so its exponent necessarily lasts longer and interacts with more gestures than would otherwise be the case.

The phonological description associated with a morpheme is constrained both by lexical information unique to the morpheme

78 *Autosegmental Representation in a Declarative Framework*

and more general information encoded as rules. As has already been emphasised, such 'rules' and 'representations' are the same: constraints on well-formedness. Constraints do *not* govern phonetic overlap or phonetic temporal precedence. Recall the discussion of the voiceless lateral in English. Such phonetic co-articulation arises from unavoidable gestural overlap conditioned by English phonetic interpretation rules. Other examples of the separation of phonetic overlap from phonological well-formedness are not hard to find. For instance consider the contextual nasalisation of vowels. Relatively speaking, French, with phonological nasal vowels disallows contextual nasalisation (overlap of nasality from a stop and a preceding vowel) while most forms of English, with no nasal vowels phonologically, allows much greater overlap. English phonetic implementation can afford a much freer licensing of nasality by nasal structures given the available contrasts. Phonetics allows a greater or lesser laxity in the temporal realisation of a sequence of phonologically valid structures, which we may explain functionally. Such laxity will derive *non*-phonological temporal coordinations of gestures, presumably a driving force behind language change.

Recall that in Attribute Value Phonology a phonological entity is simply one of a sequence of root matrices. Each matrix has some internal structure composed of attribute-value pairs, which is unordered — attributes and their values are merely atemporal properties of one or more root matrices. In reserving such notions for phonology, AVP correctly subordinates the temporal autonomy of features in favour of stressing their combinatorial characteristics. Phonologically valid structures can be realised in temporally different ways in different languages, and we do not want to assign different temporally-ordered phonological representations for all these nuances.[29]

Features are primarily features *of* segments or syllables rather than independent entities. In other words the vertical has primacy over the horizontal. These dimensions must interact, of course, and this interaction was a primary motivation for moving away from SPE-style phonology towards autosegmentalism. In AVP the interaction is indicated by *re-entrancy*, two (or more) attributes sharing a single value. Of course AP can express the overlap of features, but in any characterisation of AP such overlapping is only possible when the paths are compatible. So the question must be as to what AP gains by adding the notion of overlap *in the phonology* to the independently required one of compatibility.

Part of the job of phonology is to select those phonetically possible feature combinations that are actually present in the language, and partly to proscribe phonetically possible but arbitrarily nonphonological associations. I think it is better to interpret an association line directly as a relation defining consistent feature structures rather than an indication of an infinite number of relations of overlapping phonetic entities.

Notes

[1] Theory independent or AP features will be in *italics*, 'a *high* feature'. These are not equivalent to attributes like 'HIGH', but roughly correspond, as we will see, to paths of attributes. The articulatory definitions of features are for convenience only.

[2] Recall that each boolean sort is distinct, so *boolean* is shorthand for *boolean-high* etc.

[3] §2.2 discusses the sequential aspects of AVP in more detail.

[4] Kasper & Rounds (1986) define a feature structure as (a set of) conjoined paths. I propose augmenting their approach by assigning each set an index *i* and weakly ordering these indices. In this system paths are conjoined if and only if they are co-indexed. It follows that the indices are best formalised as intervals, but I cannot address such issues of the formalisation of AVP here.

[5] I will ambiguously call these highest-level phonological structures ROOTS when the context makes it clear that I am not talking about the root of the feature hierarchy in Autosegmental Phonology (though there is a close analogy between the two) or MATRICES when it is clear I am not talking about any arbitrary substructure.

[6] See Hayes (1990) who stresses the difference and then uses co-indexing for both relationships.

[7] See Itô (1989); Clements (1990); Cairns (1988); Fujimura (1990) for a variety of views on the primacy of segments over syllables and *vice versa*, and on some approaches to the syllable/segment relationship sympathetic to a constraint-based approach. Chapter 5 in its discussion of licensing gives further details of AVP's treatment of syllabification.

[8] Using the sort *cons* means that single extrametrical consonants

only can be accommodated. This is also true for the onset and coda. One way to deal with clusters is to use *sets* of melodies as the values of such attributes (see Rounds 1990). Another is to use more syllable functions. If it is correct that any cluster can bear only a single instance of any contrastive feature then perhaps a single melody will suffice.

[9] Though the occurrence such configurations is actually rather limited in AP (see Sagey 1986), one such case is enough to require the addition of extra machinery to handle it. See §2.5 for further discussion.

[10] Of course, a pair of attributes NASAL and NON-NASAL could be used but in that case there would be no requirement to order one before the other. In AP it is the incompatibility of [+*feature*] and [-*feature*] which forces an ordering. In AVP [ATTR+] and [ATTR-] are equally incompatible, but no suborderings are permitted.

[11] Alternatively it could be the value of a path with a composite index ij where ij is an interval equal to i and j. This detail of formalisation goes beyond the goals of this work, and so I will assume the approaches are equivalent. The important point is that no index is assigned to any structure other than the root matrix.

[12] Lombardi (1990) demonstrates the drawbacks of assuming that an affricate is a single rooted segment which consists internally of the phonological sequence of stop-fricative. In denying that such order is required, she recognises the nonsense that would result from allowing the contradictory feature specification of [+*cont*, -*cont*] in the same feature hierarchy, so she proposes a new feature *stop* to partner the familiar *continuent* and analyses affricates as [+*stop*, +*cont*]. This is just the tack AVP insists on.

[13] One could say a single path dominates it, indexed k, where the interval of $k =$ the combined intervals of i and j.

[14] This discussion can be seen as an idealisation of a historical course of events and I do not wish to imply that the order in which concepts are introduced in the text is the exact chronological order of development. The argument in this and following sections seeks to show that characterising the association relation as 'simultaneity' or 'overlap' is entirely unsuitable given its use in hierarchical phonological structures, but understandable given its origin in a theory based on two-tier analyses of tone systems.

[15] Floating tones, indicating downstep, are in fact permitted some-

times. Such superficially floating material is the exception rather than the rule, and does not detract from the position that all segmental material is necessarily associated to the skeleton and thereby syllabified on the surface.

[16] Note that the two-tier version of AP (2.17) does not actually *require* a transitive association relation.

[17] Again, any argument against Sagey's proposals must address the formal problem. Her solution is formally-based, despite the reference to interpretation.

[18] Hammond (1988) is aware of this.

[19] The diphthongisation in Québec French, "perhaps the most elaborate example of diphthongisation known to me" (Hayes 1990: 56), is highly gradient, variable, apparently allophonic and highly productive. /ɛː/ for example can be realised as [aɛ], [ae] or [ai]. If length is phonemic, then all we need to say is that either long stressed vowels describe a diphthongal gesture, while their short alternants do not, or that the diphthongal gesture is too short to involve much actual movement when realising unstressed short vowels. Such phonetic accounts of diphthongisation have to be possible unless we are prepared to countenance languages with no (or very few) phonological monophthongs, *e.g.* Cockney English (Wells 1982:49).

[20] Despite this he conflates them by defining syllable structure (his exemplar of category membership) using association (simultaneity) in his analysis of Québec French; see his (50).

[21] In the same way AVP (and AP) would define precedence ($\prec^*$) as the transitive closure of immediate precedence ($\prec$).

[22] Let me also mention Archangeli & Pulleyblank (1986: 355–362), who are not unusual in defining relationships in terms of more basic ones in order to prevent the problems I have been discussing. They propose dominance as one such extra relationship. For Archangeli & Pulleyblank, x dominates y iff $x \neq y$ and there is a path from y to a Rime node that includes x. There is a path between x and y iff x and y belong to 'a continuous set of nodes and association lines' which repeats no type of node twice. All in all they propose a very complex system, with association being a primitive relation of little consequence beyond its usefulness in the definition of other relations. By assuming that dominance and association are simple inverses the need for this complexity is

removed.

[23] An exception to this claim might be set-valued attributes; see Rounds (1990).

[24] (2.31) is a root structure with irrelevant structure elided. Substructures are bracketed, and subscripted with the path to which they are associated. More details are given below of this notational convention.

[25] Recall that this means the value is just $_{place}[\ ]$ with an internal structure no more specific than the sort assignment tells us it *must* be. For example all the terminal attributes will have boolean values.

[26] I have drawn $\mathcal{P}$ in a different place to show that this information is not significant.

[27] This sort of rule is sometimes only a default rule. Normally every constraint must hold true, but defaults, if they fail, do *not* indicate ill-formedness. Consequently defaults cannot be simple constraints. This does not mean, however, that default rules cannot be constructed from constraints or otherwise dealt with, but it would be wrong to imply that further work is not needed in this area. See Wedekind (1990) for discussion.

[28] It could perhaps be called a repair-strategy phonotactic, since it is conveniently interpreted as adding information that requires a structure to conform to the phonotactic constraints of the language.

[29] See Sagey 1986 for a discussion of differing temporal realisations of the various articulations in co-articulated segments which nevertheless are unordered phonological units.

Chapter 3

Localising Multiple Association

3.1 Introduction

3.1.1 The nature of the problem

From what has been said so far about the formalism of AVP in Chapter 2, *any* two roots may share some value for an attribute. There is nothing to prevent every like consonant or vowel in a sentence sharing a single *melody* token. Some phonological structure from the end of a sentence could unify with structure from the beginning, despite any amount of intervening material. For a simple example of what the formalism can represent if unconstrained in this way, see (3.1), a sequence of four roots, in which the second and fourth share the value of their $\mathcal{P}$ paths, as do the first and third.

(3.1)

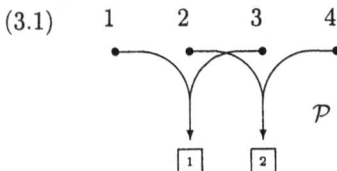

Of course, in Autosegmental Phonology the ban on crossing lines (however derived) prevents the interleaved dependencies represented in (3.1). (3.1) is a diagram of the AVP sequence in (3.2), in which the four paths are ordered *without contradiction* since the only statement of precedence is that $1 \prec 2 \prec 3 \prec 4$. The question arises as to whether this is desirable or undesirable state of affairs.

(3.2) $\{\langle 1, \mathcal{P}\boxed{1}\rangle, \langle 2, \mathcal{P}\boxed{2}\rangle, \langle 3, \mathcal{P}\boxed{1}\rangle, \langle 4, \mathcal{P}\boxed{2}\rangle\}$

$1 \prec 2 \prec 3 \prec 4$

The view taken here is that (3.1)/(3.2) is *undesirable*. The formal power an unconstrained AVP would have would be far in excess of that demanded by the data — phonological associations simply do not occur between randomly located entities. Typically, if feature F_1 shows a dependency with feature F_2, there cannot be an intervening F. Discontinuous long-distance dependencies are the currency of syntax, semantics and morphology, not phonology. Consequently this chapter seeks a revealing way to constrain association in order to restrict the formalism's expressive power.

3.1.2 Overview

The ability to associate a single feature or piece of phonological structure to more than one linear position is central to Autosegmental Phonology in all its variety, being one of its primary characteristics. Such multiple association is formalised as re-entrancy in AVP, where two or more indexed paths share a single structure as their value. This chapter investigates the constraints on the sequential proximity of such paths. As a principle of autosegmental locality the No Crossing Constraint is rejected and instead I adopt the SHARING CONSTRAINT, the force of which is to restrict re-entrancy to adjacent paths.

Multiple association is generally regarded as the appropriate formal device for representing several and various phonological dependencies. The Sharing Constraint forces a dichotomy in phonological dependencies because shared structure is limited to local applications. Local dependencies *are* recognised, however, in Autosegmental Phonology. Indeed they have a special status, for they alone display the properties of INTEGRITY and INALTERABILITY. But AP has no explanation of why multiple association consists in local and nonlocal versions; in particular it cannot derive integrity and inalterability from multiple association itself. In AVP the formal configuration of structure sharing and the properties of integrity and inalterability are co-extensive, so structure sharing can be seen as their *cause*. Once we adopt the Sharing Constraint in AVP we *predict* that multiple association behaves as it does.

3.2 Two constraints

3.2.1 The No Crossing Constraint

The NCC in its natural habitat

Part of Goldsmith's (1976) Well-Formedness Condition on autosegmental phonological representations is the No Crossing Constraint (NCC) that 'association lines may not cross'. It bans configurations like (3.3) in which $high_1$ is associated to $dorsal_2$ 'past' or 'across' the $dorsal_1$–$high_2$ association, because such a configuration exhibits a nonlocal dependency.

(3.3)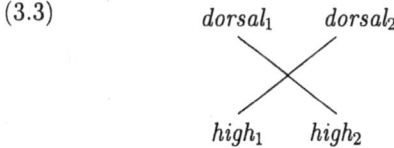

The account of locality in multiple association is founded on an account of singular associations. The $dorsal_1$–$high_2$ association divides the *dorsal–high* plane[1] into two areas such that all other associations in the plane must be located in one or other of the areas, but not both, *cf* (3.4). If (3.3) were allowed, then association would be wildly unconstrained.

(3.4)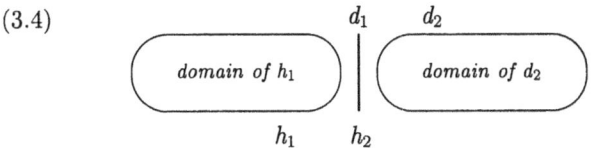

Some recent work into the proper definition of autosegmental association has resulted in the realisation that the NCC need not necessarily be an extraneous constraint on AP's representations. Instead it can follow from the way the system is set up. Sagey (1988) shows that the NCC is an intrinsic part of her formalism in which association is interpreted as overlap. Bird & Klein (1990) present a formal proof of the derivability of the NCC in a version of a Sagean framework based on event logic.

Both these approaches assume that association indicates overlap-in-time, but overlap is not necessary as an interpretation of association in order to derive these results: Scobbie (1988) shows that the NCC has derived status if association is given its original Goldsmithian interpretation of simultaneity. Scobbie points out that this result relies on the redundancy involved in the use of numerous sequenced tiers. If information about sequence is expressed once only then there is no opportunity for deriving contradictory combinations of sequences of features.

Hammond (1988) does not attempt a phonological account of the NCC, but argues for "a conception of association where autosegments are seen as issuing articulatory instructions" (p319). Consequently he assumes a characterisation of association very similar to that offered here, defining it to be transitive, asymmetric and irreflexive.[2] That some feature f is associated to a slot but not *vice versa* is parallelled in AVP, for association and dominance are the converse of each other. Hammond, however, maintains the autosegmental orthodoxy that subordinate features are sequenced independently of their association to the skeleton. This of course means that the consistency of the various sequences must be regulated if associations are made, and he adopts an Ordering Principle to do so.

(3.5)   *Ordering Principle*
Given two autosegments on a single tier, A then B, instruction B cannot be issued before instruction A.

Hammond (1988:322)

For all practical purposes (3.5) amounts to an outright statement of the NCC, except that the crossed line configuration (3.6) is

Localising Multiple Association

not ruled out as a *phonological* representation — it is just that the *interpretation* would appear to be contradictory, since "the realisation of B on x_1 would precede the realisation of A on x_2" whereas the internal relationship on the A–B tier would force the realisation of A to precede the realisation of B. (3.6) cannot be ruled out without the Ordering Principle, so Hammond makes this extra stipulation.

(3.6)
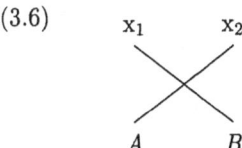

Finally note how Goldsmith (1990) uses *both* the NCC and an 'Association Convention' (3.7) to control crossing lines. The latter is so worded to avoid crossing lines at source. It restricts free association to features within one of the domains shown in (3.4).

(3.7) *Association Convention*

When unassociated vowels and tones appear *on the same side of an association line*, they will be automatically associated in a one-to-one fashion, radiating outward from the association line.

> Goldsmith (1990:14)
> (*emphasis added*)

If the NCC is a constraint on the well-formedness of all representations then one might expect the Association Convention to allow *free* association and not to need the phrases "on the same side of an association line" and "radiating outward from the association line". The NCC would govern all associations. The reason (3.7) has an in-built constraint on crossing lines is because of the different behaviour of local and long-distance associations in the face of crossed lines.

Goldsmith (1990:47) makes clear that the Association Convention offers priority to existing associations in that (3.7) does not apply to h_1 and d_2 in (3.4). There is no attempt to associate one to the other. But if some other rule adds a single association line between these autosegments (causing potentially crossed lines), this priority is *reversed*, though the ban on crossed associations remains. In fact the *original associations* (the h_2–d_1 association in (3.4)) are removed.[3] If the NCC were itself used to constrain the Association Convention then there would be no way to produce these different behaviours. Sometimes a crossing configuration acts to prevent a rule, sometimes to rescue the output of a rule.

So we can see that the precise characterisation of the NCC is uncertain. This suggests that the NCC should not be automatically adopted as the locality principle of AVP. And in fact there is a much stronger reason in that Autosegmental Phonology and Attribute Value Phonology have quite different ways of characterising *tiers*.

Why the NCC is unsuitable for AVP

The basis reason for the NCC is Autosegmental Phonology's assumption of multiple tiers, each defined as an independent ordering of features. In order that these independent statements of sequence are brought together in a meaningful way, some restriction on association is required which is sensitive to each sequence. The NCC fulfills this function because it is concerned both with sequential information from two tiers and with the sequential equations imposed by association.

Having multiple tiers demands statements of the type '$high_1$ precedes $high_2$' for one tier and that '$dorsal_1$ precedes $dorsal_2$' for the other. These statements of precedence are wholly independent. An association is just a relation between one item from each of the two tiers. When two autosegments are associated, the sequential information about each is amalgamated, so the precedence statements from each tier interact, giving rise to statements like '$high_i$ precedes $dorsal_j$' for example. Association implies some kind of sequential coordination between the autosegments, though quite what the coordination *is* is not entirely clear.[4] Each tier's inherent precedence statements must be consistent with those derived from the associations. If this is not so we have either inconsistent associations or an inconsistent tier.[5]

Localising Multiple Association 89

(3.8)

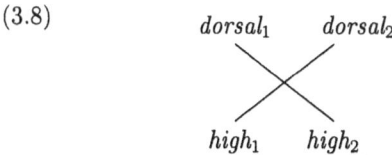

For example, in (3.8) = (3.3) association indicates that $high_2$ precedes $dorsal_2$ given the $dorsal_1-high_2$ association (and the *dorsal* tier precedences). However (3.8) also indicates that $dorsal_2$ precedes $high_2$ given the $dorsal_2-high_1$ association (and the *high* tier precedences). Since the various sources of information about the relative orderings of *high* and *dorsal* features do not concur, we have a crossing lines contradiction.

In AVP the situation is entirely different. If a substructure such as [HIGH +] is not associated to anything, then it has no sequential position.[6] In AVP just the skeletal tier is indexed, and to order two *high* features AVP orders the two corresponding *paths*. Indeed, since paths must originate from the indexed root, this is unavoidable. Information about the ordering of $high_1$ and $high_2$ is only recorded *once*, in the skeleton.

High features, being paths, necessarily mention a DORSAL attribute, since DORSAL is part of the path linking HIGH and the root:

$\langle i, [\ldots \text{DORSAL}[\text{HIGH}+]] \rangle$

Consequently, the path encoding a *high* feature has the path encoding a *dorsal* feature as a sub-path within it. This means that every *high* feature whose position is fixed at index i necessarily incorporates the 'co-indexed' *dorsal* path — the very path to which the [HIGH +] substructure is associated. No *high* path is *ever* independent from a *dorsal* path, and since a tier is nothing but a sequence of like features, the *high* tier is never independent of the *dorsal* tier.

Crossing paths in AVP

Given the differences between AP and AVP it is impossible to construct an example properly comparable to (3.8). The closest analogy to (3.8) I can construct involves four paths, two *dorsal* and two

90   Autosegmental Representation in a Declarative Framework

high. These are ordered by the (transitive) precedence relation, notated $\prec^*$. (3.9) represents a situation in which the *dorsal* paths are ordered relative to each other as are, quite independently, the *high* paths.

(3.9) $\{\langle i, \ _{r1}[\ldots \text{DORSAL}] \ \rangle,$

$\langle j, \ _{r2}[\ldots \text{DORSAL}] \ \rangle,$

$\langle k, \ _{r3}[\ldots \text{DORSAL}|\text{HIGH}] \ \rangle,$

$\langle l, \ _{r4}[\ldots \text{DORSAL}|\text{HIGH}] \ \rangle\}$

$i\prec^* j, k\prec^* l$

In (3.9) *r1* precedes *r2* and *r3* precedes *r4*. Perhaps to 'associate' in some way the matrices *r1* and *r4* and also *r2* and *r3* would give a parallel to (3.3). We can do this if we specify that $i = l$ and that $j = k$. This is contradictory, since we can derive that $l\prec^* k$ and $j\prec^* i$ by substituting indices which are equal, while (3.9) tells us that $k\prec^* l$ and $i\prec^* j$.

	Given	$i\prec^* j$	$\wedge$	$k\prec^* l$		from (3.9)
(3.10)	If	$i = l$	$\wedge$	$j = k$		'associations'
	Then	l	$\prec^*$	k		a contradiction

To equate this contradiction with crossed associations is misleading, however, for equating indices has nothing to do with AVP's interpretation of autosegmental association. It is not the case that two paths are associated in AVP if they share an index — association is a relation between (paths of) attributes and their values, not between one path and another, or one index and another. *If* it is said, in AVP, that a *high* feature is associated to a *dorsal* feature, this is just a sloppy way of saying a $_{high}[\ ]$ structure is associated to (dominated by) the path [MELODY|PLACE|DORSAL].

What then is the status of (3.9)? Here we seem to have a case where an incorrect assignment of indices results in a contradiction, but such manipulation of indices is not association. To answer this question, we must consider how phonological information from different *syntactic* constituents is combined.

Since the value of PHON is a set, set unification (Rounds 1990) is used when signs combine and their phonologies become combined. For English, when the phonology for a noun phrase combines with that of a verb phrase, a restriction is placed on the combination such that the greatest index of the noun phrase must precede the least index of the verb phrase (*cf* Reape 1991). This ensures that the NP precedes the VP. Imagine we imposed restrictions which attempted to put the final word of the noun phrase in front of the verb phrase but also the first word of the noun phrase *after* the verb phrase. The consequence would be that the type of contradiction shown in (3.9) would result. In other words a contradiction resulting from an improper treatment of indices is at the morphosyntactic level, not the phonological.

Before moving on, two points should be made to prevent confusion. If some phonological aspects of the noun phrase spread into the verb phrase by virtue of some sandhi phenomenon say, AVP analyses this by the assimilatory rules discussed above. That all nominal indices precede all verbal ones does not preclude the *place* features, say, of the noun and verb phrases being shared. Non-root structures bear no indices and are free to unify across the phrasal boundary without the phrases becoming intermeshed themselves. Secondly, free word order is modelled simply by using fewer constraints on the indices than would obtain in a fixed word order language. The greater generality of the description means a greater number of linguistic objects to which it corresponds.

3.2.2 The Sharing Constraint

AVP wishes to rule out (3.1) — repeated here as (3.11a) — and can do so by banning one of the two basic configurations to which it can be reduced.

(3.11) a.

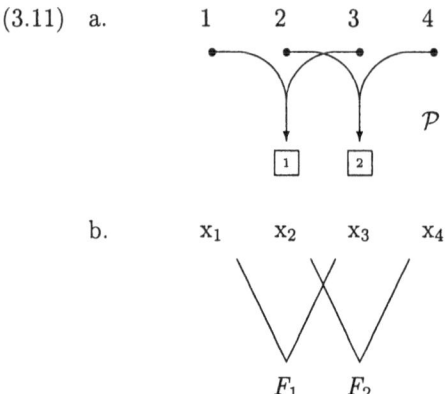

b.

Either we can ban those associations which cross in the diagram or we can ban those which are discontinuous. By now it should be clear that the former option is not viable because it only is when some structure [HIGH+] is the value of *two* paths that the possibility of a violation of a locality principle arises. A 'crossing dependency' must consist of multiply associated features.

If a structure [HIGH +] is associated to *two* paths, with indices i and k, then we have crossing dependencies if some other [HIGH +] is associated to an intervening index j. The way chosen here to prevent such an intervening path is to ban such discontinuous sharing. (3.11a) is therefore to be ruled ill-formed *not* not as a result of diagrammatically crossing associations but because $\boxed{1}$ (F_1 in the AP-style (3.11b)) is shared by two slots and 'misses out' a third at index 2.

(3.12)

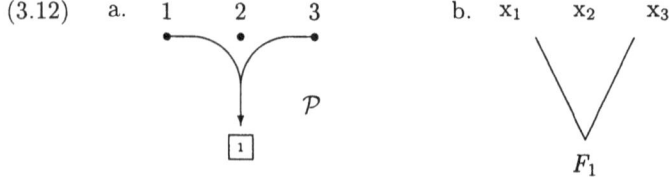

The equivalent diagrams in (3.12a,b) give the simplest version of the offending discontinuous configuration. In fact it is one which does not involve crossed lines at all! (The motivations for

Localising Multiple Association 93

this are explored below.) To ban (3.11) all we need to do is ban (3.12):

(3.13) *Sharing Constraint*
If a structure $\mathcal{M} = s^{[\ ]}$ is dominated by two paths of type $\mathcal{P}$ with indices i and j, where $i \prec^* j$, then for every index n where $i \prec^* n \prec^* j$ there is a path $\langle n, \mathcal{P} \rangle$ dominating $\mathcal{M}$.

Before moving on to consider the phonological ramifications of this characterisation of associative locality let me briefly note the benefits from the viewpoint of the phonology/phonetics interface. It seems reasonable to assume that all phonetic gestures are CONVEX. The term (van Bentham 1983:68) can be understood by analogy with a convex lens — such a lens is one in which any two points *in* the lens can be connected with a straight line enclosed *by* the lens. To say that gestures are convex is to say they are continuous, uninterrupted, unitary events. Thanks to the Sharing Constraint all phonological structures must be convex too, since they hold over an uninterrupted stretch of the skeleton (see also Bird & Klein 1990 for similar proposals). In AVP a phonetic gesture can correspond to a phonological structure in the simplest possible way.

3.2.3 AP's need to replace or supplement the NCC

AP and AVP ban the interleaved representation (3.11) by virtue of the impermissible configurations of which it consists. In AVP the parts of (3.11) congruent to configuration (3.14b) serve to rule it out. The NCC also rules (3.11) ill-formed, but the offending characteristic is congruent to (3.14a). There is therefore a different explanation of why (3.11) is ill-formed in each approach, since the

94   Autosegmental Representation in a Declarative Framework

other part of (3.14) is in both cases well-formed.

(3.14)

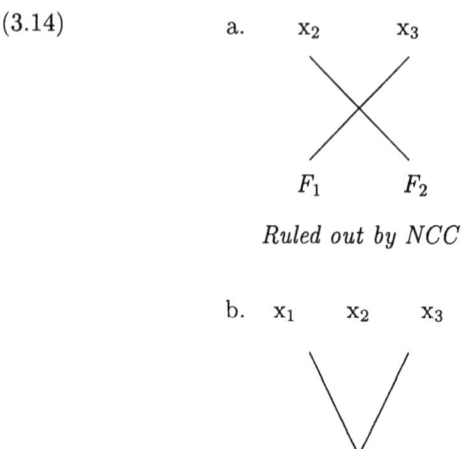

a. x_2 x_3

F_1 F_2

Ruled out by NCC

b. x_1 x_2 x_3

F

Ruled out by Sharing Constraint

Throughout the rest of this thesis I provide evidence in favour of the view that (3.14b) is the basic representation that is to be outlawed. But in this section I will first show that ruling out (3.14a), as the NCC does, is entirely the wrong approach if the idea is to account for locality of multiple association in the simplest possible manner.

It is acknowledged that the NCC provides only *part* of AP's theory of locality, that part where actual associations are involved. Kiparsky (1989:378, fn 18) notes:

> Autosegmental representations are constrained by the inviolable principle that association lines may not cross. This imposes (correctly) a locality constraint to the effect that a tone cannot be assimilated across another tone... As long as assimilation is treated by multiple linking of a tone to several tone-bearing units.

A tone or other autosegment may not be able to be associated across an association, but the NCC does not prevent assimilation when a *potential* site for association intervenes. In other words the

Localising Multiple Association 95

NCC does not rule out (3.14b) as nonlocal, which is unfortunate since it must surely do so.

It is an obvious characteristic of association that it does not miss out sites for association. The Association Convention (3.7) specifies that associations 'radiate outward' in a 'one-to-one' fashion. In consequence autosegments which remain unassociated after the application of (3.7) are always at the *edge* of the form, not in the middle.

In addition there are cases where association is actively prevented from skipping over a site specifically targeted by spreading, but which is for some reason incompatible with the value of the spreading autosegment. Archangeli and Pulleyblank (1989) provide such an example in their discussion of $[-ATR]$ harmony in Yoruba. A harmonic assimilation to $[-ATR]$ is prevented though there is *no* intervening medial ATR specification — only an intervening empty slot. (They argue convincingly that $[+ATR]$ is not present in the phonology.) This is the type of opacity which the Sharing Constraint can handle but the NCC cannot. Archangeli & Pulleyblank propose that the cause of opacity is a Feature Cooccurrence Restriction (FCR) which states that 'a $[-ATR]$ specification can be linked only to a vowel that is $[-high]$' (p175):[7]

(3.15) $[-ATR] \to [-high]$

Their $[-ATR]$ harmony spreads right to left, targeting vowels. The FCR bans association to high vowels, however. In a trivocalic word whose medial vowel is $[+high]$ and whose rightmost vowel is $[-ATR]$ the NCC does not determine whether or not the first vowel harmonises with the third. In fact there should not be harmony because a word such as *èlùbọ́* 'yam flour' is acceptable while there are no words such as * *èlùbọ́*.[8] The high vowel creates two harmonic domains in the same way as a $[+ATR]$ specification would. The NCC cannot deal with this opacity, and must be supplemented by some additional principle of locality.

> The two-domain forms... provide additional evidence that the Co-occurrence Constraint governs derivations ... [It] prevents $[-ATR]$ from ever associating to a vowel that is not specified as $[-high]$, with the result that a $[+high]$ vowel *blocks* application of

ATR spread... We attribute this opacity to the Co-
occurrence Constraint ...
*and to our assumption that the trigger and target of
a rule must be adjacent* at the appropriate level. The
first and third vowels of *èlùbọ́* are separated by the high
vowel, with the result that *ATR* Spread is blocked.

Archangeli & Pulleyblank (1989:185,6)
(Emphasis added.)

This assumption is in effect just equivalent to the Sharing Constraint. It is in addition to the NCC, however, since AP assumes *both* representations in (3.14) are ill-formed.

So we see that AP recognises that there are restrictions on locality which limit multiple associations to a local domain without recourse to crossed associations. The Sharing Constraint unites *both* types of opacity, since both are instances of (3.14b) where x_2 is *not* associated to *F*. Moreover the Sharing Constraint deals with the fact that almost without exception assimilatory rules apply to a target only if it is adjacent to the trigger. This has to be stipulated in AP because target and trigger can share structure even when arbitrarily far apart, but AVP *predicts* this adjacency.

Not only are there cases where locality is defined by means other than crossed associations, but there are cases where the presence of crossing lines fails to act as a barrier to further associations:

if a rule is formulated to add a single association line, it can, in principle, cause a line-crossing situation. In this case... the line that the rule adds remains, but *the line that formerly existed is taken to be the offending line, and is automatically erased.*

Goldsmith(1990:47)
(Emphasis added.)

In other words the crossed lines do not always define local domains within which association is contained, but are disposed of in a special manner.

Goldsmith's (1985) analysis of Khalkha Mongolian vowel harmony exemplifies the removal of an association which would otherwise have blocked unbounded spread.[9] The schematic derivation

Localising Multiple Association

in (3.16) shows how the second [+F]–V association does not serve to divide up the word into two domains of association.[10] Instead of blocking spread to the fourth slot (3.16b), the association melts away. In fact the precise mechanism used to arrive at (3.16c) is unimportant here — the point is that the appearance of crossed associations does not define locality of multiple association in AP.

(3.16)

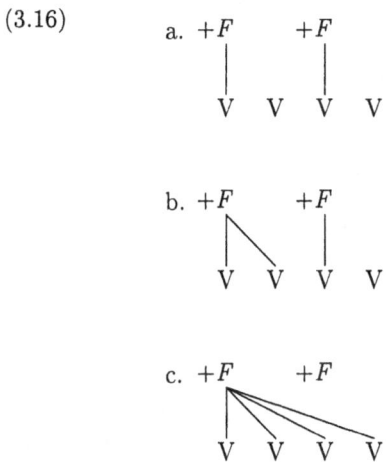

Another example where the NCC defines domains which are too restrictive is given by Cole (1987) (cited by McCarthy 1989:95). Cole discusses a glottalising harmony in Coeur d'Alène which targets only sonorants. The point of interest here is that the harmony fails to be blocked by underlyingly glottalised obstruents which would be expected to be opaque by the NCC. The theoretical device chosen to evade the NCC is to invoke *two* tiers for the feature in question (3.17). Having two tiers for [+*Cons.Glot*] allows the harmony to bypass underlying specifications without being blocked by them. Using two tiers of the same type means the analysis is MULTIPLANAR. The problem is: if an extra plane can be used every time the NCC defines locality too strictly, then the NCC is surely meaningless. Any crossing lines can be made to go away if more than one tier per feature is permitted.

(3.17)

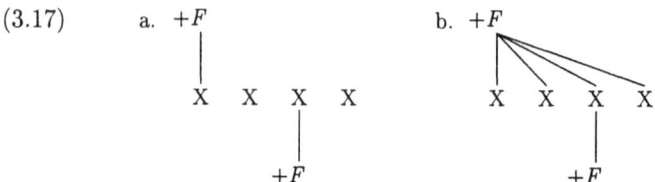

Finding differing ways around the NCC hides the common characteristic of Khalkha and Coeur d'Alène: the crossing associations involve features of the same polarity. It is a spreading [+ATR] harmony in Khalkha which is not blocked by underlying [+ATR], and a [+Cons.Glot] harmony which is not blocked by underlying [+Cons.Glot] in Coeur d'Alène. The segmental feature would seem to be *incorporated* into the domain of the harmony — the domain and the segmental specification are compatible. The NCC cannot express this idea since it is unable to differentiate the opacity of [+F] and [-F]. Both equally give rise to crossed associations.

The use of a separate plane is the maneouvre which most undermines the explanatory status of the NCC. Representations such as (3.11) would be the obvious starting point for McCarthy's (1979) treatment of Arabic nonconcatenative morphology. They are not used, of course, but only because AP prefers to permit 1 and 2 to appear on different PLANES. *Planes exist specifically to allow crossing dependencies without employing crossing association lines.* But this is a consequence of the underlying equivalence of multiplanar analyses and those using crossing long distance associations. (see a strong critique in Coleman & Local 1989).[11]

3.2.4 Summary

Phonological dependencies as indicated by association must be *local*. Nonlocality should presumably be the result of a violation of some locality principle. Autosegmental Phonology uses the NCC to achieve some locality effects, but if needs be, it can be supplemented. Moreover, when a rule needs to apply to a domain larger than that which the NCC defines, multiplanar structures can come into play, or indeed association lines can be broken. The NCC is not quite congruent with phonological locality.

Attribute Value Phonology specifically bans sharing between nonadjacent items, a much more intuitive characterisation of locality. Tangled one-to-one associations such as (3.14a) are not ruled out, since they cause no formal problems, and no problems of interpretation. Restricted by the Sharing Constraint, *all* instances of multiple association must ensure that the shared structure is convex. The basis for the ill-formedness of the interleaved (3.1) is the *discontinuity* involved.

3.3 Uses of multiple association in Autosegmental Phonology

3.3.1 The representation of length

Historically, phonologists working in a linear segmental framework had basically two choices as to the representation of long segments. Either a feature of length '*long*' can be used or a *geminate* analysis is possible, where a sequence of two identical segments functions as a phonological unit and licenses a single phonetic exponent. The geminate interpretation of length has been generally preferred for three reasons:

- Any theory must permit two identical segments to be able to appear next to each other in any case, for example in the English word *midday*.

- A feature such as *long* is different in nature from such features as *high*, *nasal* and *strident* in that it expresses quantity rather than quality.

- A long vowel is frequently classified along with vowel-consonant sequences as being 'heavy' by rules sensitive to syllable weight. This suggests long vowels are a sequence of two units. Similarly, a heterosyllabic geminate consonant correctly acts as coda and onset, just like a consonant cluster.

Certain problems arise for a linear theory using gemination to analyse long segments, however, since though all long segments can be treated as geminates, not all geminates behave like long segments (Harms 1968; Lehiste 1970; Leben 1977). In other words, though a pair of adjacent identical segments might sometimes act as a unit, this is not guaranteed. Amongst others, McCarthy

100 *Autosegmental Representation in a Declarative Framework*

(1979), Leben (1980), Clements & Keyser (1983), Steriade (1982), Schein & Steriade (1986) and Hayes (1986b) show the superiority in this regard of a nonlinear framework using structure sharing. It can furnish representations capable of capturing the differences in behaviour between *phonologically* long segments and sequences of identical segments succinctly while still employing the preferred geminate theory of length.

Autosegmental theory uses two similar representational forms. These *true* and *fake* geminates are shown as (3.18a) and (3.18b) respectively.[12] A fake geminate is the *accidental* juxtaposition of two identical feature hierarchy configurations while a true geminate is the *systematic* juxtaposition of the same. Only the true geminates are used to analyse length, so while (3.18b) is a sequence of two short vowels [aa], (3.18a) is one long, monosyllabic, heavy vowel [a:].

(3.18)   a.   b.

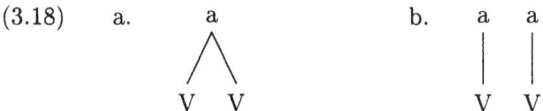

The use of true and fake geminates solves the problem that not all sequences of identical segments behave alike. For instance the example was given of the English word *midday*, which has a long [d]. Other words in English have geminate consonants, such as *penknife, coat-tails, coolly* etc. But note that in each case the geminates are heteromorphemic. This is because English does not permit monomorphemic long consonants, unlike Italian for example. Capturing this fact is simple given true and fake geminates. If we assume that fake geminates are in the unmarked case impossible due to the Obligatory Contour Principle (Leben 1973) and that the OCP's domain is the morpheme — both of which are independently supported — then it suffices to state that English has no geminates. This statement prohibits true geminates within the morpheme and between morphemes, while the OCP prohibits fake geminates within the morpheme without preventing heteromorphemic fake geminates such as [nn] in *penknife*.

Another characteristic of long segments as opposed to accidental clusters is captured by the pair in (3.18). If long segments are represented as true geminates, then a feature added to that shared melody must appear in both positions. For instance, if a long vowel is nasalised then all of it must be nasalised, not just part. And, if a long vowel could surface as either [−ATR] or [+ATR] then a true geminate correctly forces the entire vowel to have one or other value, not a mixture.

For another example, in Lithuanian (Kenstowicz 1970), both short and long mid front vowels [e] and [eː] appear as round and back [o] and [oː] before either [u] or [w]. [eou] is a possible sequence in Lithuanian, and when the [e] vowels are heteromorphemic, and hence fake geminates, [eou] does indeed arise. Monomorphemic [ee] sequences must be true geminates, so the fact that [oːu] surfaces from [eː] plus [u] rather than [eou] is predictable.

3.3.2 Assimilation

Assimilation used to be treated with the use of α-variables, at which time it was a relation of types (Chomsky & Halle 1968). Since the inception of nonlinear phonology, assimilation has generally been regarded as involving autosegmental spread, which involves a single token being associated (ultimately) to two positions. (See Goldsmith 1979; Halle and Vergnaud 1980; Clements 1976a.) A schematic progressive assimilation of [+F] would result in the shift from (3.19a) to (3.19b).[13]

(3.19) Schematic Assimilation

The advantages of the structure sharing view are that assimilation is adequately differentiated from arbitrary context-sensitive feature-filling rules. Given a rule like

$E \to F / \underline{\hspace{1em}} C$

an arbitrary rule would insert some feature F in some triggering context C with no requirement that F occurs in C. If such rules are highly marked then any rule adding a feature F in a context C would have to be assimilatory in that F would be spread from C. Indeed in most common context-sensitive rules the target becomes more like a trigger. For example, if a stop appears palatalised before a vowel, it will generally be a palatal vowel, not a round or back one.

3.3.3 Harmony systems

Clements (1976) was the first to give explicit analyses of vowel harmony using multiple association, and since then many languages and patterns of harmony have been profitably treated this way. Such autosegmental treatments typically specify a single harmonic autosegment underlyingly for the domain in question. This one unit of the harmonic tier is shared by all the appropriate vowels within its domain. The vowels are not adjacent, so the spreading results in *long distance* sharing, *i.e.* sharing between non string-adjacent targets. This theory has certain benefits lacking in previous approaches which, assuming strict segmentation, did not allow one piece of information to be shared by two others.

Firstly, it accounts for the HARMONIC SIMPLICITY: the non-arbitrary nature of harmony. A typical harmony system might involve a triggering autosegment, [+F], which if present causes all harmonic targets to become similarly [+F]. AP models this behaviour by linking a single [+F] to all the target segments.

(3.20)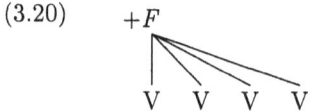

An impossible situation would be one in which every *second* vowel was [+F] while the intervening ones were [−F]. A theory of harmony using α-variables would appear to allow this by copying a token of [αF] across to one of [−αF]. If F were *round*, this might give rise to a vowel harmony pattern [i...y...i...y...i]. I know of no such case, where the harmony consists of a related pair of notes in this way: phonological harmonies are literally monotonous. The structure sharing model rules out such an impossible system since the value of the harmonic feature as well as the feature itself is the same for all harmonising segments.

A second benefit of the structure sharing, stressed by Clements (1976), is that it helps define the HARMONIC DOMAIN. Fre-

Localising Multiple Association 103

quently the spread of harmony is seen to be halted by the presence of a segment which is underlyingly specified for one or other value of the harmonising feature (see Clements & Sezer 1982). An OPAQUE association prevents further harmonisation since the multiple attachment of the harmonising feature to slots on either side of the opaque segment would involve crossed associations. The *dis*harmony between those segments preceding the blocking unit and those following is therefore nonarbitrary.[14]

3.3.4 Nonconcatenative morphology

Morphologically related forms in which the same *type* of segment appears in varying numbers and positions can be analysed instead as consisting of a single *token* of that segment melody autosegmentally associated to a varying number of skeletal slots (McCarthy 1979; see also McCarthy & Prince 1989). In Classical Arabic the consonantal morpheme *ktb* appears in various forms (3.21). Nonconcatenative theories map this sequence of segmental melodies (the 'consonant melody') onto varying numbers of consonantal slots by both local and long distance sharing of the root nodes and the material dominated by them.

(3.21) Classical Arabic verb stems, 3RD, MASC, SING, 'write'

Form	Past Active	Imperative
1	katab-a	ya-ktub-u
2	kattab-a	yu-kattib-u
9	ktabab-a	ya-ktabib-u

Since vowel morphemes such as *a* 'past active' or *ai* 'imperative' can be similarly discontinuous, segments of the vowel melody are also shared by multiple (nonadjacent) positions.

McCarthy (1979) proposes that the method by which vowel-only and consonant-only morphemes be combined is by association to a skeletal template. In order that the associations do not cross, a switch to *multiplanar* phonological representations is necessitated. A PLANE consists of one instance of each tier together with their associations. Thus the consonant plane has a *place* tier, as does the vowel plane. Each plane consists ultimately of a sequence of roots, and these are then associated to the skeleton. (3.22) shows part of the form *yukattibu*.

(3.22)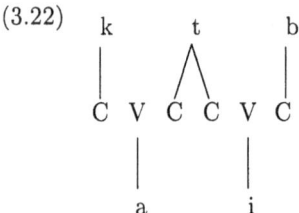

The consonant plane consisting of *ktb* is associated to the skeleton such that it has a true geminate [tː] in Form 2. The multiple appearances of [b] in Form 9 ([b...b]) are dealt with identically, except that the shared structure forms a *discontinuous* (long distance) geminate by virtue of the positioning of the segmental slots. In particular the two C slots which the consonantal melody is associated to are not adjacent, and a vowel intervenes. Regardless of the convexity of the melody following association, in both cases association has linked a single token of a melody to two slots.

3.3.5 Tone

Leben's (1973) treatment of tone provided a rich source of ideas on which Autosegmental Phonology was built. I am unable to devote much space here to tonal phenomena, however, concentrating instead on the more highly organised subsegmental feature structures. Given the historical importance of tone, however, I must mention that the long distance sharing of a tonal feature by several vowels is perhaps the prototypical multiple association. This is despite recent phonetic studies (Pierrehumbert & Beckman 1988 for example) which indicate the value of F_0 can be better predicted by phonetic interpolation than autosegmental spread.

3.4 Structure sharing in AVP

Structure sharing in AVP is more limited in its possible range of uses than it is in AP. The Sharing Constraint limits re-entrancy to paths which are adjacent in the skeleton (3.23) so discontinuous long-distance phonological dependencies like harmony, tonal spread and nonconcatenative morphology cannot involve structure sharing. It is only possible for shared structure to be used to analyse local dependencies such as those found in geminates and assimilated sequences.

(3.23) $\langle \, root_1^{[\,]} \, , \, root_2^{[\,]} \, , \ldots, \, root_n^{[\,]} \, \rangle$

3.4.1 Geminates

The shared melody of (3.24) is equivalent to the true geminate of (3.18a).

(3.24) True geminate

$$\left\langle \, root_i \begin{bmatrix} \text{MELODY} & \boxed{1} \\ \text{SYLLABLE} \, \top \end{bmatrix} , \, root_{i+1} \begin{bmatrix} \text{MELODY} & \boxed{1} \\ \text{SYLLABLE} \, \top \end{bmatrix} \, \right\rangle$$

Any feature added to the structure $\boxed{1}$ will affect both halves of the geminate equally, as is required. The fake geminate of (3.25) allows $\boxed{1}$ to be affected while leaving $\boxed{2}$ unchanged. Two different morphemes coming together can result in (3.25) (as with the [dd] of *midday*).

(3.25) Fake geminate

$$\left\langle \, root_i \begin{bmatrix} \text{MELODY} & \boxed{1} \\ \text{SYLLABLE} \, \top \end{bmatrix} , \, root_{i+1} \begin{bmatrix} \text{MELODY} & \boxed{2} \\ \text{SYLLABLE} \, \top \end{bmatrix} \, \right\rangle$$

3.4.2 Assimilated sequences

AVP is monostratal, which means that there is no way to impose different behaviour on a particular representational form merely because it results from a rule as opposed to being an underlying form — there is no such distinction. Rules are one type of constraint, they unify with other partial descriptions to reduce this partiality. The sort assignment, syllabification templates, lexical entries and feature co-occurrence restrictions are all constraints on a phonological form, some universal, some language particular, and some specific to the particular word or phrase in question.

If a rule (such as the OCP) forces two adjacent type identical structures to unify, then the true geminate that results is therefore *the same* as an underlying geminate, simply because there is no before and after in a monostratal system. The rule is a logical implication, with an antecedent and a consequent. Any partial description unifying with the antecedent must also be able to unify with the consequent to be well-formed. If we want to, we can assign a procedural interpretation of *adding* the consequential information — indeed this might be the case in some particular *implementation* of the phonology — but this derivational slant is essentially informal and not part of linguistic competence.

Partial assimilations, total assimilations, geminates and partial geminates are all analysed using shared structure. This sharing has the *same* status and properties in each case, which is exactly as is required (see for example Hayes 1986a).

3.4.3 Syllable structure

Prosodic structure (see Nespor & Vogel 1986 for a comprehensive survey) is always assumed to be convex: units such as mora and syllable cannot be associated to discontinuous stretches of the skeleton. Sometimes ambisyllabicity is analysed as two syllables sharing a segment, but the dependencies even in this case do not cross. Since syllable structure is expressed using multiple association in AVP, we capture this behaviour for free.

It is not a new idea to use attribute-value structures to represent constituency in this way: HPSG (Pollard & Sag 1987) uses attributes like PERSON with values 1, 2 or 3, but in addition a *sign* has attributes like DAUGHTERS which express constituent structure information. Syllable structure was discussed above in Chapter 2, but this is an appropriate point to discuss in more detail how the Sharing Constraint is relevant.

To ensure *full* syllabification every melody must be associated to a SYLLABLE.[15] This requirement parallels that for 'anchoring' discussed in Chapter 2:

A structure is anchored iff it is associated to

$\langle i, \ _{root}[\text{MELODY}\ ]\ \rangle$

All melodies must be anchored, and all must be syllabified:

A structure is syllabified iff it is associated to

$\langle i, \ _{root}[\text{SYLLABLE}\ ]\ \rangle$

I assume a bank of syllabification constraints are available which relate the linear segmental sequence to the syllable. Some constraints will ban particular melodies being dominated by particular syllabic roles — for instance /h/ cannot be dominated by ε-SYLL, *i.e.* it can't be syllabified into a coda. Sonority-based rules might insist that a low vowel be a syllable nucleus.[16]

(3.26) Phonotactic for low vowels

$\left(\begin{array}{c} vowel[\ ] \\ [\text{LOW+}] \end{array} \right) \longrightarrow \text{SYLL}|\text{NUCLEUS}$

In a monosyllable like *pram* the syllable structure enforces certain roles on each segment. If /p/ and /a/ are co-syllabic, then by the Sharing Constraint /r/ must be part of the same syllable too. As an example of syllable representation see (3.27).

108 *Autosegmental Representation in a Declarative Framework*

(3.27) AVS sequence for *pram*

$$\left\langle \begin{bmatrix} \text{MEL } \boxed{1}[p] \\ \text{SYLL}\boxed{5} \end{bmatrix}, \begin{bmatrix} \text{MEL } \boxed{2}[r] \\ \text{SYLL}\boxed{5} \end{bmatrix}, \right.$$

$$\left. \begin{bmatrix} \text{MEL } \boxed{3}[a] \\ \text{SYLL}\boxed{5} \end{bmatrix}, \begin{bmatrix} \text{MEL } \boxed{4}[m] \\ \text{SYLL}\boxed{5} \end{bmatrix} \right\rangle$$

$$\boxed{5} = \begin{bmatrix} \text{ONSET} & \{\boxed{1},\boxed{2}\} \\ \text{NUCLEUS}\,\boxed{2} \\ \text{E-SYLL} & \begin{bmatrix}\text{NUC}\,\boxed{3}\end{bmatrix} \end{bmatrix}$$

The entire segment sequence can be drawn in a more familiar manner, see Figure 3.1, where the re-entrancy of $\boxed{5}$ is shown by the four SYLLABLE arcs pointing to a single vertex. The skeleton is the only part of the diagram in which left-to-right ordering on the page indicates precedence.

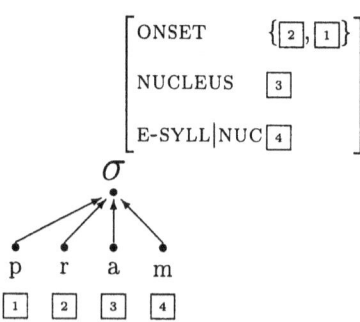

Figure 3.1: Graphical diagram of *pram*

3.5 Properties of locally shared structure

As shown in §3.3, in Autosegmental Phonology multiple association has many uses. It expresses what I will call both LOCAL and LONG DISTANCE phonological dependencies. Certain phonological properties have been recognised — INTEGRITY and INALTERABILITY — and it is essential to recognise the fact that these properties are predicated only of those configurations which make a *local* use of multiple association, namely geminates and assimilated sequences. They do not figure in discussions of nonconcatenative morphology, harmony or tonal spreading.

These properties have been identified and elucidated in work by Kenstowicz (1970), Pyle (1970), Kenstowicz and Pyle (1973), Guerssel (1977; 1978), Leben (1980), Younes (1983), and is summarised in Hayes (1986a,b) and Schein & Steriade (1986).

Integrity Long segments, even though they are formally a sequence of two identical segments, cannot be split by rules of epenthesis or have a rule apply to only one of the elements of the sequence.

Inalterability Long segments are often exceptions to rules that would be expected to apply to them if they were short.

Hayes (1986b) attempts to show that the multiple association approach to geminates in tandem with the generative architecture of AP *predicts* integrity. However, he is forced to acknowledge that this is a simplification of the problem.

> The predictions of CV Phonology concerning Integrity thus constitute a rare instance of a successful (albeit elementary) 'theorem' in phonology. [In a footnote] ...A caveat: these results appear to hold only for 'local' autosegmental linkings, such as those found in geminate consonants and long vowels ...It is clear that distinguishing the behaviour of long-distance vs. local linking is a major problem which goes beyond the scope of this article.
>
> Hayes (1986b:328)

It is my contention that such a distinction is beyond the capacity of the *theory*. The simplest solution to the problem is to limit multiple association to the expression of local dependencies. This is exactly what AVP does with the Sharing Constraint, and I will attempt to show that this is not only the simplest solution, but the best.

Hayes identifies the heart of the problem: integrity and inalterability really ought to be elementary to describe, but thanks to the omnipresence of multiple association in AP, this is far from the case. Schein & Steriade are similarly cautious:

> to our knowledge, no one has investigated the possibility of geminate blockage effects with structures resulting from long-distance partial assimilation. Such a study is obviously necessary for a better understanding of geminate blockage and as a basis for research into vowel and consonant harmony.
>
> Schein & Steriade (1986:736)

In AP multiple association appears to give a handle which can be used to account for the behaviour of local dependencies. Moreover, multiple association might even *predict* integrity or inalterability (as Hayes suggests). Unfortunately, Autosegmental Phonology is in fact unable to provide an adequate account of integrity and inalterability (as I show in Chapters 4 and 5) This is simply because, despite the recognition that they are distinct, long distance and local dependencies in AP are inextricably intertwined.

We will see that the declarative nature of AVP lends itself to an explanation of integrity and inalterability, and the Sharing Constraint means that we can posit a causal relationship between shared structure and the properties of integrity and inalterability. The local/non-local boundary is firmly drawn by limiting structure sharing to the former type. This makes it possible to derive the desired effects from a structural characteristic. These effects are thus part of the very fabric of the framework, and we are closer to Hayes's goal of that rare instance, a successful phonological theorem.

Notes

[1] Goldsmith (1990) uses the term 'chart'.

[2] He uses both the terms 'asymmetric' and 'antisymmetric' interchangeably.

[3] This difference in behaviour is discussed further below in Chapter 6.

[4] In some cases (Hammond 1988) it is explicitly a relation between the instructions which the autosegments encode, but in general the status of the sequential coordination is more ambiguous. Sagey's (1988) discussion of overlap and simultaneity as being phonological relations is regarded as being a phonetic one by Goldsmith (1990:352). Goldsmith's own view is that "from a purely phonetic point of view, the association lines represent simultaneity in time, or what we might call co-registration (though ours is not to be a purely phonetic point of view)" (p10). We are never given a non-phonetic account of what Goldsmithian association *is*, however.

[5] This latter possibility is not usually considered. I know of no instances where metathesis is used to evade crossed associations though there is no reason to suppose this is impossible.

[6] This is not to say it is 'floating'. It is accepted that floating autosegments *do* have some range of possible anchoring sites — they are 'stable' and do not just float away. This could be captured in AVP by formalising floating autosegments as an indexed path whose the index is in fact a *variable* over a certain range. The range of the variable expresses the stability. A morpheme with a floating tone cannot let the tone float onto just any anchor, and typically it lands on some segmental slot within the morpheme, or at most adjacent to it. This suggests the range of the index-variable is limited by reference to the other indices of the morpheme.

[7] The AVP constraint would be

$$\neg \begin{pmatrix} [\text{ATR}-] \\ [\text{HIGH}+] \end{pmatrix}$$

[8] Underdots indicate [$-ATR$].

[9] This analysis contradicts the spirit of the later claim that "rules of unbounded spreading will not create line-crossing situations" (1990:47).

[10] For Goldsmith the spreading feature is [$-back$], but Svantesson (1985) and Rialland & Djamouri (1984) show an *ATR* harmony is

active in the modern language. To update Goldsmith's analysis the spreading feature would be [+ATR]. See also Street (1963).

[11] See also Kitagawa (1988:80), who makes use of the equivalence between crossing lines and multiplanar analyses in the area of reduplication.

> [T]he sole motivation in the affixation approach... is to avoid the crossing of association lines... [S]uch crossing can be avoided... if we introduce the CV skeleton on an independent plane and make the association three-dimensional.

In other words, a multiplanar representation encodes just the type of dependencies the NCC tries to ban.

[12] Perhaps (3.18b) ought to be the 'true' geminate since it is undoubtedly a sequence, and indeed Paradis & Prunet (1990) make such a terminological shift. I will stick to traditional usage.

[13] Given the feature hierarchy, various assimilations are possible in addition to the simple boolean feature shown in (3.19). A class node such as *place* or indeed a whole melody can be spread.

[14] We have already seen above an indication that an account of opacity based solely on crossed associations is flawed. I offer a revised account of harmonic dependencies in Chapter 6 which accounts for harmonic simplicity and defines harmonic domains without relying on shared tokens of structure.

[15] Such full syllabification does not need to be completed at any particular stage in the derivation, since such derivational considerations are irrelevant. All that is required is that it be done sometime. Obviously all rules sensitive to syllable structure cannot apply till some structure is determined, but such intrinsic 'ordering' does not imply the theory is procedural.

[16] These constraints are for expository purposes only.

Chapter 4

The Integrity of Shared Structure

Shared structure has no special status in AVP when it comes to its resistance to destructive change. No structure can become unassociated once we have positively determined that it *is* associated. Declaratively speaking, if we know a representation involves sharing, we cannot 'unknow' it. A true geminate is subsumed by (is more specific than) a fake geminate, and in AVP we can only ever move to a more specific description. It follows that if structure is *shared* it cannot become un-shared.

The Sharing Constraint demands that structure can only be shared by adjacent paths. If there is pressure to insert material into such a configuration the Sharing Constraint demands some action be taken to satisfy it, but whatever happens, the epenthetic material cannot be accommodated by the breaking of associations. This is the account of geminate integrity in a nutshell.

In this chapter we see the benefits of the AVP approach to integrity. Those phonological dependencies realised as true geminates and partial geminates will cluster with simplex structures in resisting epenthesis rather than with long distance dependencies, since the latter are not analysed in AVP with shared structure.

114 *Autosegmental Representation in a Declarative Framework*

Integrity in AVP is due to the inviolability of individual structural units, *regardless* of the number of roots they are associated to. Mitosis — the division of one token structure into two tokens of the same type — is just not possible.

In AP integrity is seen as a property solely of multiple association. Since local *and* long distance dependencies are assigned representations using multiple association but only the former display integrity, I show that AP does not and cannot capture the proper range of behaviour.

4.1 Formal integrity and the prosodic causes of epenthesis

There are two formal aspects to geminate integrity: true geminates may not become discontinuous, and true geminates may not become fake geminates. In addition a proper account of integrity must address the question of the motivations for the phonology employing operations such as epenthesis (and cluster simplification) in the first place. We must be careful to distinguish the formal mechanism of inserting material into the root sequence from the prosodic requirement that *something* be done to handle an unacceptable sequence.

4.1.1 Formal requirements

To see how epenthesis operates let me take as an example Palestinian Arabic. Similar data to this is found in many languages: see Hayes (1986b) and Schein & Steriade (1986). Palestinian Arabic exhibits vowel epenthesis which we might describe very roughly as follows (Abu-Salim 1980):

(4.1)   Palestinian epenthesis rule

$$\emptyset \rightarrow \underset{|}{\overset{V}{\underset{i}{|}}} \ / \ C \_\_\_ \ C \ \left\{ \begin{array}{c} C \\ \# \end{array} \right\}$$

The Integrity of Shared Structure

Some rule with the general effect of (4.1) being applied from right-to-left ensures that a vowel [i] breaks up consonant clusters. Some data are given in (4.2):

(4.2) Palestinian Arabic epenthesis

Morphemic form	Syllabified form	
ʔakl	ʔakil	'food'
ʔakl-kum	ʔakilkum	'your food'
jisr	jisir	'a bridge'
jisr-kbiir	jisrikbiir	'a big bridge'

This statement of epenthesis appears to be unacceptable, however, since it incorrectly inserts the epenthetic vowel between the two Cs of a true geminate. This would produce the incorrect * ʔimim instead of ʔimm ('mother'). In order to prevent the rule applying to a true geminate some some *ad hoc* condition on the context of the rule must be articulated; for instance that the C slots in the context of this rule must not have the same melody. Of course the integrity would only be a property of this one rule.

But this is not enough: epenthesis is quite possible in this language between two segments of the same melody type, provided they are heteromorphemic. Together *fut* 'enter' and the suffix *t* '1st-SG' trigger epenthesis to give *futit*. In other words epenthesis is designed to split up clusters and fake geminates, but not true geminates. The formal structures used to express true geminates must be unable to become discontinuous.

The second formal consideration is that true geminates may not become fake. If such MITOSIS were unrestricted we would be unable to maintain the different behaviours of *futit* and *ʔimm*: in fact no true geminate becomes fake to thereby enable epenthesis. Either we must rule out mitosis entirely or attempt to give an account of why mitosis never feeds epenthesis.

A strong motivation for the absolute rejection of mitosis is that it cannot be allowed to feed rules freely: if it *were* able to do so then the distinction between true and fake geminates would be vacuous. For example it is never the case that only one half of a true geminate undergoes a rule, while fake geminates readily have this ability. If mitosis were to feed a rule affecting part of a geminate the true/fake distinction would disappear. Recall the discussion of Lithuanian Backing above in Chapter 3. When long [eː] is backed and rounded before [u] or [w] it must appear as [oː], not [eo]. When the fake geminate sequence [ee] appears in the same context, it *does* appear as [eo], since only the second of the two melody tokens is altered. If mitosis is allowed at any time to create fake geminates from true ones then an account is required of why this does not feed Backing in this instance. The only sensible course of action seems to be to assume that true geminates always remain true geminates.[1]

The two formal requirements for an account of epenthesis can be represented diagrammatically. (4.3a) shows a geminate becoming discontinuous with some epenthetic material interrupting. This is the more obvious case which must be disallowed. (4.3b) shows the mitosis which it is also necessary to ban.

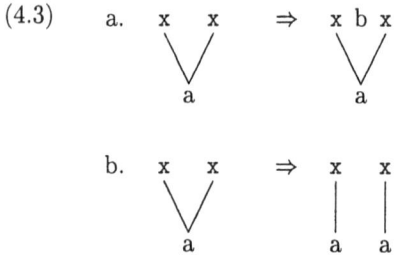

In §4.2 I will show how AVP bans the moves in (4.3).

4.1.2 The prosodic causes of epenthesis

Itô (1989) argues that a formal explanation of integrity is largely unnecessary given an appropriate *prosodic* theory of epenthesis. This account relies on the idea of exhaustive syllabification or PROSODIC LICENSING (Itô 1986), which requires all segments in a well-formed surface representation to be given a syllabic function. If it is not possible to prosodically license a segment sequence 'at the first attempt' then various strategies are used to come up with an exhaustively syllabified sequence congruent with the contrastive material:

- Epenthesis.
- Degemination.
- Cluster simplification.
- Stray erasure.

These operations add extra segments, force assimilations and restrict the appearance of optional segments in order that the string of contrastive segments can somehow conform to the phonotactics of the language.[2] In addition, syntactic concatenation can provides extra segments, which by interacting with the original string can provide a way of achieving full syllabification. This option is used in treatments of external sandhi. It is unclear in AP whether how this route to full licensing interacts with the four mechanisms given above. It is clear at least that the all-powerful mechanism of stray erasure must be held in check in cases of external sandhi.[3]

Goldsmith (1990). distinguishes representations which would be unlicensed without the operations mentioned above — those characterised by CONTINGENT EXTRASYLLABICITY — from cases in which some special statement *supplementing* standard syllable structure prosodically licenses a segment. Such LICENSED EXTRASYLLABICITY typically will be at word margins where segments accumulate (see §2.1). The operations listed above together produce compatible syllabified structures. They are attempting to remove all contingent extrasyllabicity.

Epenthesis, on this view, is an operation the intent of which is to add vowels or consonants enabling an unbalanced word to syllabify. This demands that forms be well-formed under a set of constraints on syllable structure. These constraints define possible syllables and prosodic licensing demands that every segment is syllabified.

If simple skeletal rules of epenthesis are used, then there is no automatic and guaranteed relationship between the syllable structure phonotactics and the output of the rules, but we can explain why epenthesis and the other mechanisms mentioned produce output conforming to the phonotactic constraints of the language if they apply just in case the phonotactics are not adhered to. Itô (1989) shows this to be an empirically superior and theoretically more satisfying account.

One aspect of Itô's theory concerns geminate integrity. Some languages do not allow consonants in the coda to bear a distinctive place of articulation. That consonants *do* appear in the coda is due either to their being coronal (being produced at the default place of articulation means that coronals are widely believed to need no place of articulation feature '**PoA**') or because they *share* their distinctive **PoA** feature with the following onset. Geminates and homorganic clusters are able to allow their **PoA** to fill a coda *as a side-effect*. Clusters and fake geminates, on the other hand, consist of an unsyllabifyable sequence of segments. They alone must be dealt with in some way, by means of some extra mechanism.

For example, take two vowels separated by the sequence /pk/. /pk/ has two **PoA**. /k/ can be an onset (though /pk/ cannot) but the **PoA** of /p/ means it cannot be a coda. Something must be done to ensure that /p/ is syllabified. Given the list of operations available the way chosen in this instance to solve this problem is to epenthesise a vowel — to make /p/ an onset. Now consider the case with an intervocalic geminate /pː/. Since the *single* **PoA** is linked already to the onset, somehow or other nothing then prevents a secondary syllabification to the coda. So this /p/ *is* syllabified in the coda, and there is no need to use epenthesis for the geminate. Itô's claim is that this is the explanation behind the apparent resistance of geminates to the effects of epenthesis rules – they do not *trigger* the rule. It appears that they are impervious to it, but this is an illusion.

In supposing that surface well-formedness as expressed by phonotactics is the driving force behind phonological 'derivations', Itô's approach is very much in tune with the constraint-based approach presented here. Unfortunately it is unclear how it could be possible to adopt this theory without radical alterations. It suffers both from theoretical and descriptive problems.

The theoretical machinery on which the integrity aspect of Itô (1986; 1989) relies is deeply problematic. She expresses the idea that no contrastive place of articulation is to be present in a coda with the Coda Filter (4.4) is intended to rule out all syllables with final consonants. (It mentions the *place* feature for reasons that will become clear).

(4.4) *Coda Filter* Itô (1989:224)

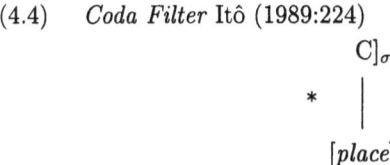

Consonants without any *place* feature (**PoA**) *obey* the filter and, parallel with open syllables, are not banned. Such consonants will typically be sonorants like glides, and obstruents with predictable **PoA** *i.e.* coronals. But how does Itô allow the **PoA** features of geminates to be linked to the coda? She uses the idea that all association lines in structural descriptions are to be interpreted exhaustively (the LINKING CONSTRAINT of Hayes 1986b: see Chapter 5) to block the application of this filter in cases which involve multiple association of the *place* node to more than one slot, *i.e.* geminates.[4]

It is wrong to say that *no* **PoA** can be associated to a coda, but this is what is conveyed by (4.4) on the face of it. In fact no *unpredictable* **PoA** can be associated. Itô is equating predictability with multiple association to enable (4.4) to be used. But of course consonants with *no* **PoA** are permitted, since the reason **PoA** is lacking is precisely that it is predictable. Itô fails to draw the proper connection between these two cases. Furthermore, the Coda Filter is a constraint on surface representations so Itô is forced to conclude that nondistinctive features are never present phonologically, which is an undefended claim. Further problems with the Linking Constraint itself and with its interaction with the Coda Filter are discussed in Chapter 5.

In addition to the practical problems attaching to her account Itô approach is flawed in that it involves a confusion of levels. Epenthesis is just one formal solution to a prosodic problem of failed syllabification. Integrity is a formal property of geminates making then resistant to epenthesis; it is not a comment on the remarkable syllabifiability of geminates. Because Itô collapses the formal property of 'resistance to epenthesis' and 'resistance to the prosodic cause of epenthesis' her theory only deals with integrity in languages which *permit* geminates in the epenthesis context.

Epenthesis is one particular mechanism "by which phonological strings are brought in conformity with Prosodic Licensing" (Itô

1989:220). Geminates are already in conformity, so are never split: they show integrity as a consequence of *not being subjected* to the rule. But in a language where geminates are *ill-formed* in the same context as that in which clusters are ill-formed, and where epenthesis splits up the latter, then Itô can only stipulate that epenthesis is not allowed as an operation on the geminates to render them well-formed. Degemination or another of the mechanisms listed above, not epenthesis, is used. For Itô an independent account of integrity is still required to explain why epenthesis is impossible to syllabify geminates. Well aware of this problem, she cites the cases of Turkish (Clements & Keyser 1983) and Tangale (Kenstowicz & Kidda 1985) as problematic for her approach:

Turkish uses epenthesis to break up impermissible consonant clusters and degemination in the remainder of cases. In particular, word-final geminates are unsyllabifyable and are degeminated. This ought to be due to the restrictions of integrity. But Itô can only derive the integrity of geminates from the well-formedness of geminates. Clearly she has to resort to a second, *formal*, account of integrity. Itô (1989: 234) admits

> it is not clear whether it is possible to maintain that ...[integrity] should always follow from syllabification conditions

and leaves the problem open. The examples cited are of word-final clusters which are either broken up or degeminated: *devir* 'transfer' from /devr/ and *hak* 'right' from /hakk/.

Tangale inserts epenthetic /u/ after C_1 in triconsonantal sequences. If the first two consonants share place of articulation then some form of cluster simplification takes place. Consider what happens when *-no* 'my' is suffixed to CC-final words: *bagud-no* 'my pigeon' has an epenthetic /u/ (see *bagda* 'pigeon') but *lan-no* 'my dress' has not (see *landa* 'dress') and similarly *mol-no* 'my brother' has failed to undergo epenthesis (see *molle* 'brother'). Geminates or homorganic clusters cannot syllabify and this triggers some remedial action as the prosodic theory demands. But crucially epenthesis is available only for nongeminates thanks to integrity.

It is impossible to equate epenthesis (one way to get proper licensing) with the necessity *for* proper licensing. In showing that geminates have a special ability to be licensed when clusters are not Itô claims, wrongly, that this is the full account of integrity. The implication of those cases where *geminates* are ill-formed is not fully comprehended.

In sum, Itô's account is inadequate in two respects:

1. Applying the Linking Constraint to the Coda Filter is theoretically unsatisfactory.

2. It is not explained why epenthesis cannot be the remedial measure for geminates which are ill-formed.

Goldsmith (1990) offers the possibility of a more attractive theoretical approach to epenthesis than the use of the Coda Filter but it is nevertheless still subject to the second criticism above.[5] In Chapter 5 I offer a description of a framework of licensing similar to Goldsmith's, and so I postpone any further discussion of the prosodic approach to syllabification. I will now turn to the analysis of formal integrity offered here.

4.2 An AVP account of formal integrity

4.2.1 The role of the Sharing Constraint

The true geminate in AVP is a sequence of root matrices which share melodic structure. Fake geminates do not have these token identical melodies. The relation of transitive precedence $\prec^*$ between the root matrices does not necessitate absolute adjacency (as immediate precedence $\prec$ would). If $\prec$ were used then integrity would be dealt with already, but incorrectly, since *any* two roots could resist epenthesis, regardless of any shared structure.

A true geminate is shown in (4.5a) and the corresponding fake geminate in (4.5b). For sake of clarity, the geminates discussed will be /mː/. Note the geminate is necessarily hetero-syllabic.

122   *Autosegmental Representation in a Declarative Framework*

(4.5) a. $\left\langle \underset{root_i}{\begin{bmatrix} \text{MELODY} & \boxed{1} & \text{`}m\text{'} \\ \text{SYLLABLE} & \boxed{4} & \end{bmatrix}} , \underset{root_j}{\begin{bmatrix} \text{MELODY} & \boxed{1} & \\ \text{SYLLABLE} & \neg\boxed{4} & \end{bmatrix}} \right\rangle$

b. $\left\langle \underset{root_k}{\begin{bmatrix} \text{MELODY} & \boxed{2} & \text{`}m\text{'} \\ \text{SYLLABLE} \top & & \end{bmatrix}} , \underset{root_l}{\begin{bmatrix} \text{MELODY} & \boxed{3} & \text{`}m\text{'} \\ \text{SYLLABLE} \top & & \end{bmatrix}} \right\rangle$

Epenthesis corresponds to adding extra information to the skeleton; information that there is a root matrix $\langle n, S \rangle$ where, to take the case of (4.5a) first, $i \prec^* n \prec^* j$. The Sharing Constraint would impose the additional condition that in S the value of [MELODY] is $\boxed{1}$, *i.e.* /m/. Immediately we see that this makes it impossible to epenthesise a consonant into a true geminate vowel or a vowel into a true geminate consonant. The Sharing Constraint insists that the new segment has the same melody as the geminate and so it gives us the bulk of an account of integrity for free.

A rule epenthesising a fully specified /m/ into /m:/ would never be suggested — there would be no point. But we have inserted an empty slot because an epenthetic segment is usually assumed to be completely unspecified as to melody. Its melody is supplied by the context, or it is given a default value. In the particular circumstances of insertion into (4.5a) the slot's melody by necessity must unify with that of the geminate. All material shared by the geminate's roots is shared by the intervening slot. Epenthesis does not *fail*, it is merely useless; exactly as useless as inserting /m/ into /m:/ would be.

In the case of (4.5b) the empty melody need not unify with its neighbours, and so epenthesis is able to make a difference. It affects the chances of the sequence's ability to syllabify, which is what epenthesis is intended to do.

A slightly more complex case is that of the partial geminate, such as the nasal-stop cluster /mp/. This cluster involves sharing of the value of PLACE. Epenthesis of an empty slot results in a structure which is no more than an *extension* of its neighbours. What they share, it shares. It has no structure other than that which they share.

4.2.2 The OCP and degemination

Although again epenthesis is a dead-end, we must deal with the consequence of its application. Where we had a sequence of two identical structures, now we have *three*. These three structures are unusual in that the epenthetic segment is not DISTINCT from the others. In fact it consists of what they have in common. The Obligatory Contour Principle 'OCP' (Leben 1973; Goldsmith 1976; McCarthy 1979) bans such sequences, for they do no more than assign vacuous indices to structure. A typical statement of the OCP is "in a given autosegmental tier, adjacent identical segments are prohibited" (McCarthy 1979:238). Let us see how AVP can make use of the OCP.

The OCP says, in effect, that phonological units in the sequence of units are analogous to members of a set. In set theory the set $\Sigma = \{\text{apples}\}$ and the set $\Sigma' = \{\text{apples, apples}\}$ are identical. In phonology it is quite possible to have the same unit repeated: a syllable appears more than once in *banana* and *dada*. But this is because phonology consists of a *sequence* of units. What we find, again and again, is that it is impossible to have identical elements when they are *adjacent*. So *ttttttop* and *oooooo* are impossible words. This requirement for a continuously modulated phonological description is a very strong tendency. The epenthesis of a slot into a geminate does nothing more than spread the melody of a segment by assigning it a new index. No new material is added. Consequently there is no *contour*, and the sequence is treated *as if it did not exist*. All other things being equal, (4.6) holds.[6]

(4.6) Index OCP

$$\left(\boxed{1}\right)_i \wedge \left(\boxed{1}\right)_j \stackrel{def}{\Longrightarrow} i = j$$

(4.6) rules out a syllable such as /ppppa/ *automatically*, since /pp/ → /p/ unless we have reason to believe otherwise.

(4.6) works with reference to the range of available segment structures and syllable functions. It forces two paths sharing a value to have equal indices, if possible. If the indices are equal, then the paths must be too, for an attribute-value structure is a *set* of conjoined paths. No structure can have two instances of the same attribute. When two indices are equated by (4.6) any remaining distinction between the roots 'goes away'. They become the same object at the same location. In this way some of the effects of deletion rules can be copied by *adding* the information that $i = j$. Unless a prosodic role is available, we witness an apparent deletion.

The OCP serves to turn tri-geminates into normal geminates not by arbitrarily counting root nodes. It forces each slot to be *incompatible* with its neighbour, for there to be a contour. Otherwise they collapse together. In the case of geminates, which share a melody, the contour must come in the choice of syllabic function. I suggested in §2.2 that in the initial acquisition of a morpheme, a sequence of segments of the language is assigned to it. Geminates and other complex segments have certain extra constraints imposed on them from this stage. The slots of a geminate consonant must be heterosyllabic, meaning that while the value of SYLLABLE on first slot can be labelled $\boxed{1}$, the value of SYLLABLE on the second must be $\neg\boxed{1}$. Long monophthongal vowels consist of the same melody being shared by two functions. Since such a vowel is tautomorphemic the OCP *can* cause the collapse of the sequence of roots into a single structure. How many indexed structures are required to represent this is irrelevant so long as the requisite phonological roles are represented. A long vowel becomes even more like a segment in AVP since it can be represented by a single root matrix structure:

(4.7) $$\begin{bmatrix} \text{MELODY} & \boxed{1} \\ \text{SYLLABLE} & \begin{bmatrix} \text{NUCLEUS} & \boxed{1} \\ \varepsilon\text{-SYLL}|\text{NUCLEUS}\boxed{1} \end{bmatrix} \end{bmatrix}$$

Questioning of the integrity of this structure is like questioning the integrity of short vowel. That short segments show integrity is so obvious as not to require mention, and so treating long and short vowels are identical structures in which the former merely has double re-entrancy makes this connection quite dramatically. This is a radical departure from the intuitive interpretation of root matrices as phonemes. I see no reason to accept that to analyse long vowels we must add a new root matrix adjacent to the matrix in (4.7), whose content is identical to (4.7) — see (4.8). Surely the sequence of two identical structures ought to be a mere notational variant of a single structure.

$$(4.8) \quad \left\langle \begin{bmatrix} \text{MELODY} & \boxed{1} \\ \text{SYLLABLE} \boxed{2} & \begin{bmatrix} \text{NUCLEUS} & \boxed{1} \\ \varepsilon\text{-SYLL}|\text{NUCLEUS} \boxed{1} \end{bmatrix} \end{bmatrix}, \begin{bmatrix} \text{MELODY} & \boxed{1} \\ \text{SYLLABLE} \boxed{2} \end{bmatrix} \right\rangle$$

Note that (4.6) collapses *adjacent* structures without having to specify this. If the root matrices were not adjacent then by the Sharing Constraint they could not be sharing any structure. Versions of the OCP in autosegmental theory need to specify adjacency, so again the Sharing Constraint is playing a useful role in reducing redundancy.

4.2.3 The OCP: gemination and dissimilation

In addition to its index-equalising aspect the OCP performs a slightly different function: forcing fake geminates to be true. In AVP this amounts to ensuring that structures which seem only to be type-identical are in fact token-identical (within morphemes at least). To do this AVP again does not need to mention adjacency. This aspect of the OCP can be characterised as forcing everything to share structure. In the last section we saw the OCP try to collapse shared structure by attempting to prevent two indices where one could do.

In both its roles the OCP cuts redundancy, forcing the phonological skeleton to consist of a sequence of *distinct* structures. Together these aspects can be informally characterised as a Sharing Principle:

(4.9) *Sharing Principle*

All structure that can be shared is shared.

The OCP sometimes holds over nonadjacent segments, *i.e.* over long distances such as the word. AVP predicts that shared *tokens* cannot be involved in such dependencies. OCP-like patterns such as Greenberg's (1950) observations on the structure of Semitic roots *can* be resolved by resorting to structure sharing — in the consonant-only morpheme. But in cases where only one feature is permitted per word, say, intervening segments mean that the OCP cannot turn fake geminates into true geminates in order that the rule be respected. The only solution AVP can offer is type differentiation: DISSIMILATION. *This is exactly what is found.*

Steriade (1987b) discusses Latin r/l alternations in which the adjectival suffix *-alis/-aris* selects /r/ or /l/ depending on the identity of the preceding non-nasal sonorant. If no non-nasal sonorant is present, then we get *navalis* 'naval', but there is dissimilation in *militaris* 'military', *solaris* 'solar'. And when the root has both /l/ and /r/, it is adjacency on the *lateral* tier which counts. Thus we get *floralis* 'floral' and *reticularis* 'of the net'.

This is clearly an OCP effect. Standard AP could abide by the restriction by assimilating the *lateral* features, but this is wrong, even within the morpheme: see the case of *flor*. Steriade's explanation of the long-distance OCP effect is that nothing on the *lateral* tier intervenes, so the features in question are 'adjacent' and subject to OCP control. But if nothing intervenes there is no possibility of assimilation resulting in a line crossing violation. Surely assimilation would be expected in this model? Why does dissimilation exist at all? AVP, which does not permit such assimilation, *predicts* dissimilation in cases such as this, where a phonotactic affects items adjacent on their tier, but not adjacent skeletally.

4.2.4 Summary

In AVP the well-formedness or ill-formedness of the geminate *cannot be altered by an epenthesis rule* since it leaves everything as it finds it. Note how this is similar to Itô's view: if a geminate is well-formed, she would say the rule is not triggered. In AVP, if it is well-formed then epenthesis will apply vacuously. Itô's position is problematic when the geminate is ill-formed, since the impossibility of epenthesis is not accounted for by her system of integrity. But in AVP when the true geminate is ill-formed, then the epenthesis of an extra melody again is vacuous, and some other course of action is required to achieve full syllabification.

The Sharing Constraint, proposed to prevent an associative free-for-all, derives the behaviour of true geminate integrity. A true geminate involves sharing, and *sharing must remain local*. In the case of the fake geminate (4.5b) no sharing is involved so epenthesis is free to apply.

The other formal aspect of integrity discussed above is that mitosis should not be allowed to feed epenthesis. Since mitosis involves two token-identical structures becoming merely type-identical it is ruled out in AVP. Mitosis is a nonmonotonic operation in that information is removed and we move from one representation to another which properly subsumes it. This is not possible in a unification-based framework since we collect information (constraints) from different sources and move inexorably towards a more specific description. We unify the melodies in a fake geminate to create a true geminate, so to go the other way — to 'de-unify' — is impossible. Thus the idea that a melody cannot be split as a prelude to epenthesis is part of the very fabric of AVP. We will see that this is not so in the No Crossing Constraint account of formal integrity.

4.3 Formal integrity and the No Crossing Constraint

In this section I will discuss the formal account of integrity which Autosegmental Phonology requires in addition to a theory of full syllabification.

4.3.1 Deriving integrity from crossing associations

An early attempt to capture the behaviour of geminates was Guerssel's (1978) Adjacency Identity Constraint (4.10), though see also Kenstowicz & Pyle (1973). It imposed a description of the two aspects of integrity I have discussed onto a theory which, since it lacked structure sharing, was unable to encode in its representations the dependency existing in the geminate structure.

(4.10) *Adjacency Identity Constraint*
Given a string $A_1 A_2$, where $A_1 = A_2$, a rule alters the adjacency of $A_1 A_2$ if and only if it alters the identity of A_1 or A_2.

The connection established in (4.10) is that the ability to alter only one part of a geminate co-exists with its interruptibility — both characteristics which ought to follow from the use of shared structure in the differentiation of true and fake geminates. But Guerssel was working in a linear framework which could not provide the appropriate representational distinctions. Autosegmental Phonology *does* provide the appropriate starting point, and the purpose of this section is to show that it cannot capitalise on this. Unlike AVP it must add stipulative constraints in order to describe integrity adequately.

The basis of the current AP account originates with an observation of Kaye (personal communication cited by Halle and Vergnaud 1980) and independently Kenstowicz, Bader and Benkeddache (1982). Think back to the example of the Palestinian Arabic word *?imm* which would be expected to undergo epenthesis to become the ungrammatical * *?imim*. When some segment [i] is inserted into a true geminate (4.11a) the true geminate cannot house the epenthetic vowel without a crossing lines violation (4.11b,c).

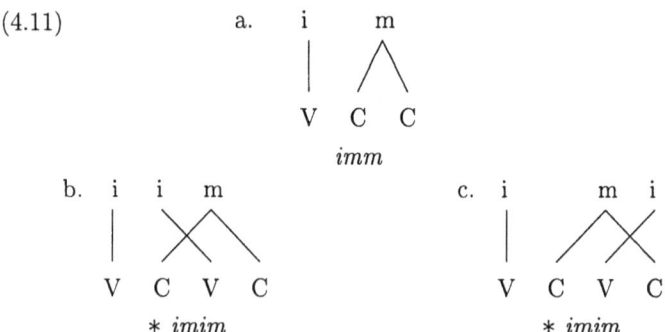

Since such configurations are ruled out the conclusion is that the epenthesis rule is *prevented* from applying. In other words the standard autosegmental theory of integrity relies on the No Crossing Constraint. Although this seems a very simple proposition, there are severe difficulties with this approach. In fact this is generally known, see Hayes (1986b), Schein & Steriade (1986), Itô (1989). Indeed Itô's motivation for an account of integrity based wholly on the requirement for full syllabification is that "it avoids the problematic appeal to the No-Crossing Constraint for blocking

The Integrity of Shared Structure

epenthesis in linked structures." Since we have just seen that a structural account of integrity is still required to explain why unsyllabifyable geminates never undergo epenthesis, we must return to the account of integrity based on the NCC and investigate its potential advantages and shortcomings more closely.

4.3.2 Problems with the NCC approach

How to stop lines from breaking

First of all there is a very obvious problem which has not been sufficiently stressed. The AP solution, or the 'crossing' solution as I will call it, has no value unless it can be explained why the crossed lines in (4.11) cannot be broken. The multiple linking of a local true geminate (4.11a) is safe from epenthesis only if we assume that the line crossing contradictions in (4.11b,c) cannot be evaded in any way, for instance by turning the true geminate into a fake geminate (MITOSIS) in the process of accommodating the epenthetic vowel (4.12).

(4.12)
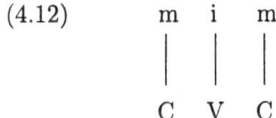

In AVP, once two structures have been declared as token identical it is impossible to then move back to the less specific type identity. But in AP it is perfectly permissible to non-monotonically delink autosegments in order to produce a well-formed structure from an ill-formed one such as (4.11b,c). Deletion is an operation available anywhere and everywhere in the phonology. Recall that in §3.2.1 we saw that Goldsmith (1990:47) define what is possible in such cases, namely that any single (*i.e.* nonharmonic) association line added by rule which would cause line crossing results in the offending *original* lines being "automatically erased." It is therefore difficult to maintain that an epenthesis rule would be blocked by the ill-formedness of (4.11b,c) since it would appear that these configurations could automatically trigger mitosis to produce the well-formed (4.12).

A solution to this would involve the claim that 'epenthesis does not qualify as a rule-type able to trigger mitosis and automatic erasure', but this begs the question. AP has no formal reason to bifurcate associations into 'harmonic' and 'single' sub-types other than the necessity to account for integrity. AP *must* make this distinction though, since mitosis can only be made available to relieve crossing line violations in the harmonic cases. Otherwise the NCC would *never* block a rule. The NCC acts as a preventative principle in single linkings like those in epenthesis and as a repair strategy in harmonic linkings. This clearly requires that we know what type each association is, but it is unclear how AP can do this.

The 'harmonic cases' on which AP can use mitosis are non-local in AVP — they never use structure sharing in the first place. There is a fundamental distinction between the two types of phonological relationship which AP is implicitly forced to recognise. Of course it has no explanation of why the NCC acts as it does — but AVP's monotonicity easily accounts for the different behaviours. Integrity follows from structure sharing itself.

The same-plane assumption

Mitosis is an operation which turns token identical structures into type identical ones, as was seen above. What protects AP's true geminates from mitosis? The answer is that it is generally assumed that mitosis is not available except in a restricted range of cases. Archangeli & Pulleyblank (1986:135) define mitosis (or 'fission') such that it cannot be explicitly and individually addressed: "tier conflation, merger and fission are not processes that can be manipulated by the phonology. There are no functions such as *conflate*, *divide* or *merge*." Mitosis only arises in order to circumvent a line crossing violation (or similar) due to another non-manipulable part of the phonological derivation, *i.e.* arising from a device of universal grammar.

One situation which gives rise to mitosis arises in multiplanar treatments of nonconcatenative morphology systems. In such analyses multiplanar structures are collapsed together into a single plane at some point in the deriviation, a process called PLANE CONFLATION (see Younes 1983; and Chapter 6 below). The aspect of plane conflation of interest here is that a consonantal melody at-

The Integrity of Shared Structure 131

tached to two nonadjacent slots must undergo mitosis when there is an intervening vowel. (This vowel is on a different plane to the consonants before conflation.) Thus in the derivation of a form like Tigrinya *räqqiχ* 'thin' derived from the consonantism /rq/ the multiplanar (4.13a) undergoes conflation into (4.13b).

(4.13) a.   b.

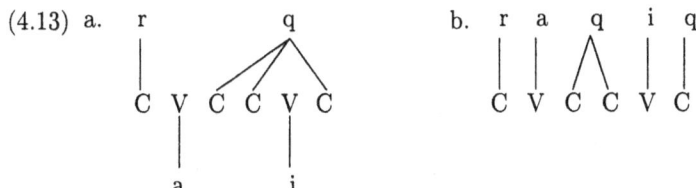

Note that the /q/ melody undergoes mitosis in (4.13). This is to avoid crossed association lines in the formal derivation, but it has the practical consequence that it allows a simple phonological treatment of a spirantisation rule. The final /q/ is realised as [χ] *independently* of the medial geminate [qq] (see Schein 1981). The requirement that these nonadjacent consonants do not share a token melody is shown by the medial geminate which does not spirantise while the final stop of the same underlying type does do so.[7] AP allows a single token /q/ to be shared in the multiplanar stage and uses mitosis to reach the desired surface representation in (4.13b) with two independent /q/ tokens.

It should be clear by now the assumption that is required if the crossing lines explanation of integrity is to be maintained. First recognised by Steriade (1982) and Kenstowicz, Bader and Benkeddache (1982), it is necessary to assume (to stipulate) that an epenthetic segment has its melody on the same plane as the material it is being epenthesised into. Otherwise (4.14a), the multiplanar post-epenthesis form, could be turned into (4.14b) by plane conflation applying automatically.

132 *Autosegmental Representation in a Declarative Framework*

(4.14)

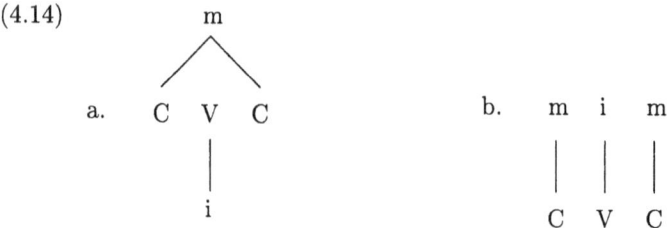

a. C V C
      |
      i

b. m i m
    | | |
    C V C

There is nothing ill-formed about epenthesising on a different plane in the wider scheme of operations AP makes use of, which is why it has to be explicitly ruled out. The reason it must be banned is that (4.14) constitutes a *discontinuous* geminate (like that in the analysis of *räqqiχ*). Such a configuration triggers plane conflation which in turn triggers mitosis. A discontinuous geminate can be split, and a normal true geminate cannot — but this position can be held only if epenthesis is banned from producing multiplanar representations.

The default rule assumption

Consider the formal possibility of epenthesising just a segmental slot. This is a natural rule for autosegmental theory, for a language's epenthetic vowel or consonant is usually taken to be maximally underspecified in order to account both for 'different' epenthesis rules all inserting the same vowel and for epenthetic segments taking on characteristics of adjacent segments. It was noticed by Schein & Steriade (1986) that the epenthesis of an empty V-slot into a true geminate is not ruled out by the crossing lines approach to geminate integrity. If a slot alone (which has no associations of course) is inserted, no crossed lines can arise. No new lines have been introduced into the representation.

Consequently Goldsmith (1990:79) claims that the crossing lines explanation of integrity must assume a vowel melody in conjunction with a slot, despite the facts which often show the melody is predictable. He notes that the crossing lines account of integrity "depends on an assumption that is not at all certain — that epenthesis rules insert a particular vowel quality." To rely on the insertion of a particular melody is to nullify one of the central

The Integrity of Shared Structure 133

characteristics of Autosegmental Phonology. Consequently I will assume empty slots must be epenthesised.[8]

If the crossing solution to integrity is to be maintained then some way must be found to handle empty slot epenthesis. Schein & Steriade (1986) offer a potential solution to the problem. Their presumption is that no real harm is done by the creation of the discontinuous true geminate straddling an empty nucleus. The successful epenthesis is only a temporary stage in the analysis, not a surface form, and all possible surface forms derivable from it are, they claim, ill-formed. The act of specifying default features and values for the slot necessarily introduces crossing lines it would seem, so the very use of default rules will be ruled out by virtue of their potential for introducing ill-formedness. Since empty slots are presumably not able to reach the surface (though we could argue with the position given the characteristics of glottal stops and unstressed centralised vowels) by extension the epenthesis itself is ruled out:

> the V-insertion process, epenthesis itself, would not be blocked from applying into a geminate sequence: only the later process whereby the V slot acquires segmental specifications would be blocked in the case of split [*i.e.* discontinuous — J.M.S.] geminates, since at that point the crossing lines problem would occur.
>
> Schein & Steriade (1986:692, fn 1).

In fact this is incorrect.

Archangeli & Pulleyblank in their discussion of underspecification and default rules (1986:150, fn 26) are quite clear about the theoretical power of default rules: "a rule or process supplied by universal grammar applies obligatorily, producing a result consistent with principles like ... the Crossing Constraint" (1986:140). We have seen that plane conflation causes mitosis in order to conform to the NCC. For A&P this is because it is a universal process. For them default filling is similarly universal (in that the rules themselves can be predicted given the underlying alphabet and the universal Redundancy Rule Ordering Constraint governing their application). Default rules are also able to use mitosis to avoid line crossing violations. So when an empty slot is subject to default rules which give rise to crossing lines it is *not* that case that the default rules are blocked. Rather mitosis causes the breaking of the original associations of the geminate, though this is exactly the opposite of what we desire. In the case of normal, arbitrary, language particular phonological rules, consistency is achieved by preventing the application of any rule which would produce ill-formedness.[9]

Goldsmith (1990) also presumes that if an empty slot is epenthesised, nothing can prevent the destructive power of default rules. It would appear that Schein & Steriade's position is untenable and that to maintain an account of integrity based on the NCC we must ban the epenthesis of empty slots, a move which flies in the face of the majority of the evidence.[10]

More support for the power of default rules comes from any analysis of a harmonic process involving a restricted projection of targets or with transparent targets. In such a case there will be slots unspecified for a value of the harmonic feature while being flanked by segments sharing a harmonic feature. When the default rules apply, crossing lines are prevented by mitosis at which time the original associations are broken by those resulting from default rule application.

For example, consider the neutral /i/ vowel of Khalkha Mongolian (Svantesson 1985; Rialland & Djamouri 1984). /i/ is transparent to an *ATR* harmony affecting all vowels. In a word such as ɔrxi-yɔɔ 'let's throw it away', the voluntative suffix must be [−*ATR*] and not realised as the [+*ATR*] variant *yoo*.[11]

(4.15)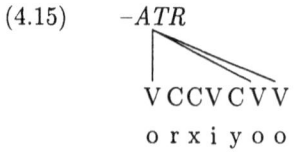

The /i/ vowel, which is [+*ATR*], does not block the harmony since it gets its [+*ATR*] specification by default. The addition of this default feature would cause a crossing lines contradiction (4.16a) unless the default value were able to accommodate itself by causing mitosis of the harmonic feature, (4.16b).

(4.16) a.

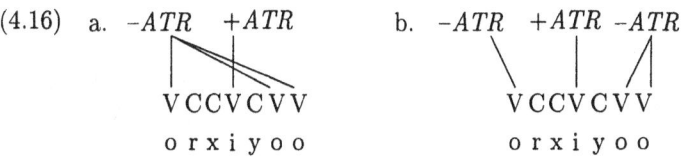

4.4 Summary

In AP, formal integrity is supposed to result from the No Crossing Constraint. Any attempt to insert material into a geminate fails because crossing lines result. This account only works given two assumptions which cannot be independently justified. The first is that epenthesised melodic material must be on the same plane as the geminate. The second is that *some* melodic material is inserted in addition to the skeletal slot.

These two assumptions block processes which would cause the roots of the true geminate to become nonadjacent while being otherwise well-formed. In other words they conspire together to prevent the the progression (4.17). (The dotted association line indicates the possibility of a melody on a different plane.)

(4.17) Necessary prelude to successful mitosis

In effect this progression *itself* is being banned, because no mechanism is available to save the true geminate once it is discontinuous, whatever may be causing the discontinuity, be it the epenthesis of a slot that is empty or one that has a melody on a different plane. *Once discontinuous, the true geminate is effectively a fake geminate.* In order to prevent the true geminate becoming discontinuous the two *ad hoc* and counterproductive assumptions discussed above are essential.

One hope for AP is that there is one source for the two assumptions. If there were could AP use it directly to account for the badness of the change in (4.17)? Recall that the mitosis of a melody results in mere type identity. Type identity cannot prevent epenthesis so we must prevent mitosis. Back one step, some discontinuity of structure sharing is necessary to trigger mitosis. We must prevent discontinuity. Discontinuity, in turn, arises as the result of epenthesis — but we are in a circular chain of dependency here. In AP we cannot prevent the transition in (4.17) in any principled way: *in AP both types of true geminate exist anyway*. The only difference between them is the string adjacency of the slots.

The attribute-value approach to phonology outlined above proposes a simple constraint on representations: all structures have to be convex. In consequence only adjacent roots can share structure and discontinuous structures involving token identity are not permitted. In addition, AVP is a unification-based formalism, and is therefore declarative and monotonic. No structure (and hence no structure sharing) can be destroyed, and structure sharing never occurs nonlocally. Taken together these basic aspects of AVP mean that no special theory of formal integrity is required.

Notes

[1] In Chapter 5 we will see moreover that when part of a geminate is unable to undergo the rule because some filter or constraint, *none* of it may. This shows mitosis never applies to allow rule application in a context which partially blocks it.

[2] I am aware of no general proposals as to how these strategies interact, however, or indeed how distant the sequence of contrastive segments may be from the surface representation. I assume that there will be a maximum amount of contrastive material buttressed by a minimal amount of prosodic padding.

[3] In AVP all influences are equal. The underlying forms for syntax — the output of the lexicon — will be affected by phonological constraints and adjacent word forms equally and in no derivational order. If English *far* has an underlying optional /r/, then given a maximisation meta-principle /r/ will be chosen over ∅ in all cases where /r/ can be syllabified. It is not the case that /r/ is 'deleted' and lost *before* a following (vowel-initial) word has the chance to be added, but that the ∅ option is chosen only *if* there is no follow-

ing word. AVP does not start with ill-formed structure and move towards well-formedness but deals with underlyers which can be made more specific in different ways in different contexts.

[4] This ingenious use of notation comes originally from Prince.

[5] On the second point Goldsmith (1990:120,121) suggests that degemination is "preferred" to epenthesis, where preference is expressed by ordering the rules. This apparently is not "truly sequential ordering" but "logical precedence rule ordering." I am at a loss as to what is intended, and doubtful that Goldsmith is doing more than restating the problem in a novel vocabulary.

[6] Since (4.6) is clearly not an implication, I have notated it with '$\stackrel{def}{\Longrightarrow}$' — it is a default. Defaults are complex entities in a constraint-based formalism. They are not simply constraints for they do not *need* to apply. For more discussion see Wedekind (1990) and below.

[7] That the medial geminate does not spirantise is an example of the phenomenon of inalterability. See Chapter 5.

[8] Alternatively raw syllable structure with an empty nuclear position is constructed over the unsyllabified consonants.

[9] Note the rather surprising fact that default rules go ahead whatever happens while nondefault rules get blocked.

[10] At this point I should note that Goldsmith's solution to the problem is to claim, with Itô, that no epenthesis rule will apply to geminates. Again the problem is that this approach only works when the epenthesis location *permits* geminates. If they are ill-formed (as in Turkish and Tangale) they must degeminate and *this is due to integrity*. As noted, Goldsmith's theory of syllabification is more articulated than Itô's use of the Coda Filter and indeed it offers the beginnings of a much more radical approach based on 'syllabic licensing' (1990:335, fn 16). See Chapter 5.

[11] The analysis cited here is based on Archangeli & Pulleyblank (1987) and many others, though I change the feature on which the harmony is based from the historically accurate *back* to the synchronically accurate *ATR*: see Svantesson (1985); Rialland & Djamouri (1984) for justification.

Chapter 5

Inalterability and Licensing

It has long been known that, even though they have the same type of underlying melody, the phonotactic distribution of geminates and nongeminates is different, and the allophones chosen for a particular position often differ. The special behaviour of geminates occurs because the choice of allophone is frequently sensitive to the prosodic role or linear position of a melody, and a geminate fills *two* prosodic roles and *two* linear slots.

This chapter describes the various methods used by Autosegmental Phonology to deal with geminates, broadly grouped under the terms INALTERABILITY and LICENSING depending on the formal treatment used. The special distributional behaviour of geminates has several different solutions in AP, but below I propose a unified account based on constraints. Such constraints are applicable, moreover, whether or not the melody is geminated. The presence of geminates may prompt a particular constraint to be included in the phonology, but they do not alter the way in which constraints apply. I do not propose, therefore, to augment AVP with any formal apparatus to handle geminates. The machinery set up in Chapter 2 to define well-formed structures is sufficient, the same

140 *Autosegmental Representation in a Declarative Framework*

conclusion reached in the preceding chapter on integrity. This is a consequence of adopting the Sharing Constraint.

5.1 Introduction: different conceptions of the problem

5.1.1 Blocking

Inalterability. We saw in Chapter 4 that in AP (and AVP) gemination expresses quantity. The shared autosegmental melody is therefore an abstraction from quantity. Some operations on a melody will, therefore, apply regardless of quantity, as we saw above in the case of Lithuanian Backing; other cases are discussed below in §5.4.4. In certain circumstances, however, nearly all instances of a particular melody m in context r are modified — 'nearly all' because *geminate* melodies are unaffected. The normal approach to such distributional patterns in generative phonology has been to postulate a rule (5.1) *universally* modifying m in context r.

(5.1) A rule dependent on melody and prosodic context

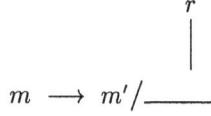

The problem of geminate distribution is now transformed into the formal problem of preventing (5.1) from applying to geminates, *i.e.* the problem of INALTERABILITY.

Given this perspective, geminate behaviour is summed up:

(5.2) *Inalterability*
Long segments often resist the application of rules that *a priori* would be expected to apply to them.

Hayes (1986b:321)

Rules are the theoretical statement of a linguistic generalisation, and the cases in which the generalisation is *wrong* are dealt with by modifying the way in which the structural description (SD)

Inalterability and Licensing   141

of a rule matches to the input.[1] I call this the BLOCKING approach
to inalterability.[2] One way to prevent (5.1) applying to geminates
is to adopt a matching algorithm (determining whether some input MATCHES the rule) which requires STRONG SATISFACTION, as
opposed to WEAK SATISFACTION. I discuss the specific proposals
below, but roughly, a structure or sequence of structures weakly
satisfies a rule if (the SD of) the rule subsumes the input. This
means that part of the input can be replaced by the SD without this
making any changes to the input.[3] (The rule then modifies the part
of the SD which is on the left of the rewrite arrow.) A structure or
sequence strongly satisfies a rule if the SD weakly matches the input
and does so 'exhaustively'. The actual definition of this exhaustive
matching differs depending on which account of strong satisfaction
is adopted — the LINKING CONSTRAINT of Hayes (1986b) or the
UNIFORM APPLICABILITY CONDITION of Schein & Steriade (1986),
as we will see.

Geminate phonotactics. Since there are generalisations which
cannot be captured in any formal way by manipulating underlying
forms by a bank of rewrite rules, it is generally accepted that a separate body of PHONOTACTIC rules are required by a phonological
theory. The problem is that rewrite rules cannot formally express
generalisations about their *output*. Kisseberth (1970) demonstrates
just such one CONSPIRACY in Yawelmani: certain rules conspire to
produce compatible surface forms, yet do not express this pattern
formally. Concrete phonotactic constraints on surface forms (formally distinct from rewrite rules) are needed to to handle such
generalisations (see §1.2).

Amongst others Steriade (1982), Prince (1984), Itô (1986;
1989) and Goldsmith (1990) have discussed certain patterns of distribution, called CODA WEAKENING, in which the coda permits
fewer cluster types than the onset. That the data in question is
phonotactic is not in doubt: if rewrite rules were used, a conspiracy would be the result. Furthermore the data is not centred on
alternations, but nonalternating distributions. The important observation these authors have made about coda weakening is that
geminates and nongeminates have to treated as special cases. Not
only is there a formal requirement for a class of phonotactic rules,
but *geminates seem to form a special case for these phonotactics*

too. Some additional formal modification is required to alter the behaviour of the phonotactics in AP in order that the aberrant behaviour of geminates is dealt with.

One way to approach the behaviour of geminates in systems of coda weakening is to again shift the emphasis away from an account of a complex distribution. Instead, a simplified set of phonotactics can be proposed, on the assumption that are *blocked* just in case they would apply to geminates. This Blocking approach is proposed by Itô (1986;1989).[4] Itô's suggestion is that phonotactics are also required to be strongly satisfied by the input. As we will see in §5.3.4 there are very serious problems with this approach, and I argue that it has to be rejected. If rejected, there can be no unified Blocking approach to the interaction of geminates with the 'generalisation-expressing' machinery of Autosegmental Phonology.

5.1.2 Licensing

Goldsmith (1990) adopts an entirely different approach to the problem of geminate phonotactics: AUTOSEGMENTAL LICENSING. A domain (essentially the main syllabic roles) 'licenses' one occurrence of a feature within the domain. This occurs when the segment is syllabified into the appropriate role. Geminates interact with this approach to phonotactics since the features of which they are composed can be licensed by the onset, and once licensed, these features can then syllabify into the coda without the coda necessarily being a licensing domain for them.[5] In this way a domain not licensing a feature F can nevertheless syllabify an instance of F, just in case F is part of a geminate. This is the interaction of geminates and phonotactics which is required.

Such licensing is discussed in greater detail in §5.5, where I propose an interpretation of licensing which does not require any additional machinery. Itô's position is that F cannot be syllabified into a coda, whereas I interpret Goldsmith's as an alternative phonotactic that F *must* be syllabified into an onset. This interpretation allows F to *also* be dominated by the coda, which is the main intent of Goldsmith's proposals. In order not to misrepresent Goldsmith I should make it clear that he may not see licensing in this way, but nevertheless it is valid to classify AVP and Goldsmith (1990) alike as exemplars of the licensing approach.

Finally note that, in an attempt to present a unified approach to the distribution of geminates, which is lacking in AP, Goldsmith tentatively suggests that the cases of rewrite-rule inalterability can instead be treated by autosegmental licensing, but he gives few details and the discussion is informal and inconclusive. We will see that my approach to licensing develops out of AVP's constraint-based account of inalterability given below and does indeed constitute part of a unified account of the well-formedness of phonological representations. In AVP phonotactics of varying specificity are used to express *all* generalisations. The cases of blocking are dealt with in this way, so inalterability as 'rules being blocked' ceases to exist. The constraints apply in the same manner whether or not a geminate is affected and are ideal for the treatment of coda weakening.

5.2 Data

5.2.1 Cautionary remarks

In (5.2), repeated here as (5.3), inalterability is characterised relative to 'expectations', presumably of individual phonologists who posit a rule to express whichever analysis of the language they prefer.

(5.3) *Inalterability*

Long segments often resist the application of rules
that *a priori* would be expected to apply to them.

Hayes (1986b:321)

This is unfortunate because an *a priori* expectation held by one may not be held by another, with the consequence that the body of inalterability data is highly variable. This is particularly so when we come to contrast the advocates of Blocking (characterised by Kenstowicz 1970; Pyle 1970; Fidelholtz 1971; Guerssel 1977; Leben 1980; Hayes 1986a,b; Steriade 1982; Schein & Steriade 1986; Itô 1989; Goldsmith 1990 *etc*) whose position is a descendant of the Generative Phonology of Chomsky & Halle (1968) ('SPE'), with the

Licensers, as exemplified by other sections of Goldsmith (1990) and AVP itself.[6]

5.2.2 Examples of inalterability

In the case of Lithuanian Backing discussed above in §3.3, long and short vowels alike were backed by assimilation. In AVP, assimilation is modeled using re-entrancy — a single value is shared by the MELODY attributes in the case of a geminate. Trivially there is also only one value in the case of the short vowel. One might say that it is the value of MELODY which is addressed by the rule, regardless of how many paths this structure is the value of. The examples discussed below are, on the contrary, ones in which it appears that the number of dominating paths is crucially important in determining whether a substructure is well-formed. While it is necessary to bring out the potential importance of inalterability for AVP, the discussion by necessity must work from the perspective of procedural Autosegmental Phonology.

Latin lateral allophony

In Latin there were two allophones of /l/, a plain palatal [l] and a dark velarised [ł] (Schein & Steriade 1986). The dark [ł] appeared in the coda, according to Roman grammarians, and conditioned various sound changes. Backing, raising and rounding testify to the diachronic assimilation of a dorsal articulation from the lateral to preceding vowels. Short /e/ and /i/ developed into /o/ and /u/ respectively, while /o/ was raised to /u/. Traces of these changes can be seen here:[7]

(5.4) Latin vowel changes

	Assimilation to ł	No assimilation
a.	sepułchrum	sepelio
	'grave'	'bury-1ST-SING'
b.	facuł	facilis
	'easy-NEUT'	'easy-MASC/FEM'
c.	vołtis/vułtis	velim
	'want-2ND-PLU'	'want-OPT-1ST-SING'

Inalterability and Licensing

Unassimilated forms are those in which there is no dark [ɫ] for the vowel to assimilate to. In *sepelio*, *facilis* and *velim* the lateral can be syllabified into the onset, where it is always light.

The sound change mentioned above failed to affect certain vowels even when they preceded a *coda* lateral. This was not due to a failure of vowel assimilation, but because the lateral in question was never dark itself. From (5.5) it can be seen that the light coda laterals were all part of geminates.

(5.5) Light and dark coda laterals

	Light	*Dark*
a.	pollen	puɫvis
	'fine flour'	'powder'
b.	velle	vuɫtis
	'to want'	'you want'

In addition to the evidence from the failure to trigger the vowel changes observed, we have the testimony of the Roman grammarians, who noted that the exponents of /lː/ were different from those of the coda /l/ in that only the latter were 'plenus' (heavy). If a three-way distinction was used, the geminate was noted to be the lightest lateral, and if a two-way distinction was used, /lː/ was clearly stated to belong to the light class (Sturtevant 1940). The conclusion we must draw is that an allophonic rule with the effect of (5.6) adds dorsal articulation to /l/ when it appears in a coda but fails to apply when the lateral is part of a geminate structure.

(5.6) Latin ɫ rule

$$/l/ \rightarrow Dorsal\ /\ \underset{|}{\overset{Coda}{}}$$

In other words, if we propose (5.6) as the means to express the behaviour described, then we must contend with the inalterability of the geminate lateral.

Semitic spirantisation

1. Tigrinya. Among the first attempts to use structure-sharing to account for inalterability were analyses based on data from Tigrinya, a Semitic language of Eritrea (Schein 1981; Kenstowicz 1982). In Tigrinya dorsal obstruents such as the /k/ of *klb* 'dog' appear as fricatives postvocalically (5.7a) and as stops elsewhere (5.7b).[8] Generally this is analysed as the postvocalic spirantisation of underlying stops /k/ and /k'/.

(5.7) Tigrinya Spirantisation
    a. ʔaxalɨb   'dog-PLU'
    b. kälbi   'dog-SG'
    c. fäkkärä   'he boasted'
       *fäxxärä   *no change due to inalterability*
       *fäxkärä   *no change due to integrity*
    d. mɨraxka   (from mɨrak-ka) 'calf-2SG.MASC'

If the underlying stops are geminates, neither the whole stop nor the immediately postvocalic portion spirantises (5.7c) (the latter behaviour showing the integrity of the geminate). In the case of fake geminates, what happens to the postvocalic melody has no effect on the following onset melody (5.7d). AP requires a rule resembling (5.8) to ensure the spirantisation happens after any vowel, but the question again arises of how to block it from applying to true geminates.

(5.8) Tigrinya Spirantisation

$$/k/ \rightarrow [+cont] \;/\; \overset{\displaystyle V\;\;C}{\underset{\rule{2em}{0.4pt}}{\;\;\;|\;\;\;}}$$

2. Tiberian Hebrew. In Tiberian Hebrew a similar spirantisation rule, applying to six obstruents /ptkbdg/, created six fricative allophones [fθχvðɣ] not otherwise found in the language at the time. The fricatives are found in postvocalic position in complementary distribution with the stops with which they alternate (5.9a). The stop allophones are found post-consonantally or initially. The exception is that stops are always found if they form part of a geminate (5.9b) (see Sampson 1973; Leben 1980; McCarthy 1981) and (5.10) has to respect this.

(5.9) Tiberian Hebrew Spirantisation

a.
	Not postvocalic		Postvocalic	
/k/	kâθav	'he wrote'	mixtâv	'letter'
/t/	mixtâv	'letter'	kâθav	'he wrote'
/k/	malku	'queen'	melex	'king'

b.
	Obstruent melody attached postvocalically			
	Nongeminate		Geminate	
/d/	gâðal	'he became great'	giddêl	'he magnified'
			*giððêl	(inalterability)

(5.10)

$$[-son] \rightarrow [+cont] \Big/ \begin{matrix} V & C \\ & | \\ & \underline{} \end{matrix}$$

McCarthy (1986) offers some data which would appear to contradict the picture of spirantisation and inalterability given. The form malχê 'kings of', cognate to melex, shows a fricative in a post-consonantal position. Presumably at this stage of the language's development the fricative~stop alternation was no longer allophonic. The form itself arose due to a rule of schwa syncope applying between two consonants in this genitive construction, so historically the /χ/ was in postvocalic position: maləχê. Evidence for this is that the syncope failed to apply if it brought two homomorphemic type-identical consonants together: harərê 'mountains of', * harrê. Similarly, the form təβaareχχáa 'she will bless you' has a fake geminate fricative. It arises from schwa syncope in the pronominal suffix -(ə)χaa, historically -əkaa. That the consonants were hetero-morphemic allowed syncope despite the fact that two type identical segments are adjacent as a result.

Coda weakening

1. Hausa. Klingenheben's Law in Hausa can be viewed as a phonological rule, and if so it must be unable to affect geminates (Klingenheben 1928; Hayes 1986b). Historically, coda obstruents have become sonorants with a predictable place of articulation; velars and labials have become /w/ and alveolars a trill /r/. Geminate obstruents were not affected, however, so words like the intensives *bubbuga* 'to beat mercilessly' and *kakkama* 'to catch a lot of' *do* have an obstruent in the coda. If a sonorantisation rule (5.11) is posited, geminates are exceptions to it — they must be inalterable.

(5.11) Klingenheben's Law rule (Hayes 1986b:334)

$$[-cont] \rightarrow [+son] \;/\; \underline{} \overset{\displaystyle C)_\sigma}{|}$$

The current distribution of obstruents is really what is worthy of note in Hausa, since Hausa permits coda obstruents just so long as they are part of a geminate or a partial geminate (a nasal which is homorganic with the following consonant onset). A coda can also be a glide, a liquid or /s/, the default obstruent. Structure sharing is of importance here since otherwise (excepting /s/) obstruents are banned from the coda. This general pattern of stops being banned from the coda is called coda weakening. The fact that geminate consonants are not subject to this ban in Hausa suggests inalterability.

It so happens that a rule (5.11) has been proposed which '*a priori* would be expected to apply' to geminates, so thinking of this phonotactic distribution in terms of inalterability may seem acceptable. The next set of data, however, ought to raise questions about the propriety of studying the distribution of geminates by postulating rules that in fact are intended *not* to apply to geminates — if these doubts have not surfaced already.

2. Axininca Campa. This Peruvian Arawakan language (Payne 1981; data here from Goldsmith 1990) allows only a homorganic nasal in word-internal codas. The only nonvocalic feature permitted in the coda (independent of structure sharing) is *nasal*:

(5.12) Weak coda in Axininca Campa
    antari   'large-ANIMATE'
    impoke 'he will come'
    saŋko   'sugar cane'

The complex phonotactics of the geminate in Axininca Campa *could* be analysed using a rule like Klingenheben's Law. This rule would remove obstruents' place of articulation features ('**PoA**' for short) from the coda. Since geminates and homorganic nasal-stop sequences *are* possible, the **PoA** of these sequences must not be subject to the rule. If such an analysis were proposed, in which geminates were not subject to the rule, against the linguist's expectations, then the data would constitute evidence for inalterability. The phenomenon (being one of 'expectations') is dependent on the analysis chosen. If we do not choose to analyse Axininca Campa with a rule like (5.11) then we have no evidence for inalterability.

Glide/vowel alternations

Hayes (1986b) also discusses various glide/vowel alternations (in Berber, Arabic, Sanskrit and Micmac) which affect only short segments. As an example of this type of data consider Sanskrit Glide Formation. The vowels /i/, /u/ and /r̥/ appear as glides prevocalically. If a rule such as (5.13) is used for this alternation, then it must affect the short vowels but not their geminate counterparts; /iː/ and /uː/ must not be turned into [yi] and [wu].

(5.13) Sanskrit Glide Formation

$$V \rightarrow C \Big/ \begin{matrix} [-low] \\ | \\ \rule{1em}{0.4pt} \end{matrix} V$$

5.2.3 Summary: inalterability as a unified phenomenon

I have presented a selection of rules of varying types which must exhibit inalterability in order to be observationally adequate. These rules are adduced as evidence by the proponents of the theories discussed below. We can group the examples into three classes:

- standard rules (such as spirantisation, Latin dark /l/),
- coda weakening,
- glide/vowel alternations.

This shows how inalterability arises in many typologically different areas. Any approach to inalterability should capture this universality. Hayes and Schein & Steriade ensure this with their assumption that standard phonological rewrite rules operate in each of the three classes, and that it is the *form* of such rules that is the cause of inalterability.

Rather than being advantageous, the assumption of a ubiquitous analytic approach undermines the uniformity of any current treatment of inalterability. This is because recent developments in moraic and prosodic phonology strongly suggest it is not possible to depend on the all-pervading availability of standard rewrite rules such as (5.6), (5.8), (5.10), (5.11) and (5.13). In addition recent research has indicated the superfluity of the C/V skeleton used in some of the rules (Hyman 1985; McCarthy & Prince 1989; Hayes 1989; Itô 1989; Waksler 1990). In particular, glide/vowel alternations are now understood to operate quite differently from the manner indicated above: they are *prosodic* phenomena, dealt with using *phonotactic constraints* (Zec 1988; Goldsmith 1990; also Waksler 1990 for a unification-based account). Moreover we will see that coda weakening is a prime candidate for a prosodic/phonotactic treatment. This leaves just the standard rules as a class which can motivate inalterability, since only in this class do the rules have some degree of support.

In retrospect the universality of inalterability may well seem to be an artifact of a defunct method of analysis. Rewrite rules have greatly diminished in importance since the days of SPE. Consequently the only class in which inalterability can now be presumed to operate is the 'standard rules' class. I will therefore concentrate on the Spirantisation rules and the Latin example in the next two sections in order to exemplify the Blocking approach to inalterability and to show that even in these cases the Blocking approach is inadequate.

Inalterability and Licensing 151

5.3 Standard rule-blocking approaches to inalterability

If the rules in §5.2 are accepted as valid, then an account is required of the inalterability associated with them. The Blocking approaches to inalterability hold that, in order that these rules can give rise to the proper results, the theory of rule-application must be tightened up. They change the way in which rules operate to deal with geminates.

What it means for a rule to match an input in Autosegmental Phonology originates in Chomsky & Halle (1968: 391). Their definition says that rule R "is applicable to" a string D if, basically, the structural description (SD) of the rule "is contained in" the string. For the SD to be contained, the column of feature-value pairs of each element in the SD must be a *subset* of the corresponding column of elements in the input, and the precedence relationships between elements must be respected. This procedure has been assumed to be valid in AP and the analogous autosegmental procedure requires that the input WEAKLY SATISFIES the SD.

The Blocking approach claims that the input must STRONGLY SATISFY the SD. Without strong satisfaction, the rules above overapply, the consequence of which is that both geminates and short segments are being affected by rules designed to affects nongeminates only. I will discuss below the two proposals for defining strong satisfaction and employ this term in order to be able to talk of the two together.

5.3.1 The Linking Constraint

Rules which *do* alter geminates (like Lithuanian Backing) refer to a single tier — the melodic quality tier in that example. Another case might be an alteration of quantity which affects all vowels, regardless of quality. In AP such a rule would (correctly) affect diphthongs and long vowels alike. Those cases which *are* bound by inalterability feature an *interaction* of melodic quality and either linear position or prosodic function. In other words rules which are triggered by a combination of quality and quantity information must only match against input which possesses *both* the appropriate quality and quantity.[9] Hayes's account of inalterability relies

152   *Autosegmental Representation in a Declarative Framework*

on the fact that to represent both melodic and skeletal/prosodic information autosegmentally, the associations which hold *between* these tiers (5.14) must be included in the rule also.

(5.14)   prosodic information

                    ↕ *associations*

                    skeleton (linear information)

                    ↕ *associations*

                    melodic information

Hayes (1986b) suggests that the necessary inclusion of association lines in the rule is the factor required to get a handle on inalterability. He offers (5.15) as a constraint on the application of rules.[10]

(5.15) *Linking Constraint*

Association lines in structural descriptions are interpreted as exhaustive.

In other words Hayes is saying that input to a rule cannot merely be a subset of the SD of the rule. Under the Linking Constraint a rule whose structural description refers to a single association between the skeleton and melody tiers cannot apply to geminates, because the geminated melody has *two* associations to the skeleton. Although one of the associations regarded individually would weakly satisfy the structural description, this is insufficient: the numbers of associations in the target and the rule must match exactly.

For example, in the cases of Semitic spirantisation discussed above, the rule (5.8) contains a single association line. The Latin ɼ rule (5.6) does so also. (5.8) is given again here as (5.16).

(5.16) Tigrinya Spirantisation

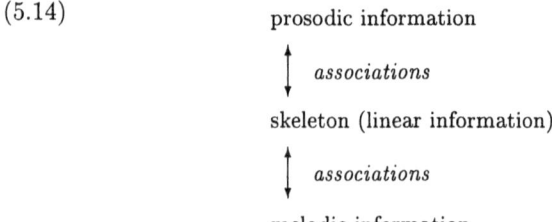

Inalterability and Licensing 153

The structural description matches against the underlined part of a word like ʔ*akalib* to give ʔaχ*alib*. It must not match, however, against *fäkkärä* despite the fact that both words contain the sequence 'äk'. The reasoning is as follows. In SPE the feature set for V is a subset of the bundle for ä, and k is a subset of itself, so the input weakly satisfies the SD. The Linking Constraint means, however, that there can only be a single association between the matched C slot and the root tier, and only a single association between the matched root and the skeleton. Because it is geminate, the root of /k/ in *fäkkärä* is associated to *two* slots (5.17) and the rule passes by.

(5.17) Double linking of /k/

To illustrate this informally we can draw a window round the part of the input which weakly matches the rule. If weak satisfaction were in use (as in SPE and AVP) then the fact that the structural description subsumes the input is enough. But for Hayes it is essential that no associations of the type mentioned in the rule link an element of the input which is within the window to some other element *outwith* the window. In (5.18) n is linked to C_2, which is on the same tier as C_1 but outside the window, so (5.18) is not an instance of strong satisfaction.

(5.18)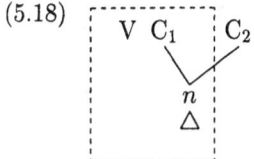

One potential problem with the Linking Constraint arises when no associations are mentioned at all linking T_1 a tier mentioned in the rule and some other tier T_2 (as in the case of a rule applying only on a single tier T_1). The rule must match against any number of lines between T_1 and T_2. This raises the question of how to refer to a tier which may have *no* associations to it. Although a special notation (5.19) is available in AP to indicate an autosegment 'a' with no associations at all, so far as I am aware there is no way to force an absence of associations between two particular tiers.

(5.19)

To summarise: quantity and quality are independent in AP because multiple association is permitted. In SPE such configurations were impossible. Geminates are best analysed as involving multiple association, but consequently their single melody would be subjected to rules intended for simple segments unless the way in which rules apply is changed (or different rules are proposed). If a rule refers to the skeleton to fix the *location* or the *prosodic function* of a particular melody, then the rule must mention both quality and quantity tiers. The hypothesis behind Hayes's account of inalterability is that elements mentioned on those tiers are treated as units by the rule. In the Linking Constraint, Hayes formulates the convention that, when used to specify the prosodic function or location of a quality, a rule necessarily specifies quantity too.

5.3.2 The Uniform Applicability Condition

indexUAC Steriade (1982) and Schein & Steriade (1986) choose a blocking approach which is based more on the *meaning* of rules than their form. They leave open the possibility that a geminate could fulfill the skeletal conditions on a melody because the relationship between geminate quantity and skeletal/prosodic function is not rigidly fixed. On this view it does not necessarily matter that there *is* an autosegment outside the window of (5.18). All that is required is that any such autosegment fulfill every requirement predicated of its tier-mates inside the window. The advantage of this approach is that it is closer to the intuitive explanation of why a geminate is not prey to, say, Semitic Spirantisation. It is not merely the fact that a geminate has an extra slot: it is that the location (or prosodic function) of the second slot is *not compatible* with the rule's requirements. Schein & Steriade state their constraint on rule application as the Universal Applicability Condition (UAC):

Inalterability and Licensing

(5.20) *Uniform Applicability Condition*

Given a node n, a set S consisting of all nodes linked to n on some tier T, and a rule R that alters the contents of n: a condition in the structural description of R on any member of S is a condition on every member of S.

Schein and Steriade (1986:727)

Although one of the two slots of a postvocalic geminate is immediately postvocalic, the other must be regarded as immediately post-consonantal. Without this difference between the slots the geminate and nongeminate versions of a melody would be indistinguishable. If, therefore, some feature is being added onto the melody of a geminate on the express condition that n is associated to a slot which is postvocalic, then inalterability results unless all slots associated to n are immediately postvocalic. This is impossible for a geminate.[11]

The use of a window-representation is not so suitable to exemplify the operation of the UAC, so (5.21) shows n, the target melody of the rule, and identifies the set S each member of which must be adjacent to a vowel position. The rule (5.16) imposes the postvocalic condition on each member of S.

(5.21)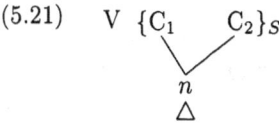

As with the Linking Constraint, there is a lack of explicit detail about the workings of the UAC. It is difficult, for example, to see how the UAC handles rules intended to apply only to geminates. Each of the two slots mentioned by such a rule could be seen to impose a condition on every member of the set S. But such a literal approach seems to force each slot, wrongly, to fulfill its own conditions *and* the conditions on the other slot. With the Linking Constraint we are at least certain that two associations means 'two and only two'. Furthermore the UAC cannot be taken literally when it deals with a total absence of associations between two tiers. Just as with the Linking Constraint (for which no mention of associations in the rule can match any number in the target) the UAC does not interpret a lack of associations as a condition that there *be* no associations. A special means is required to force an absence of associations (5.19).

To summarise: the structural description of (5.16) says that the *k* melody must be associated to a slot which is postvocalic. In order that it does not apply to *fäkkärä* the UAC demands that the *k* melody must be linked to *only* postvocalic slots. It is not the uniqueness of the slot together with its position that matters but simply the position. Any number of slots are possible, just so long as each is postvocalic.

5.3.3 Apparent differences between the Linking Constraint and the UAC

Menomini lowering

The Linking Constraint and the UAC would behave differently if the two slots of some geminates could be identical in every way *other* than the very existence of the two slots. In such a circumstance the UAC would allow a rule to apply to the geminate, since the conditions laid down on the slot in the SD would be fulfilled by both geminate slots. The UAC permits any number of nodes in S as long as each satisfies all the prosodic conditions that the others do. The Linking Constraint does not allow the set S in (5.21) to have more members than the rule mentions (except the case in which the rule mentions none at all). To properly compare these approaches to strong satisfaction we need a suitable prosodically conditioned rule.[12]

I have unfortunately been unable to discover any really reliable data to test the different predictions made by the Linking Constraint and UAC about the role of prosodic/functional constraints on rules. This is because of the number of independent variables involved. For example Schein & Steriade provide an apparently appropriate example with the rule of Menomini Lowering (5.22) which shows just how many assumptions have to be fixed before the UAC can confidently be said to behave any differently from the Linking Constraint.

Inalterability and Licensing 157

(5.22) Menomini lowering

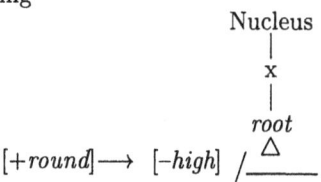

The rule ensures a nuclear round vowel is specified as [*-high*]. The rule does not affect the round glide /w/ and therefore, Schein & Steriade argue, it must in its structural description mention an association between the nucleus (indicating vowels) and the melody [*+round*], see the SD of (5.22) in (5.23a). During a derivation, the length of the target vowel ought to be irrelevant since in Menomini both long /o:/ and short /o/ are found rather than /u:/ and /u/. Theoretically the consequence of this is that the structural description given in (5.23a) has to be able to match a geminate. The Linking Constraint cannot handle this case because a single line in a rule can never match two in the target, but the UAC can, *if we allow a specific analysis of geminate vowels.* This argument demands that they look like the structure in (5.23b).[13]

(5.23) a.   b.

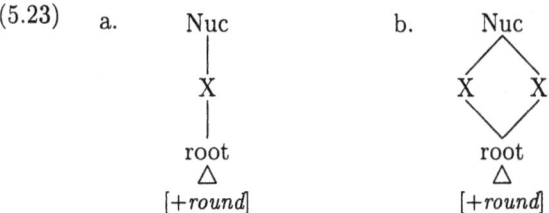

The UAC treatment of Menomini requires that the same function is assigned to both parts of a long vowel, a theoretical assumption which is highly controversial. Usually it is important to identify a syllable nucleus and a glide position of some kind. Diphthongs consist of a nuclear vowel melody paired with a glide, and glide melodies are always a subset of the vowel melodies — in the glide position some of the vowel contrasts are neutralised. If a diphthong/long vowel were analysed as a sequence of two equal nucleii this would radically obscure the unequal systems of vocalic contrasts.

Given the rule in (5.22), the UAC, just like the Linking Constraint, wrongly predicts inalterability unless the controversial theory of the syllable in (5.23b) is used. Unless the SD of the Menomini rule is of a very particular type, the example is meaningless.[14]

One can also criticise the rule itself. The inclusion of the Nuclear node in the SD is necessitated by the assumption that the /w/ glide would otherwise be lowered to a nonsyllabic /ŏ/. Such glides are marked and it is reasonable to suppose that there are independent reasons why only vowels are affected by Lowering. In those Amerindian languages with a vowel system /ieao/, if the decision is made to make the underlier of /o/ be [+*round*] and assign it a lowering rule such as (5.22), then the requirement that the rule does not affect glides can be achieved in AP by pre-specifying glides as [+*high*], either prosodically by virtue of their position, or underlyingly. Lowering, which appears to be a default rule, will not apply to glides thus removing the need for a SD like that in (5.22) and the structure in (5.23b).

It would appear that it is impossible to assess quite how these characterisations of inalterability differ in their predictions given the wealth of uncertainty in other areas of the theory. Although a rule looking for (5.23a) will match against (5.23b) if the UAC is used but not if the Linking Constraint is used, there are no good examples of such a rule. In Menomini it is highly doubtful whether either (5.23a) or (5.23b) is motivated other than by the exigencies of differentiating the two approaches.

The diacritic use of strong satisfaction

Schein & Steriade (1986:734–736) claim that

> the UAC predicts geminate blockage from aspects of the rule that must be invariant under any formalization... On the other hand, the aspect of structural descriptions on which the Linking Constraint focuses — the number of association lines mentioned — can be arbitrarily manipulated so as to nullify any predictions made about geminate behaviour ... The UAC, then, makes the easily falsifiable claim that geminate blockage can always be predicted from independently observable properties of a given rule.

Inalterability and Licensing 159

Schein & Steriade are claiming that an *independently required* aspect of the rule α is responsible for blocking. In fact the only reason α is ever included in the rule is to prevent geminates being affected. Of course inalterability is 'predictable' given an expression of a rule — the rule has been constructed in that way simply because the geminates do not alternate.

Imagine a pattern of data facing a phonologist in some language L. The phonologist notes a potential process which affects melody m in a certain context (post-vocalic, say) if and only if m is not geminate. A rule can be devised which includes the appropriate structure to capture this process. For example m has some feature $[+F]$ to identify it. Now if we make reference to the skeleton, the rule (5.24) will not match a geminate.

(5.24) Rule in L

$$[+F] \rightarrow [+G] \quad / \quad \overset{\displaystyle V \quad C}{\underset{\rule{1.5em}{0.4pt}}{\mid}}$$

The reason the rule is stated as being post-vocalic in the first place is to rule out application to geminates. *This is not an independent part of the rule.*

Schein & Steriade may criticise Hayes for having no independent reason for including associations in the rule, but they miss the point that there *are* no 'independent' aspects of the rule that determine inalterability. Inalterability is the result of, first, choosing a certain rule to represent the distributional facts, and second, including in the rule enough information to prevent it applying to geminates, given a strong satisfaction account of matching. Recall that there seems to be no reason other than inalterability to use a structural description like (5.23a), so in what way does it 'predict' inalterability?

Hayes does admit a purely diacritic use of association lines, however. He gives three examples (1986b:334) in which he includes 'an otherwise unnecessary association line' to ensure inalterability: Spanish Spirantisation, Berber Spirantisation and Lithuanian /o/-Lowering. For example in Berber /ptkbdg/ are spirantised in all contexts, unless they are geminates. No context statement is required, but Hayes can add an association to an unspecified slot and block the rule applying to geminates.

5.3.4 The application of strong satisfaction to phonotactics

Itô (1986; 1989) strongly argues for the use of constraints on well-formed surface structure for the analysis of coda weakening. In those languages with coda weakening and geminates, the geminates interact with coda weakening in ways that may be '*a priori* unexpected'. In particular if coda weakening is analysed as a *ban* on coda consonants, then this ban must not apply to geminates.

Codas are WEAK in that they often allow a smaller range of contrasts than the onset does. In other words some melodies are not permitted in the coda, although they are found in the onset. However this does not seem to apply to melodies which are part of geminates — a bigger range of segments can appear in the coda when the melody is part of a geminate. In effect, then, there is a requirement in many languages that codas may only be the first part of a geminate or a homorganic nasal-stop cluster (Steriade 1982; Itô 1986; Prince 1984; Goldsmith 1990). For example forms like those in (5.25a) are well-formed in Japanese. In these forms the coda consonant shares structure with the onset. Those in (5.25b) are ill-formed and no structure is shared. (The full stop indicates the syllable boundary.)

(5.25) Japanese coda weakening

    a. kap.pa   'a legendary being' b. * kap.ta
        tom.bo   'dragonfly'   * tog.ba
        gak.koo 'school'   * tog.ba
        kaŋ.gae 'thought'

Syllabification of the nongeminate obstruents /p/ and /g/ in (5.25b) to the coda is impossible. Japanese has no epenthesis rule to insert a third syllable nucleus and thereby enable syllabification. The forms in (5.25b) are therefore not possible Japanese words.

Itô's analysis of these distributional facts does *not* use a rewrite rule such as that given in (5.11), which Hayes (1986b) uses to encode Klingenheben's Law in Hausa. Klingenheben's law turned obstruents into sonorants with a predictable place of articulation when they were in the coda. But geminates were inalterable, so words like *kakkama* 'to catch a lot of' *do* have coda obstruents. Rather than postulating a rule removing underlying consonants from the coda such as (5.11), for which there is presumably no evidence in Japanese, Itô (1986, 1989) opts for a well-formedness constraint; the Coda Filter:

(5.26) Coda Filter, Itô (1989:224)

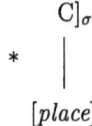

Itô (1989:224) writes:

> The Coda Filter [(5.26), her (5)] rules out syllables with final consonants. This may seem overly restrictive since we want to allow the first part of a geminate or homorganic cluster to close the preceding syllable. The solution lies in the doubly place-linked nature of geminates and homorganic clusters...

Itô effectively suggests that, if strong satisfaction is the means by which rules match input, *filters* should only match input which strongly satisfies them. Since geminates are doubly-linked, and since the Coda Filter refers to a single association line, the Linking Constraint is used as the means by which the filter fails to ban geminates from the coda.

A major problem with this approach, as shown in Chapter 4, is that it does not account for formal integrity. Another problem is the very use of the Linking Constraint as a blocker of phonotactic constraints rather than a blocker of rewrite rules. Itô's theory demands adherence to the extraordinary position that an ill-formed structure is well-formed just in case it achieves geminate status. For example Latin did not permit a dark lateral /ɫ/ in the onset, and this can be expressed with a filter (5.27).[15] The problem is that

162   Autosegmental Representation in a Declarative Framework

(5.27) does not apply to the geminate /ƛ:/, though it ought to since there was no [ƛ:] in Latin.

(5.27) Latin Onset Filter

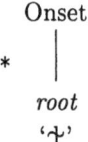

For another example, consider a language with nasal consonants but no nasal vowels. In an analysis it would be reasonable to suppose a filter like (5.28) were active. Itô's approach would have such a filter being subject to the Linking Constraint with the consequence that there were no short nasal vowels while long ones did occur.

(5.28) Nasal vowel filter

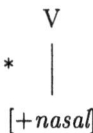

As far as I am aware there is no language like this. The system of long segments tends to be a reduced version of the short system, not a larger version as Itô predicts.

The trouble with using the Linking Constraint to relativise the import of phonotactic constraints is that any filter dealing with a random gap in a distribution is only *contingently* successful. Filters are intended to ban a particular configuration *necessarily*, regardless of the larger structures of which it is part.

For example, in nonrhotic English, [r] cannot appear in the coda. If a coda filter is used to express this distributional gap are we liable to see it contravened by *geminate* [r:]? The answer has to be yes, unless a constraint is used to ban geminate [r:], and at once we must wonder why no *tri*-geminate [r::] can evade *that* filter, and so on. This may seem frivolous, but if we allow side-stepping of a constraint on well-formedness just because the structure in question is multiply-linked, then we are allowing rampant nonlocality and nondeterminism. An ill-formed structure could become well-formed merely by adding more information at some point, so we would never know for sure that a representation was ill-formed.

Filters as absolute bans on certain configurations are fundamental to phonological theory (for just one example see Kiparsky (1985) on Structure Preservation) and *especially* in any phonological theory which directly expresses surface distributions. If, as Itô suggests, input had to strongly satisfy a filter, the consequences would be very far reaching. Though Itô is prepared to accept the (mostly unknown) ramifications of this move, I think that the burden of proof lies with Itô to show that such a radical interpretation of filters has no detrimental effects elsewhere in phonology.

It should be noted that Itô's prosodic theory of epenthesis depends on some theory of coda weakening, not the Coda Filter one in particular. I will offer an alternative below. Moreover, despite my rejection of her claim that the theory can fully explain integrity, nevertheless it is clear that much of Itô (1989) is of great value, and is directly adopted by AVP.

5.3.5 Demanding non-geminate input is a redundant way of avoiding inherently ill-formed output

We have seen how, in AP, input to a rule must strongly satisfy its structural description. This has to be slightly qualified, however. It is not every rule, nor every part of a rule, that requires strong satisfaction. At least, this is the position of Schein & Steriade. Recall that the UAC applies to 'a node n', not the the structural description of a rule. This node is the FOCUS of a rule, and is the part that is generally placed to the left of the arrow. The UAC applies to all associations in the SD which emanate from this node. Other associations are *not* required to strongly match the input. These associations describe the CONTEXT of the rule.

The claim that the context is indiscriminately long or short is supported by a group of rounding rules in Tigrinya (Leslau 1941). One rule, described by Schein & Steriade spreads [+*round*] from both [w] and [wː] onto a [ə] assimilating it to [u].

(5.29) Tigrinya ə-Rounding

a. yə-wläd → yuwläd
'engender-JUSS-3SG-MASC'
b. yə-səwwär → yəsuwwär
'carry-REFL-IMPF-3SG-MASC'

Under the UAC the rule can apply despite the glide being part of a geminate because the rule does not alter the glide's melody. The glide melody is not the focus of the rule, merely the context, and as the context of a rule is not subject to strong satisfaction, the geminate glide matches.

Hayes, however, is uncertain as to whether a rule should be blocked by a contextual geminate. The issue is rather peripheral in Hayes (1986b), and though the Linking Constraint, as stated, does *not* allow contextual geminates, in effect Hayes leaves the issue open. Goldsmith (1990) sides with the view that only the focus shows inalterability, so when he adopts the Linking Constraint, he modifies it accordingly. His CONJUNCTIVITY CONDITION deals only with the focus:

(5.30) *Conjunctivity Condition*
If a rule R has the effect of *modifying the feature specifications of a segment S*, or deleting a segment S, and if the rule explicitly refers to a chart C (*i.e.* association lines linking two autosegmental tiers), then segment S will undergo the effects of the rule only if all of its association lines in C are explicitly mentioned in rule R.

Goldsmith (1990:39)
(*emphasis added*)

Given the lack of evidence to the contrary and the preference in the literature (except for Hayes's uncertainty) I think it is up to those who claim that on rule application should treat focus and context *alike* to find a case where a geminate fails to be the context of a rule (assimilation say) purely by virtue of its geminateness. There are cases where focus and context *do* act alike: geminateness in either is no bar to the rule's application (see §5.4.4). Consequently I agree with Schein & Steriade and Goldsmith.

Inalterability and Licensing 165

The important change to the Linking Constraint which Goldsmith makes is shown in italics in (5.30). Basically only rules altering the content of S are subject to strong satisfaction. S is the focus, therefore, and only associations made to the focus are relevant. This mirrors the UAC (5.20) which deals with a rule that "alters the content of n". This definition not only means that the context (which is not altered) is able to match a geminate, but rules which simply add association lines to S can apply even when S is geminated. Goldsmith's justification for this is that "a number of examples suggest that such rules are not subject to the kind of constraint we are discussing here" (fn 13, p334). Goldsmith is presumably talking about harmony rules.[16] These specify a focus, but apply even if the focus is a geminate.

There is, in fact, a good reason why these Blocking analyses are applicable to geminates which are in the focus of a rule, but not applicable to geminates in the context. Recall what the context *is*. It is precisely that which is *presupposed* by a rule — its prior existence is required by the rule. Its well-formedness is therefore *independent* of the rule. The well-formedness of the focus, on the other hand, is defined by the rule's successful application. The UAC is not sensitive to the number of associations in a rule's context, because the rule cannot create a bad context, or any kind of context. What was before, remains. Geminateness, however, matters for the focus. The rule

$$\iota \to \omega / \_\_\_\_ \kappa$$

designed to produce output ω from the focus ι in context κ would produce two outputs, ω and $\omega\omega$, unless the input was required to strongly satisfy the focus. The requirement for strong satisfaction prevents $\iota\iota\kappa$ being a suitable input. But more importantly, it prevents the output $\omega\omega$.

Now, suppose $\omega\omega$ were never found, never output from any other rule, never part of an underlying representation. Would we not feel that the effort expended in preventing some rule from applying to $\iota\iota$ was misplaced? A condition banning $\omega\omega$ would do this for us, at no cost. In fact, in preventing the rule's focus from matching a geminate, we create a CONSPIRACY, a redundancy of effort intended to create the same result over and over. Let's take two examples of such a conspiracy.

Latin [ɫ]. In the discussion of Latin [ɫ] above we saw that there is no geminate [ɫ:] in Latin, either underlyingly or as a result of some other rule. Nor does [ɫ] ever appear in the onset. Velarising the geminate /l/ would break both these generalisations. AP needs a constraint banning [ɫ] in the onset in any case, so why not let it block the rule? If we did this, then the rule can be simplified to a default rule: 'l→ɫ'.

Tigrinya [x]. In Tigrinya there is no post-consonantal [x] underlyingly or as the result of any rule. It is therefore no surprise that the geminate /k:/ does not undergo spirantisation: if it did so there would be a side-effect of creating such an otherwise unattested form. From the form of the spirantisation rule it is impossible to predict that [x] *never* appears post-consonantally. Given a phonotactic constraint banning [x] from this position, however, the 'inalterability' behaviour is accounted for.

It would be bad enough if just a few of the cases of standard rule inalterability were attributable to the independent ill-formedness of the potential geminate output of the rule. Such a conspiracy removes much of the motivation for a strong satisfaction approach to inalterability. But in fact, in *every case* the output ωω would be ill-formed. It is not that ωω *could* be valid, but just not here, not as a result of *this* rule — the configuration is never acceptable.

5.4 A constraint-based approach to inalterability

5.4.1 Introduction: the explanatory power of constraints

In procedural, derivation-based phonological frameworks, well-formedness is defined by the *rules*. Whatever structures they yield are by definition well-formed, at least at that particular stage in the derivation. Well-formed *surface* structures are the final step in a mechanical progression from underlying forms, a derivation consisting of the repeated application of rewrite rules. In some frameworks

Inalterability and Licensing

there may be in addition *constraints* (also called filters) which are conditions on surface form — phonotactic statements which must always be adhered to. Any analyses which include statements of the kind: 'configuration C is ruled out as output of the rule since it is of a type not otherwise found in the language' exemplify this position. Two questions immediately arise. Are both rules and constraints necessary, and if so, how do they interact?

Why phonotactic constraints are essential

In a criticism of the views of Chomsky & Halle (1968), Sommerstein made a strong case for the inclusion in the phonological canon of constraints on surface representations:

> [SPE] had no place for two notions which had long played an important role in phonological thinking. One was the notion of a set of principles directly determining the class of possible surface representations... — the *phonotactics*. ... [T]he other was the notion of the syllable ... The present chapter is about the rehabilitation of these two neglected notions. Its title [Phonological Templates] makes the point that segments are not, as it were, anarchic individualists; they appear in fixed syntagmatic patterns, almost in slotted frames, and the effects of some phonological rules are not fully comprehensible without consideration of the principles on which these frames or templates are structured.
>
> Phonological rules in GP are single isolated entities. Rules which exhibit certain types of structural similarity are "collapsed" into schemata; other rules cannot be. The theory thus makes the implicit claim that where two (or more) rules can properly be regarded as aspects of a single process, they will always be structurally similar... [F]urther, ... facts about permissible and impermissible segment sequences at the output level are nonsignificant, the fortuitous product of the restrictions on underlying representations plus the phonological rules.

Both these claims are untenable; but their denial involves far-reaching modifications of established GP theory.

Sommerstein (1977:193,194)

Indeed the modifications are so far reaching that the process is not yet complete. So, although phonologists again accept the syllable as a fundamental unit of phonology to the extent that the segment has passed somewhat into disfavour (see the papers in *Phonology* **6/2**, 1989: *The atoms of phonological representation*), the parallel but more gradual rehabilitation of the phonotactic constraint has not really threatened the rewrite rule. Goldsmith, in a discussion of Sommerstein (1974), re-iterates this view:

> ...to write separate rules where each specifies the particular *way* in which a phonotactic can be violated — and to call that, then, the 'structural description' of the rule, as if it were that *particular* sequence that caused the rule to apply, rather than the representation's failure to satisfy the phonotactic — is to miss a string of important generalisations.

Goldsmith (1990:322)
(original emphasis)

For example, it was noted above that a whole regime of rules such as epenthesis and cluster simplification are available whose purpose is to produce fully-syllabifiable output which is phonotactically well-formed to the same criteria of well-formedness as apply to other structures in the language. Given the heterogeneity in any one language of the inputs to epenthesis and cluster simplification rewrite rules, a rule schema is impossible, and therefore no generalisation forthcoming of any kind. All that remains is to note the conspiracy.

If these operations were to be triggered by the necessity to conform to well-formedness statements then the generalisation would be captured. When people meet for a party their starting points and routes have nothing in common. It is the destination which is shared. So it is with the syllabification of the contrastive elements making up morphs. The mechanisms for ensuring proper

Inalterability and Licensing

prosodic licensing of these elements vary. The combinations of elements themselves vary. But the end result in all cases is constrained by a common pool of phonotactic statements, and this pool goes to form the phonology of the language.[17]

Rule/constraint interaction

In Chapter 1 I discussed the problem of the interaction of rules and constraints. I indicated there that the resolution of the problem can be achieved if we abandon rules. The suggestion is not so radical as it might at first appear. Itô (1989), for instance, follows just this path in her exemplification of the benefits of using constraints in the treatment of syllabification using phonotactic templates. She does so to the exclusion of rewrite rules. More generally, syllable templates are widely accepted and force each syllable to match the templates in order to be well-formed — rules which would be able to create new types of syllable throughout the phonology are dispensed with. If constraints do not replace rules in this way there will be tension between the ability of rules to create syntagmatically novel representations and the purpose of constraints to impose syntagmatic limits.

Inalterability facts are relevant in this respect because in some cases a rule fails to apply. I claimed at the end of §5.3 that in each case of inalterability, the rule's outputs would have been ill-formed. If the rule is prevented from applying to a geminate by the Linking Constraint, say, this is merely a conspiracy. Instead we might expect AP to use a phonotactic constraint on output to somehow block the rule. Before considering the data, let me show the general pattern.

In (5.31) is a schematic view of the possible outputs of a rule turning a into α before b. Let us assume a statement of the rule making use of the appropriate tiers and associations such that strong satisfaction allows only the derivations in (5.31a,b). In these a is non-geminate. The generalisation I wish to discuss is that the configurations not produced, namely (5.31c,d), do not occur elsewhere in the language. In all cases where such a rule is prevented from applying (5.31c,d) to the input, I claim that the *output* is ill-formed in any case: * $a\alpha b$, * $a\alpha bb$.

(5.31) Modifications of strings including ab
 a. $ab \Rightarrow \alpha b$
 b. $abb \Rightarrow \alpha bb$
 c. $aab \Rightarrow \alpha\alpha b$
 d. $aabb \Rightarrow \alpha\alpha bb$

Suppose we use constraints to ban the output configuration in (5.31c,d). It is not that a *rule* is blocked from applying to geminates, instead the *pattern* that would be produced by the rule applying is banned. No Linking Constraint or UAC is needed if we assume rules do not give rise to structures constrained somewhere in the grammar to be invalid. We cannot tell, given the Blocking approach to inalterability whether geminate $\alpha\alpha$ (5.31c,d) is or is not independently prohibited in the language in the context in question. But such independent ill-formedness ought actually to be the source of the inalterability phenomenon.

This can be achieved, if, given a rule (5.32a) intended to produce some particular structure and a constraint (5.32b) partly defining the possible sequence of structures, the rule fails just in case it would be in conflict with the constraint.

(5.32) a. $a \longrightarrow \alpha\ /\ \underline{\quad}\ b$

 b. $\neg\alpha\alpha$

This supposes AP can furnish a proper account of how rules and constraints interact in all cases. Perhaps the simplest way is to say that constraints can never be violated, and that rules will apply only so long as all phonotactics are observed. In this respect rules would resemble *defaults*.

In the next section I will attempt an AP analysis of one of the patterns of inalterability using this approach, and we will see that instead of providing a coherent picture of how rules and constraints interact, AP almost ends up doing away with the rule altogether.

5.4.2 Inalterability rules as defaults

In standard AP, both rules and constraints are allowed. I will examine how this framework develops if inalterability is handled

Inalterability and Licensing

in the way suggested, *i.e.* by using a phonotactic constraint on surface form rather than making use of strong satisfaction in order to prevent the rule applying to geminates.

A constraint-based approach to inalterability in Autosegmental Phonology is to treat, say, Semitic Spirantisation as a rule which need not apply if its output is banned by a filter (rather in the way a default rule can be blocked). The filter in question places an absolute ban on [x:].

In Tigrinya /k/ will be a voiceless velar obstruent unspecified for continuancy. To characterise such underspecification AP would assign the feature *cont* no value: [18]

$$/k/ = [\emptyset \ cont]$$

A (default) spirantisation rule picks '+' as the value of *cont* when *cont* is post-vocalic. Note that the rule will have some indication of velar place of articulation but this has been omitted for expository purposes.

Rule 1. $[\emptyset \ cont] \rightarrow [+cont]/V\_\_\_$

The constraint FCR 1 bans geminate [x:].

FCR 1. $*[xx]$

If the spirantisation rule is triggered by the first half of a geminate /k:/, [x:] would be produced. But this contravenes FCR 1, so the rule does *not* apply.

Note that there are further restrictions on the appearance of the structure representing [x] and these are also expressed by constraints.

FCR 2. $*[Cx]$

FCR 3. $*[\#x]$

Since FCR 2 is more general than FCR 1 we only require FCR 2. FCR 3 says that [x] is not found initially, FCR 2 that no [x] is found post-consonantally, which includes the second half of the geminate form. These constraints leave something to be desired, however.

There is a loss of generality since these constraints, making the disjunctive pair

$$*[\left\{\begin{array}{c} C \\ \# \end{array}\right\} x]$$

do not directly express the fact that [x] is only found after a vowel. What is needed is a conditional constraint

[x] → [Vx]

which forces every [x] to follow a vowel segment of some kind.[19] This constraint should *not* be confused with a rewrite rule epenthesising V in front of x: it is a logical, conditional constraint.

But now note that there is no need for the context in Rule 1. We have moved to a position of using constraints on surface well-formedness, not contexts for derivation. We now need simply to note the default value for *cont*:

Rule 1'. [∅ *cont*] → [+*cont*]

At this point it is appropriate to consider what has happened to (i) the spirantisation rule and (ii) the inalterability. The original rule has gone, together with the necessity to block it. There are therefore two major differences between the analysis I have developed here and the traditional analysis:

1. The defeasible Rule 1' is a familiar default rule.

2. The analysis is based on surface distributions.

Inalterability-displaying analyses use rules such as Tigrinya spirantisation (5.8) which are triggered by a certain context. The rule must then be prevented from applying if the input contains a geminate, simply because the geminate output would be ungrammatical. The original rule did not express a true generalisation in the sense of Hooper's (1976) True Generalisation Condition. In common with the other rules said to show inalterability, spirantisation can be made a context-free default rule if constraints on ill-formed surface structure are added to the phonology.

The addition of phonotactics to the AP analyses makes them resemble closely the constraint-based form of AVP. In AVP, a structure which is ill-formed by virtue of the common pool of constraints

Inalterability and Licensing

is not going to become well-formed just because it is part of a geminate structure, and yet this is the behaviour the Blocking approach has been trying to achieve.

In AVP, if some structure $\mathcal{S}$ (5.33a) is ill-formed, then it is ill-formed regardless of how many paths it is a value of (5.33b).

(5.33) a. b.

In standard AP, an underlying structure $\mathcal{S}'$ is ill-formed in the sense that some rule must apply to it to make it a well-formed surface form. Current approaches to inalterability presume that the number or type of nodes that the structure $\mathcal{S}'$ is associated to *can* alter its well-formedness at the surface, since if it is a geminate form, then the rule must be prevented from applying. The well-formedness of some structure $\mathcal{S}'$ is *different* depending on factors outwith the structure itself.

5.4.3 Excursus: default and conditional constraints in AVP

Above we saw that inalterability rules were blocked by an ill-formed output. Default rules have the same property. Given an adequate set of constraints for Tigrinya the inalterability rule is revealed as a simple default rule. The conclusion I have drawn is that rewrite rules in inalterability analyses express default feature assignments which happen to be invalid for geminates. Since the inalterability rules and default rules are functionally the same, we only need to solve one problem about how such rules are dealt with in AVP, a problem which needs attention in any case.

In a declarative framework it is not immediately obvious how to interpret the claim that rules are blocked if the output they would produce is ill-formed. All rules must hold if they match the input. If applying the rule produces ill-formedness, this is an indication that the input was ill-formed. The solution is to equate the rules used in inalterability analyses with default rules: if we make them formally identical then whatever solution is provided for a formalisation of defaults should carry over into the analysis of rules subject to geminate inalterability.

In AP a default rule is one which need not apply. In order to analyse this in AVP — a declarative framework in which all constraints are obligatory — a default rule can either be a special kind of constraint, or a compound constraint. The former case is exhibited by a conditional constraint $a \to b$ which is interpreted as 'if a matches the input, *and b can unify with the input*, then unify b with the input'. The italicised part of this interpretation of the default allows the default to succeed (with no effect on the input) in those cases where a conditional constraint under a normal interpretation would fail to unify with the other constraints in the pool.

The latter case does not directly make use of such a novel interpretation for constraints. It analyses a default rule as a constraint with a disjunctive consequent, one disjunct of which is identical to the antecedent. The other disjunct serves as an indication of the default value. The default rule is a tautology because the identity disjunct can be satisfied even if the more specific disjunct is not consistent with the other constraints in the pool.

(5.34) $[\text{ATTR}\,boolean] \longrightarrow$

  $([\text{ATTR}\,+] \lor [\text{ATTR}\,boolean])$

The sort *boolean* is equivalent to a disjunction of '+∨−'. The default rule, that all F attributes have a value '+' (if possible) is compatible with a structure containing [F−] since the second disjunct *boolean* has the subsort '−'.[20] This 'default' rule is an obligatory constraint. Where both disjuncts are applicable the final representation which the pool of constraints defines will include two representations the first of which subsumes the second in which the value of ATTR will be +. In order that default rules behave as intended, the more specific representation must be chosen.[21]

I will adopt the second approach to defaults outlined above in the course of the text, but do not want to claim that this is a satisfactory approach, nor that others are impossible (see Evans & Gazdar 1990). At times I will use a special default rule format '$a \stackrel{def}{\Longrightarrow} b$' in order to distance myself from any particular approach. The problem of defaults is a recurring one in Unification-Based

Inalterability and Licensing 175

Grammar and further consideration would take me too far from the concerns of this work (see Wedekind 1990.) The point is that defaults are not just constraints. They are quite different. Using a notation like '$\stackrel{def}{\Longrightarrow}$' is in many ways a 'black-box' approach to the formal problem. Whatever solution is chosen, the behaviour of the 'default' relative to the rest of the system can still be examined.

At this point it is useful to review how conditional constraints operate in AVP since they are used below. Given a conditional constraint, if the antecedent unifies with any structure, then the consequent must do so too. If its antecedent does not unify with anything, so be it. The constraint still holds of the structure since logically a false antecedent can imply any consequent. Feature Cooccurrence Restrictions (FCRs) are one way of notating constraints:

$$\neg S$$

Such an FCR banning S is logically equivalent to a conditional constraint whose antecedent is S and whose consequent is $\bot$, the inconsistent structure:

$$S \longrightarrow \bot$$

Any structure matching the antecedent S must necessarily match the consequent as with any other conditional constraint. But to match the consequent $\bot$ the structure must be ill-formed. So 'there is no well-formed structure S' is equivalent to 'if there is some structure S, then it is ill-formed'.

Here is an example of the usefulness of this logical approach. It shows how constraints can replace generative rewrite rules. In AP there is usually a ban on

$$[+high, +low].$$

Either two rules can be used to effect a conspiracy:

$$[+high] \to [-low] \quad and \quad [+low] \to [-high],$$

or a single constraint can be used

$$*[+high, +low].$$

The latter approach is exclusively used in AVP. However, because the implication

$$\neg[F+] \leftrightarrow [F-]$$

holds for all boolean attributes, the single constraint

$$\neg([\text{HIGH}+], [\text{LOW}+])$$

actually is logically equivalent to the pair of conditional statements:

$$[\text{HIGH}+] \rightarrow [\text{LOW}-]$$

$$[\text{LOW}+] \rightarrow [\text{HIGH}-]$$

Thinking procedurally, such conditional constraints do nothing to a form if its description does not fit, but if it does fit, then the change in the rule is performed. Thinking logically, if the antecedent unifies with a structure, then the consequent must do so too or the form is ill-formed.

To save space a structure can be expressed using the B_{ss} notation described above. This enables us to mention only the relevant substructures S_1-$S_n = B$ that we are interested in. If the path dominating B is not just the null path, or if the index is important, then the subscript ss expresses this. In a conditional constraint, the antecedent and consequent can be expressed in this form. B itself can be omitted from the consequent if it is a copy of the antecedent.

An example of a constraint on prosodic structure is (5.35), which bans all consonants from the coda, and a sequential constraint is (5.36), which ensures that a back fricative is post-vocalic.

(5.35) $\quad \neg \left(\;\; cons^{[\;]} \;\; \right)_{\text{SYLLABLE}|\varepsilon\text{-SYLL}}$

(5.36) $\quad \left(\begin{array}{c} [\text{CONT}+] \\ [\text{BACK}+] \end{array} \right)_i \rightarrow \left(\;\; vowel^{[\;]} \;\; \right)_j \quad\quad j \prec i$

Inalterability and Licensing 177

5.4.4 AVP analyses

In this section I present a representative sample of the 'standard rule' type of inalterability. The analyses below employ phonotactic constraints and default rules. They do not deal specifically with 'inalterability'. They constrain the universe of possible phonological structures and sequences of structures so that the only well-formed representations coincide exactly with the requirements of the language.

The distribution of Tigrinya [x]

The Blocking account of Tigrinya spirantisation says that an underlying voiceless velar stop must become a fricative. Somehow this statement must be prevented from affecting geminates.

As an alternative I will suggest an analysis made up of components each of which is a true generalisation, a constraint. There will be no 'except clause' other than the use of a default (a conditional constraint which has a disjunctive consequent, one disjunct being maximally general). The consequent of this default rule is like any other disjunction in that if one of the disjuncts is not permitted the *other* must be. Inalterability here is reduced to general principles and no special provision is made to prevent a geminate from matching against the focus of any rule.

The analysis rests on two main observations, one prosodic/functional and one sequential.

(5.37) a. [k] must be associated to an onset.

b. [x] must follow a vowel.

The underlier /K/ is a structure specified to be a voiceless velar obstruent, *i.e.* its continuancy is unspecified: [CONT *boolean*]. A default rule selects '+' as the default value for CONT. The default rule (D1) is a normal constraint, so must always be true, even when CONT has the value '−'. The consequent therefore consists of a disjunctive pair one member of which is identity.

178   *Autosegmental Representation in a Declarative Framework*

$$(5.38) \quad D1 \quad \left(\begin{bmatrix} \text{DORSAL} \begin{bmatrix} \text{HIGH} + \\ \text{BACK} + \end{bmatrix} \end{bmatrix} \\ [\text{SPREAD.GLOTTIS} -] \end{array} \right)$$

$$\longrightarrow ([\text{CONT}+]) \vee ([\text{CONT } boolean])$$

D1 says that for some index i, if the path MELODY dominates each of the substructures in the antecedent, then that MELODY path at index i must dominate one of the disjuncts in the consequent too. The constraint is still true if applied to [k] since the null path in [k]'s root matrix does dominate [CONT*boolean*].[22] In order not to go beyond the bounds of the data being discussed I have restricted D1 to voiceless velars only. It could well be that a full analysis of the language would employ a simpler default rule.

Let's see how the analysis works. Underlyingly, all we know about the value of CONT for any unvoiced velar is that it is either + or −. In other words the underlyer for /K/ is [CONT*boolean*]. The data tells us that we must never assign the more highly specified description [CONT+] if the structure /K/ is part of a geminate sequence /K:/. Similarly this description is not well-formed when it is used to refer to a realisation of /K/ which is post-consonantal or word-initial. This is the observation of (5.37b) above. AVP uses (5.39) to express this. For convenience I will refer to complex structures such as the antecedent of R2 as $_{mel}[\text{x}]$ etc.

$$(5.39) \quad R2 \quad \left(\begin{bmatrix} \text{DORSAL} \begin{bmatrix} \text{HIGH} + \\ \text{BACK} + \end{bmatrix} \end{bmatrix} \\ [\text{CONT} +] \\ [\text{OBS} +] \end{array} \right)_i \longrightarrow \left(vowel^{[\ ]} \right)_j$$

Conditions : $j \prec i$

Recall that the sort *vowel* is a subsort of *melody*. It identifies the vowels. In a geminate [x:] the second root matrix [x] (index i) *immediately* follows another [x] ($j \prec i$). [x] may not be a vowel in

Tigrinya, so it does not unify with the consequent — any representation incorporating a geminate (5.40) would be ill-formed.

(5.40) Ill-formed geminate [xː]

$$\left\langle {}_{cons}\begin{bmatrix} \text{MELODY}\boxed{1} \end{bmatrix}, {}_{cons}\begin{bmatrix} \text{MELODY}\boxed{1} \end{bmatrix} \right\rangle$$

$$\boxed{1} = {}_{melody}\begin{bmatrix} x \end{bmatrix}$$

Because a specification of [CONT+] on /Kː/ would result in ill-formedness, the disjunct [CONT−] must be selected for the geminate so that [kː] is found rather than ∗[xː]. Rule R2 (5.39) does more than this, however. If /K/ is post-consonantal or word initial, then [CONT+] is similarly impossible. The rule makes the continuancy specification of /K/ more precise by ruling out one of the two possible values in a variety of cases. These are the cases to which the spirantisation rule traditionally used does not apply. No claim is made here that '*all* post-vocalic /K/ are [x]', so it is hardly surprising that there are no exceptions to this generalisation. Instead AVP uses a default rule D1 of the kind already motivated by much work in AP.

Before a consonant or word-finally the stop [k] is impossible as a realisation of /K/ unless it is part of a geminate. How is this to be handled? If we were constructing a Blocking analysis we would use a constraint to ban [k] in these contexts, and then use the Linking Constraint to prevent the constraint from applying to geminates. This is what Itô (1989) does in her treatment of coda weakening. I argued above that such an approach is flawed. Other means are necessary to properly describe the data Itô addresses. In any case AVP could not employ a constraint which operated in this manner.

Instead of banning [k] from the coda, AVP takes a line more in sympathy with the distributional requirements of the language. If [k] is chosen as the allophone of /K/, then the analysis must ensure that in all circumstances this structure is dominated by an onset (5.37a). If [CONT−] is chosen as the more specific version of [CONT *boolean*] then the rule R1 (5.41) must be satisfied.

180   *Autosegmental Representation in a Declarative Framework*

(5.41)   R1 $\left(\ _{melody}[k]\ \right)$ ⟶ SYLLABLE|ONSET

Recall that only roots are part of any sequence, not melodies. If $_{melody}[k]$ is to be part of a phonological representation, it must be associated to the skeleton; a value of MELODY. R1 says that $_{melody}[k]$ must also be the value of SYLLABLE|ONSET. The rule is saying that $_{melody}[k]$ can be part of a root matrix only if the path mentioned in the consequent dominates it. (MELODY is guaranteed to dominate this structure already given the interpretation of the notation given above.)

Other paths can dominate $_{melody}[k]$ too, and the rule does not deal with these. As [k] being dominated by an onset is impossible pre-consonantally or word finally, the rule has the effect of forcing /K/ to be [x] in these contexts.[23] In a geminate, the substructure matching $_{melody}[k]$ *is* dominated by a coda, but this is not a problem: *it is dominated by an onset too*. R1 is therefore satisfied when the [k] melody structure is shared by an onset and coda.

One final case has not been dealt with. Intervocalic /K/ is compatible with being either [x] or [k]. Each is possible in an onset, each is possible post-vocalically. I suggest that the default rule takes care of this case. All other things being equal, the most highly specified form will be sent to or extracted from the phonetic interface. Since the default rule *can* pick the more specific [x] without inconsistency, it will do. If the default rule does not apply, intervocalic /K/ remains '[x] *or* [k]'. If the identity disjunct of the default rule is picked when [x] *is* possible then this is not the same as picking [k]. The default offers a choice of 'x or (x or k)'. If both [x] and [k] are permitted, then choosing the latter disjunct '(x or k)' clearly does *not* amount to picking [k]. As [x] is the more highly specified choice (+ being a subsort of *boolean*) it is selected.

To conclude I want to re-emphasise the difference between this approach and the Blocking approach. In AVP the voiceless velar geminate is seen primarily as being a post-consonantal [k] (with a predictable post-vocalic part) not a post-vocalic [k] (with a predictable post-consonantal part). Only if the latter view is adopted does it make any sense to search for a theory of inalterability, since there is no simple statement about post-vocalic velars. In AP, a

Inalterability and Licensing

rule like 'all post-vocalic voiceless velars are fricatives' must somehow be squared with the fact that some are not.

Tiberian Spirantisation

The analysis of Tiberian Hebrew is similar to the analysis of Tigrinya except that the rules concern all obstruents not just velar obstruents. The rule parallel to (5.41) is (5.42).

(5.42) R1 ([CONT−]) ⟶ SYLLABLE|ONSET

It expresses the generalisation that the [CONT−] of a stop must be dominated by an onset path wherever it appears. In addition there is a post-vocalic condition on the fricatives (5.43) and a default D1 rule similar to that given above.

(5.43) R2 $([\text{CONT}+])_i \longrightarrow (\text{ vowel}^{[\ ]})_j$

$Conditions: j \prec i$

(5.44) D1 $(\top) \stackrel{def}{\Longrightarrow} ([\text{CONT}+])$

The distribution of the allophones of Latin /l/

A traditional AP analysis of the Latin lateral would say that /l/ in the coda is velarised, *except when geminate*. The analysis given here again shows the benefit of a more surface oriented approach.

In Latin [ɫ] is impossible in the onset. This can be expressed with an FCR (5.45), which bans the features all being dominated by that path.

(5.45) R2 $\neg \begin{pmatrix} [\text{LATERAL}+] \\ [\text{HIGH}+] \\ [\text{BACK}+] \end{pmatrix}$ / SYLLABLE|ONSET

This constraint accounts for the lack of velarisation on all onset laterals, whether part of a geminate or not. Word initial, post-consonantal and geminate laterals cannot be velarised and remain consistent thanks to (5.45). A parallel FCR, that non-velarised

182 Autosegmental Representation in a Declarative Framework

lateral cannot appear in the coda, would result in a Blocking analysis. AVP would need to prevent application of such a FCR in the case of geminates, which partly consist of a light lateral in the coda. Instead of this Blocking approach a conditional constraint is required, parallel to (5.41) and (5.42) which expresses the rule that a light lateral melody must be dominated by an onset:

(5.46) $\quad$ R1 $\quad \begin{pmatrix} [\text{LATERAL}+] \\ [\text{BACK}-] \end{pmatrix} \longrightarrow \text{SYLLABLE}|\text{ONSET}$

The only case not yet dealt with is the intervocalic lateral, just as happened with the spirantisation analyses above. There the syllabification did not distinguish between [k] and [x]. Both were possible in the onset, both were possible post-vocalically. The default choice of [x] picked it out as the one to appear. In Latin, the intervocalic lateral is light if an onset, is dark if a coda. The syllabification given to the lateral will co-vary with this choice, rather than being picked by a light lateral default. Generally intervocalic consonants are onsets, and the light [l] form will correctly be chosen on the basis of such onset preference, however this is encoded. Such a default can be over-ridden, in English for example, where the choice of light or dark allophone of /l/ may be determined by stress-sensitive syllabification. The forms *volume* [vɔɫ.jum] and *voluminous* [vɔ.lju.mɪ.nʌs] with dark and light laterals respectively show that the velarisation of /l/ is dependent on syllabification.[24] Consequently I feel that relying on syllabification is a valid move and that the general preference for an onset consonant will lead to the nonvelar pronunciation.

Note the difference between Latin and Tigrinya. In Latin the 'onset form' [l] occurs intervocalically, but in Tigrinya the 'coda form' [x] appears. Of course, [x] is a post-vocalic form, not a coda form, which is the source of the difference.

Alterable geminates

Can this account deal with the cases when geminates *are* alterable? The answer is yes — because no special means are used to describe inalterability other than the use of phonotactics.

Inalterability and Licensing 183

1. Lithuanian Backing. The case of Lithuanian Backing mentioned above was one in which geminate /eː/ and nongeminate /e/ surfaced as [oː] and [o] respectively before a back glide [w] or high back vowel [u]. This is handled by an assimilation rule stating that any sequence of mid-vowel plus following high round segment must share the value of their *round* paths. A constraint says $\boxed{1}$ must be dominated by MELODY at i:

(5.47) $\qquad \left(\begin{matrix} [\text{HIGH}-] \\ [\text{LOW}-] \end{matrix} \right)_i \wedge \left(\begin{matrix} [\text{HIGH}+] \\ [\text{ROUND}\boxed{1}+] \end{matrix} \right)_{i+1} \longrightarrow (\boxed{1})_i$

Since both [o] and [oː] appear in other contexts there can be no chance of process being described by a rule applying only to the nongeminate vowel. If there were no [oː] an analysis bent on showing inalterability could be designed to demonstrate this.

2. West Greenlandic Lowering. West Greenlandic (Aagesen 1987) has a productive system of uvularisation which affects consonants and vowels. /i(ː)/ and /u(ː)/ are realised as [e(ː)] and [o(ː)] before the back [ɴ(ː), q(ː), χ(ː)]^25 Uvularised coronals and labials also trigger the allophony. As with the example above a stipulation is made, assuming that the uvular consonants are [−*high*], that a vowel and following consonant share the value of their *high* paths.

3. West Greenlandic Palatalisation. West Greenlandic has an allophonic rule which realises /t/ and /tː/ as affricates [tʃ] and [tʃː] only and always before [i] and [iː]. Again a statement that each member of the sequence /ti/ must share the value of their *high* paths covers the /ti/, /tti/, /tii/ and /ttii/ cases.

4. Luganda Palatalisation. Luganda optionally palatalises /K/ and /g/ before /i/ or the cognate glide /j/ (Hayes 1986b) to the affricates [tʃ] and [dʒ]. The geminate stops also palatalise to a (long) affricate. A rule like that given in paragraph 3 above is used.

5.4.5 Summary

In this section have I offered an approach to inalterability which contends inalterability arises as a result of the type of analysis offered in the literature. The normal constraints on well-formedness give rise to inalterability effects without stipulation. In fact inalterability is not even an issue specifically of geminateness — except that the multidominance of a structure gives a greater chance of full syllabification.

I do not want to suggest that the role of shared structure in the data discussed under the title of inalterability is unimportant. It should be noted that in the analyses offered, shared structure is crucial. In the analyses presented of cases which are said to show inalterability a constraint of the form

(5.48) $\mathcal{S} \longrightarrow$ SYLLABLE|ONSET

was part of the analysis. This constraint forces a certain pattern of syllabification for the structure $\mathcal{S}$. Normally a melody will appear in any prosodic position compatible with its sonority but if $\mathcal{S} = {}_{melody}[\ ]$, (5.48) forces the melody to be syllabified into the onset. Shared structure is important because a geminate version of the melody can be associated to an onset, satisfying (5.48), *and* to the coda too. Nongeminate melodies cannot appear in the coda given the constraint (5.48), but in a very particular sense, the geminate is immune. This is not due to the mode of applications of a rule as AP suggests. It is the true geminate representation itself which allows melodies to appear in unsanctioned positions.

5.5 A constraint-based approach to coda weakening

I identified three classes of inalterability rules above in §5.2, namely 'standard rule' inalterability, coda weakening and glide/vowel alternations. Having considered the first class I now move on to sketch an approach to coda weakening. Note that I am not going to discuss the glide/vowel patterns in connection with inalterability — because of recent developments in moraic phonology, any arguments based on skeletal rewrite rules like 'V→C' are at least highly suspect.[26] This section aims to show that coda weakening phenomena and 'standard rule' inalterability differ only in the size of the class of segments affected.

5.5.1 Analysing defective distributions

Inadequacies of the blocking approach

It is highly doubtful that the rewrite rule approach to inalterability can be extended to encompass the phenomenon of coda weakening, because there is little to motivate the use of rewrite rules in this area. The nearest we can get to a unified approach is to witness the extended application of the Linking Constraint to filters, as proposed by Itô (1989). It is unclear, however, to what extent Itô's filter-based approach can be taken as an extension of the rewrite-rule approach to inalterability. If 'filters' are different from 'rules' in AP, as the terminology would suggest, how can Itô assume without further argument that they act so alike? The ability of the Linking Constraint to over-ride the Coda Filter raises unanswered questions about the inter-relationship of rules, representations, and constraints on representations in Generative Phonology. Itô's Coda Filter has already been discussed (§5.3.4) and that approach to coda weakening rejected because of the problems it causes for filters elsewhere in the phonology.

Licensing in Autosegmental Phonology

Goldsmith (1990) proposes a theory of coda weakening which, since it appears to be non-derivational, might be compatible with AVP's constraint-based approach to inalterability. Goldsmith's approach is called AUTOSEGMENTAL LICENSING, and in this scheme, distinctive features are 'licensed' (by a licenser — a node of syllable structure). While *prosodic* licensing is, roughly, the requirement that every melody be syllabified, *autosegmental* licensing allows only particular parts of syllable structure to syllabify a given feature. By permitting the onset to license more features than the coda, this forms the core of Goldsmith's approach to coda weakening.

The type of diagrammatic account Goldsmith provides for autosegmental licensing is shown in Figure 5.5.1.

Note the features F_1-F_n which comprise the contrastive features of the language. While all these features are listed on the syllable node, only a subset are listed on the Coda. A prosodic node may license those features which are listed on it, thus the syllable node licenses all the features of the language, but the coda is a

186   Autosegmental Representation in a Declarative Framework

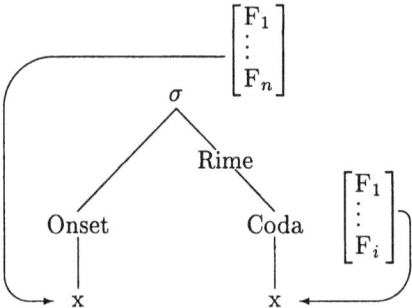

Figure 5.1: Goldsmithian Licensing.

SECONDARY LICENSER, licensing just those members of the subset F_1-F_i ($1 \prec i \prec n$). Licensing is indicated by the curved arrow, and defined as follows:

> A given licenser can license no more than one occurrence of the autosegment in question. This unique licensing can be graphically represented in terms of a non-branching path that can be traced from the licenser to the autosegment (or feature) in question [see Figure 5.5.1].
>
> Goldsmith (1990:123,4)

The motivations behind this view of licensing are sound enough. Goldsmith refers to Fujimura (1976; 1990) and Hirst (1985) to support his claim that the onset-nucleus and the coda typically each bear only a single instance of any contrastive feature. Moreover each licenser corresponds to a metrical weight unit. Finally, this approach provides, in the notion of secondary licenser, a way to talk about the defective distribution of contrasts in the coda.

Geminates interact with this system in an interesting way. In coda weakening languages the coda licenses very few features — it may be unable to license stops, for example. Yet stops will still be able to appear in the coda, *but only if they are part of*

Inalterability and Licensing 187

a geminate. Goldsmith's account says that since such geminates are syllabified into the following onset as well as the coda, their content, once licensed by that onset, is free to syllabify elsewhere — in particular into the non-licensing coda constituent.

5.5.2 AVP's constraint-based approach

Prosodic licensing forces melody structures to be syllabified (5.49). They must be dominated by MELODY *and* SYLLABLE.

(5.49) *Prosodic Licensing ('full syllabification')*
($mel^{[\ ]}$) $\longrightarrow$ SYLLABLE

Autosegmental licensing statements limit the range of syllabic functions available for a given type of melody. In a typical case, place of articulation features (**PoA**) may not appear in a coda unless licensed elsewhere, in the following onset. Instead of introducing a new relation of 'licensing' to analyse these distributional patterns, I propose to treat them as more specific versions of (5.49). The **PoA** feature which is 'licensed' by the onset but not the coda is, in AVP, a feature subject to a conditional constraint obliging it to appear in an onset:

(5.50) *Licensing of* **PoA** *by onset*
($place^{[\ ]}$) $\longrightarrow$ SYLLABLE|ONSET

In Hausa, coda weakening means that a contrastive **PoA** does not appear in the coda. This is captured by (5.50). Since **PoA** can only be licensed by the onset, I interpret this as a constraint that **PoA** *must* be associated to the onset in order to be prosodically licensed, *i.e.* syllabified.[27] (5.50) forces every $place^{[\ }$] to be dominated by the onset, which is just what is required. Moreover, nothing in such a constraint bans the melody in question from being dominated by some further syllable function. A shared melody (as found in a geminate) raises the possibility of (5.50) being satisfied despite the fact that part of the geminate is syllabified into the coda. Since Hausa does in fact permit coda obstruents just in case they are also onset obstruents, the conditional constraints can be seen to be a satisfactory means of dealing with coda weakening. In a sequence of structures (5.51) where 1

$_{place}$[ ] is the **PoA** specification of a geminate, the licensing requirement (5.50) is met because $\boxed{1}$ is indeed dominated by the path [SYLLABLE|ONSET].

(5.51)
$$\left\langle \begin{bmatrix} \text{SYLL}|\varepsilon\text{-SYLL}|\text{CODA}|\text{PLACE}\boxed{1} \\ \text{MELODY} \quad \boxed{2} \end{bmatrix}, \right.$$
$$\left. \begin{bmatrix} \text{SYLL}|\text{ONSET}|\text{PLACE}\boxed{1} \\ \text{MELODY} \quad \boxed{2} \quad \begin{bmatrix} \text{PLACE}\boxed{1} \end{bmatrix} \end{bmatrix} \right\rangle$$

Note the difference between the AVP approach and Goldsmith's. Goldsmith has added notions to AP such as 'nonbranching path', 'licensed features' and 'licenser'. AVP analyses coda weakening in a language by adding further more specific versions of the Prosodic Licensing constraint (5.49). In both cases stipulations must be made about onsets being the better licenser — in both cases a proper theory of the onset/coda asymmetry is required. But AVP has introduced no new machinery to handle the phenomenon. We could have constructed a body of theoretical apparatus to express the generalisation:

- Only path $\mathcal{P}$ may LICENSE structure $\mathcal{S}$.

This would require a definition of the new relation LICENSE. Instead familiar theoretical machinery is used. All autosegmental licensing statements will be of the form:

- Path $\mathcal{P}$ must dominate structure $\mathcal{S}$.

5.5.3 Linking coda weakening and inalterability

Recall that in the analyses presented of inalterability facts an important part of each was the claim that one of the distributional variants was obliged to appear in the onset. For example in Tigrinya, the voiceless velar stop must be associated to the onset regardless of whether it is geminated or not; see (5.41), repeated here

Inalterability and Licensing

as (5.52). Such a constraint can now be seen as a specific statement of autosegmental licensing.

(5.52) $\left(\; _{cons}[k] \; \right) \longrightarrow$ SYLLABLE|ONSET

My claim is that in Tigrinya the onset licenses [k], but the coda does not. In AVP, coda weakening is handled using the self-same conditional constraints that formed the basis of the treatment of standard rule inalterability. Consequently inalterability and coda weakening receive a unified treatment, which was one of the goals set out for a proper treatment of these phenomena. The difference between them is purely in terms of degree. The inalterability distributions do not deal with such regular classes of segments.

Goldsmith is aware of the continuum from very general coda weakening phenomena right down to idiosyncratic cases usually dealt with by inalterability. In various footnotes he states that he believes the licensing approach can be extended to handle "a large proportion" of cases of inalterability (see his footnotes on pp336, 353–355). He still assumes a blocking approach, however, in the rest of his monograph, and his proposals to extend licensing to inalterability are fairly imprecise. It is most interesting, therefore, that the constraint-based treatment of inalterability given above, which is based on surface distribution, can so easily turn its hand to the analysis of coda weakening data.

Goldsmith's rather oversimplistic table of types of coda weakening, Table 5.1 shows some of the data a theory of licensing has to handle. Each entry allows a subset of the segments in the coda of the entry below it, and this might give the impression that the patterns of coda weakening are limited to such a relationship.

Having seen already that the segment-particular cases of inalterability are in fact obscure cases of autosegmental licensing, we should treat Table 5.1 with caution. In AVP the antecedent of a conditional constraint can be any structure, defined as the intersection of individual features. This gives it the expressive power to go beyond the confines of Table 5.1. AVP is, in principle, equally able to control the CV syllable structure of Hawaiian as the distribution of [h] in English. There is a continuum from the [x]~[k]

190   Autosegmental Representation in a Declarative Framework

Type of syllable	Example
a. $CV_i(V_j)$	diphthongs and contrastive vowel length: Hawaiian.
b. CVX (no P of A)	nasal or obstruent permitted in the coda if it is homorganic with the following consonant or has otherwise predictable **PoA**: Selayarese, Luganda, Irula, Axininca Campa.
c. CVX (X = sonorant)	like (b), but also glides and liquids allowed in rime: Standard Hausa.
d. CVX	Coda can have anything the onset can.

Table 5.1: Possible coda contrasts   Goldsmith's (18)

alternation of Tigrinya through to phonotactic distributions such as German final-voicing neutralisation which affects all obstruents.

5.5.4 Summary

Goldsmith (1990) offers two alternative ways of analysing inalterability: a Blocking approach and a Licensing approach. The latter is the result of a study of patterns of coda weakening — it being unilluminating to treat them as the Blocking of rewrite rules. Any elegant phonological theory would seek provide a single analytical basis for these two phenomena, and Goldsmith holds out hopes that autosegmental licensing can be extended to deal with such cases of inalterability as Semitic spirantisation.

Attribute Value Phonology, because a Blocking analysis of inalterability is unavailable, adopts a constraint-based approach which appears to be ideally suited to the characterisation of coda weakening. Moreover, the constraint-based analyses of the standard cases of inalterability avoid a conspiracy, in common with other phonotactically-based analyses.

Clearly more work needs to be done, whichever framework is selected as the means to study the generalisations evident in the syllabic patterning of contrastive features. Nevertheless, the constraint-based approach of AVP has shown itself equal to the task of expressing the appropriate distributional generalisations in a unified way. The Sharing Constraint has the consequence that geminates and nongeminates alike are composed of attribute-value structures. Constraints on the well-formedness of these structures apply to each type of segment equally, and the behaviours discussed at length above are dealt with succinctly without any need for further elaboration of the framework.

Notes

[1] The structural description is only roughly the elements to the right of the slash '/', since rules are subject to a notational convention (Chomsky & Halle 1968). If the elements to the left of the arrow replace the '_____', then in (5.1) the r–m configuration is the structural description.

[2] The term 'inalterability' originally presupposed a blocking account; I am attempting to separate the problem from the range of solutions, however. AVP's solution for inalterability does not depend on geminates 'failing to alter', but it is useful to keep the term.

[3] Such subsumption is the only form of satisfaction permitted in AVP when the antecedent of a constraint is matched against other constraints. See §2.6.

[4] She credits the suggestion to Alan Prince.

[5] Why onsets license more features than codas, and how this is to be represented, is a separate issue which I will ignore here.

[6] The Licensers make use of the syllable-based phonotactic, which is a historically recurrent phonological notion. It is for this reason that I interpret Goldsmith's terminology in the way indicated above. Probably the approach closest to licensing as conceived here is that of Natural Generative Phonology (Venneman 1971, 1974; Hooper 1976). Indeed Hooper's insightful study is much more compatible with the views expressed here than the mere coincidence in the use of the term 'constraint' might suggest. NGP's True Generalisation Condition for example is valid for AVP since it follows from AVP's monostratal approach. See §1.2.

[7] The allophonic variation [l]∼[ɫ] was no more indicated in the orthography of Latin than it is in English — ɫ is used here in the

orthography for expository purposes only.

[8] In an excellent Firthian treatment, Palmer (1957) gives the affricate ejective [qχ'] as the postvocalic realisation of underlying ejective /k'/ rather than a glottalised fricative [x']. That a glottalised fricative and an ejective affricate have both been found is hardly surprising.

[9] Putting it this simplistic way demonstrates that the 'problem' of inalterability is the perfect exemplar of the failure of *linear* phonology, where inalterability was first discussed. The introduction of a structure sharing representation ought to have solved the problem — and indeed it can do if the SPE-style analyses that have been outlined above are dropped. The data itself holds no real problems for the representational side of AP other than the use of multiple association in both local and long distance dependencies, while inalterability affects only local dependencies.

[10] Goldsmith (1990) adopts a slightly revised version under the title the 'Conjunctivity Condition' as part of a change of terminology. (In his scheme the 'Linkage Condition' is the name given to the principle that all autosegments are anchored.)

[11] This is so if we assume the associations are not to two *nonadjacent* postvocalic slots. The Sharing Constraint gives us this behaviour for free, while the NCC does not. See Chapter 6.

[12] Positionally conditioned rules will not do: it is impossible for both slots of a geminate to follow *and* be adjacent to some segment, say.

[13] AVP does not distinguish (5.23a) and (5.23b) thanks to the OCP, see Chapter 3. *Some* contour of information must exist to justify the extra slot. In the OCP is active in this way then the Linking Constraint and the UAC are identical in import.

[14] If a moraic analysis of long vowels is used then again the UAC would not work as required. The nuclear mora must be distinguished somehow from the rhymal mora other than by position, otherwise there would be an enormous amount of redundancy from constraints on the content of the coda/second mora. They would need to individually refer to the 'rightmost of two co-syllabic morae' rather than μ_2 (as distinct from the differently labelled μ_1). In order to avoid /w/, the SD of the rule would need to mention μ_1.

[15] I omit the predictable internal structure of /ʉ/.

[16] This is another example of AP treating local and long dis-

Inalterability and Licensing 193

tance associations differently. AVP does not use shared structure in harmony, so harmony cannot be expected to show inalterability. That in AP long distance harmonic dependencies must be explicitly excluded from the UAC and Conjunctivity Condition is again indicative of the need for a version of the Sharing Constraint. See Chapter 6.

[17] Kiparsky (1985) is concerned with Structure Preservation, the requirement that constraints on well-formedness are obeyed throughout the phonology. He suggests that rules are subject to phonological constraints lexically but not necessarily post-lexically since segments appear which do not form part of the phonotactic alphabet of the language. This dichotomy is echoed in AVP in the supposition that phonological structures are ruled well-formed by reference to a pool of constraints, but that phonetic gestural alignment may construct apparent contradictions to such phonological structures. It is not a question of constraints being side-stepped post-lexically. In AVP the phonetic gestural score is not subject to phonological constraints. Phonetic and phonological descriptions are not part of a continuum with more constraints at one end than the other.

[18] I have avoided using '*boolean*' in order to prevent confusion with AVP and used '[$\emptyset cont$]' rather than '[*cont*]' to suggest that *some* value for *cont* will appear. It should be noted how AVP's use of a sort hierarchy would help here. In AVP there is no ambiguity over whether the lack of a feature means that the feature cannot appear or that the feature's value is only unspecified.

[19] This is different from saying [x] must appear in the coda, note. Postvocalic [x] can appear in the onset: *ʔaxalib* 'dogs'.

[20] I could use any identity structure, say the maximally general structure T as the second disjunct.

[21] This might be done at phonetic implementation, where the most specific representation was selected. This could be a difficult computational problem, especially if the default value is needed as the antecedent of some other conditional constraint since a complex web of interdependencies can arise.

[22] It may actually dominate [CONT−], but '−' is a subsort of '*boolean*'.

[23] An onset at these positions is impossible due to there being no following nucleus.

[24] This example is taken from speakers who pronounces *lute* as

[ljut]. The same distinction obtains for those who have [vɔ.lju.mɪ.nʌs], but the segmental context differs slightly with the syllabification.

[25] Note that the short uvular fricative is in fact voiced though the geminate cognate is voiceless.

[26] Glide/vowel alternations are, however, a phenomenon ideally suited to a unification-based phonotactic analysis (Waksler 1990). A nongeminate G/V melody is syllabified in a phonotactically determined way, geminate G/V melodies (the 'inalterability case') being dealt with in the same way. If the language in question permits no glide-glide sequences, then this is simply stated by a phonotactic constraint.

[27] The nucleus would also be a licenser: I ignore that complication here.

Chapter 6

Long Distance Dependencies

6.1 The spreading and sharing of phonological information

One particularly important consequence of the Sharing Constraint is that it enables a simple formal definition of LOCAL DEPENDENCIES: they are instances of structure sharing. AVP predicts, because of the limitations on sharing, that the body of phenomena analysed in Autosegmental Phonology using multiple association consists of two incompatible subparts. Although AP *could* distinguish local and long distance dependencies pretheoretically (see §3.4), the universal availability of multiple association entails that the pretheoretic difference is not valid theoretically.

In Chapters 4 and 5 I examined some of the phenomena which Autosegmental Phonology uses multiple association to describe. Because any local multiple association can be made nonlocal, AP struggles to make sense of formal integrity, the sole purpose of which is to prevent such a transition. Inalterability is basically a formal problem dealing with a fundamental distinction between single association and multiple association (whether local or nonlocal, as we will see). Attribute Value Phonology proposes, in the

Sharing Constraint, a different distinction from the single/multiple association one. In AVP, the association of some value to some attribute is subject to the pool of constraints on well-formed structures, and re-entrancy is employed in the analysis of geminates, but it does not follow that the definitions of well-formed structures must change. The simplified treatment of geminates that results counts as positive evidence that the multiple association of Autosegmental Phonology must in fact comprise *both* structure sharing *and* another means of expressing dependency, which I will call SPREADING.

In this chapter I argue that only a certain type of evidence could motivate non-local structure sharing. After a critical examination of it, I conclude that the distinction between sharing and spreading (more accurate terms might be 'associative' and 'non-associative' phonological dependencies) is more explanatory than the Autosegmental dichotomy between single and multiple association. There are, however, two deficiencies in my account which must be made clear at the outset.

Firstly, I do not intend to present a clear alternative account to nonlocal association as the formal expression of long distance dependencies. Moreover I limit myself to demonstrating the basic point with reference to harmony phenomena and nonconcatenative morphology. Some tentative proposals are presented, and I suggest that long distance dependencies should be handled by the morphological system.

Secondly, given the focus of this work on segmental phonology, I will not be addressing tonal or intonational phonology. It should be noted, however, that recent results from the study of Japanese (Pierrehumbert & Beckman 1988) show quite conclusively that it is no longer possible to accept without argument the multiple association analysis of tonal behaviour as incorporating the nonlocal attachment of a tone feature. Although the phonetic correlates of tone (particularly F_0) are continuously present to some degree, their actual values are best predicted by a phonetic interpolation function which is given *singly attached* contrastive features. Such results are compatible with the basic contention here that long distance segmental phenomena consist of a dependency between individual tokens of structure rather than the multiple attachment of a single token over a multi-syllable domain.

Long Distance Dependencies 197

6.2 Nonconcatenative morphology and multiplanar phonology

In Chapter 3 I gave AP's rationale for using multiple association in nonconcatenative morphology. Forms like *samam*, with different token /m/'s of the same type, derive ultimately from a morpheme which, by the OCP, is allowed only *one* token of any given type; *sm*. Autosegmental association is a readily available means of ensuring that a single token /m/ appears on different slots. These slots may form a geminate, or individual segments. In either case association is used to link slot and melody. This association-based analysis forces AP to employ DISCONTINUOUS GEMINATES and a MULTIPLANAR PHONOLOGY in order that the association of consonant melodies around vowels (and *vice versa*) does not result in crossing associations.

6.2.1 Discontinuous geminates

The spirantisation rules of Semitic (discussed in Chapter 5) are good candidates for rules which might apply to multiplanar structures. Hebrew *sibbeβ* 'to turn' and Tigrinya *räqqiχ* 'thin' would be given multiplanar representations like those in (6.1) in which each morpheme is assigned its own PLANE.[1] The second consonant of each word (/b/ and /q/ respectively) is associated to nonadjacent slots.[2]

(6.1) Discontinuous geminates

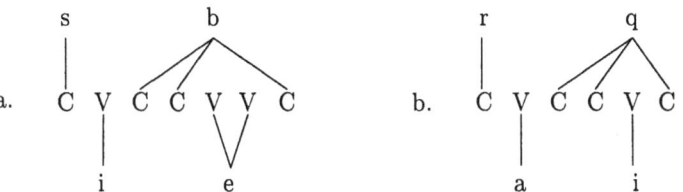

Another form of interest is Tigrinya *mäsäxaxärä* 'witness-frequentative', (not illustrated) in which there is a discontinuous geminate /x...x/ but no true *local* geminate. In AP it is assumed that Tiberian Hebrew and Tigrinya have spirantisation rules, as we have seen above, which apply only to simple post-vocalic stops, *not to geminates*. In Chapter 5 I concentrated solely on local geminates. We now see that autosegmental phonology allows discontinuous sharing of structure, and we need to address its properties. In particular we need to determine whether this 'phonological' representation is subject to any rules; spirantisation for instance.

Two spirantisation rules which operate in Hebrew and Tigrinya prevent the 'underlying' forms *sibbeeb*, *räqqiq* and *mäsäkakärä* from surfacing, in favour of *sibbeeβ*, *räqqiχ* and *mäsäxaxärä*; see (5.7).[3] In the case of *mäsäkakärä*, the relevant part of the structure (6.2a) shows part of the consonantism doubly linked to the skeleton. We could imagine that the spirantisation rule affects the unique /k/ melody in a 'two for the price of one' operation (6.2). Both positions are postvocalic, so the phonological rule could be allowed to apply to the discontinuous geminate.

(6.2) Operation of a multiplanar phonological rule

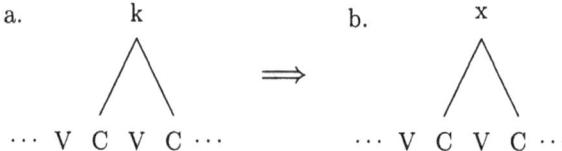

Note that Hayes's Linking Constraint says the mapping in (6.2) is impossible, since the *two* association lines in (6.2a) do not strongly satisfy the *single* line in the structural description of the rule in question (6.3) =(5.8).

(6.3) Tigrinya Spirantisation

$$/k/ \rightarrow [+cont] \ / \ \begin{array}{c} V \ C \\ | \\ \underline{} \end{array}$$

The Linking Constraint therefore predicts that all rules applying to multiplanar structures will behave differently, in that a form like *mäsäxaxärä* will fail to be affected by a rule just in case the foci form a discontinuous geminate. I am aware of no such rules. If AP adopts the Linking Constraint, then no phonological rule will ever apply to the representations in (6.1). Discontinuous geminates would not be phonological entities since no phonological rule would apply to them.

The UAC, however, *would* allow the rule to apply, judging from Steriade (1982:35) and Schein & Steriade (1986). The UAC is only interested in whether each of the /k/-melody's slots complies with the structural description of the rule. For this word (*mäsäxaxärä*) the UAC acts as if there were no discontinuous geminates. If *all* examples were like this one, there would be no reason to permit rules to apply to multiplanar structures, and again we would query the *need* for phonologically discontinuous geminates.

If multiplanar representations are not to be redundant, there must be some ways in which the discontinuous geminate is the cause of behaviour which does not simply mimic that of monoplanar representations.

6.2.2 How to test for a multiplanar phonology

There are two ways in which the application of rules to multiplanar structures would not be vacuous. Either a rule is prevented from applying to a target that would normally undergo the rule in a monoplanar framework, by virtue of a nonlocal association — this I call NONLOCAL INALTERABILITY — or a rule could do precisely the opposite, and cause a SIDE-EFFECT in a melody that would not normally be expected to undergo the rule. We must find and evaluate analyses that posit such rules.

(6.4) shows, schematically, the type of thing required. It shows nonlocal associations (in a multiplanar representation) on the top row and the corresponding independent segments on the bottom row (which would be required by a monoplanar architecture). To motivate multiplanar phonology we must find a case where slots are affected by a rule in a different way. We must look at discrepancies between the upper and lower row in the ways in which a slot matches ('*yes*') or doesn't match ('*no*') a rule.

(6.4) Multiplanar satisfaction and monoplanar satisfaction

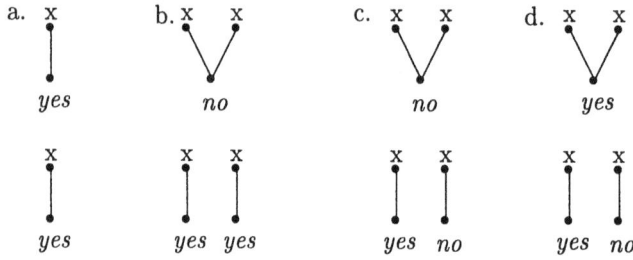

(6.4a) shows that single associations act no differently, matching to the rule (or not matching) in each case. (6.4b) shows the non-existent case, discussed above, in which a rule does not apply to a discontinuous geminate although each individual slot *would* undergo the rule itself. This is the behaviour the Linking Constraint predicts. (6.4c) shows a more interesting case of nonlocal inalterability. A discontinuous geminate fails to undergo a rule because although one slot matches, the other does not (as we can see from the lower row). A slot that would undergo the rule in a monoplanar phonology does not do so. (6.4d) is the analogous case, except that the discontinuous geminate *does* undergo the rule despite one slot not matching; this (rightmost) slot undergoes the rule as a side-effect.

Before discussing the data which bears on this issue (§6.2, §6.3) it is worthwhile reinforcing the idea that, without such evidence, there is no basis for adopting a multiplanar phonology. To see why, let us look closer at the phonological properties of the discontinuous geminates in Tigrinya and Tiberian Hebrew.

6.2.3 Are discontinuous geminates fake geminates?

In Tigrinya and Hebrew the spirantisation rule under discussion cannot be permitted to apply to the multiplanar forms of (6.1). They therefore fail to provide the evidence we are seeking, and are entirely typical in this. In *mäsäkärä* both velar positions are spirantised, making it empirically possible to allow a rule to affect the shared melody. The consonants of *sibbeeb* and *räqqiq* do not all act alike, however, for though the final C-slot spirantises, the medial geminate surfaces as a stop. The rule must not, therefore, apply to representations like those in (6.1) — either a final β in *sibbeβ* would be prevented (nonlocal inalterability), or the geminate would be spirantised (a side-effect), since the changes to the melody would appear in every position.

Since it assumes that the discontinuous geminates *do* exist in Semitic, AP must ensure that they are removed or broken up before the rules of spirantisation apply. They must therefore exist only at a relatively abstract stage in the derivation. Note that this breaking of association lines indicates discontinuous geminates have no integrity (§4.3.2). Once association lines linking the slots of the discontinuous geminate to its melody are removed, and 'mitosis' (see below) ensures two tokens of the consonant melody instead of one, we contain two independent segments.

The inalterability of /bː/ in *sibbeβ* is explained by AP in the usual way: it must be due to the sharing of melody information between the two slots. This indicates that when association lines are broken in the removal of discontinuous geminates, this operation does not affect *local* true geminates. In order to show inalterability later, the true geminate must show integrity at the point when the associations of discontinuous geminates are broken. The operation that performs this task on discontinuous geminates must miss local geminates out — in AP terms, they are inalterable even here.

In Tigrinya and Hebrew, since the relevant associations are removed before any phonological rules can apply to them, there is no content to the claim that the multiplanar structures are phonological. It is as if, phonologically, the discontinuous geminates did not exist. Their behaviour is identical to that of fake geminates.

6.2.4 Plane conflation

Before the spirantisation rules in Tigrinya can apply, (6.1a,b) must have become something like (6.5a) at least; or perhaps (6.5b). The broken associations (relative to (6.1)) in (6.5) are taken to be as a result of an operation which confounds one of its motivations, namely to ensure that the sharing of structure is intimately related to integrity and inalterability. This is indeed the case in (6.5), but

202 *Autosegmental Representation in a Declarative Framework*

to get there AP posits a stage of pseudo-phonology (6.1) in which everything appears normal, except that structure sharing does *not* entail integrity and inalterability; at the very least in the face of the operation turning (6.1) into (6.5).

(6.5)

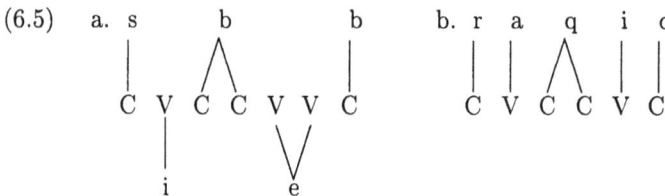

AP supposes, however, that an independent factor of grammar splits just those melody tokens which need it. This would account for the fact that discontinuous geminates appear to act like fake geminates. The operation of MITOSIS is driven exclusively by an avoidance of line-crossing violations when the multiplanar representations of (6.1) are shuffled together into a monoplanar structure like (6.5b). (Contrast this with (6.5a) in which mitosis cannot have been triggered by crossing lines since it is still multiplanar.) This operation of monoplanarisation is PLANE CONFLATION (Younes 1983; McCarthy 1986a, 1989).

Why is plane conflation required? First of all note that it is not required in order to discover the linear relationships between different autosegments on different planes (McCarthy 1989). This can be dealt with indirectly via the skeleton. Another possibility (rejected since Cole 1987) is that plane conflation could be identified with bracket erasure. The reason it is required is to render representations like (6.1) suitable for phonology. The question is: why do we need multiplanar representations in addition to monoplanar representations?

McCarthy claims that there are two valid sources of evidence (1989:96) for plane conflation (and thus for the multiplanar structures which are conflated). One is the integrity of local geminates as opposed to long distance geminates — conflation is required to make discontinuous geminates look as if they were fake. This *may* be taken to be a valid source of evidence for plane conflation, but it is better evidence *against* multiplanar phonology.[4] The best way to handle discontinuous geminates is to assume that they *are* fake.

The other factor is the one identified above, that discontinuous geminates may behave differently than their parts would lead us to suspect. McCarthy only deals with nonlocal inalterability, and does not consider side-effects, though these too require multiplanar representations, and I turn to these in §6.3. Nonlocal inalterability can motivate multiplanar phonology, but I am only aware of a single example of this hypothesised phenomenon; McCarthy's analysis geminate devoicing in Chaha.

6.3 Chaha

6.3.1 Background description

Chaha is a south Ethiopian Semitic language, a dialect of Gurage.[5] (see Leslau 1941, 1948, 1950; McCarthy 1983, 1986b.) The case of Chaha geminate devoicing provides a unique motivation for plane conflation as a operation mediating two *phonological* derivational stages.

First of all we need to motivate the multiplanar architecture of Chaha. McCarthy argues that rules of palatalisation and velarisation require such independent vowel and consonantal planes. In Chaha, the impersonal verb and the verb form (in any tense) for a second person feminine singular subject involve palatalisation. The impersonal also exhibits labialisation. The patterning is as follows: palatalisation affects the last root consonant (if it is coronal or velar) (6.6), labialisation affects the rightmost root consonant (if it is labial or velar) (6.7).[6]

(6.6) Chaha palatalisation

Masculine	Feminine	Gloss
nemad	nemaĵ	'love!'
nekes	nekeš	'bite!'

(6.7) Chaha labialisation

Personal	Impersonal	Gloss
danaga	danag^{w}a	'hit'
nakasa	nak^{w}asa	'bite'
masara	m^{w}asara	'seem'
nätär	nätär	'separate'

204 *Autosegmental Representation in a Declarative Framework*

In the impersonal both labialisation and palatalisation occur. If both palatalisable or labialisable consonants are missing, the impersonal form does not change (6.8a); if both are present (where the final form is coronal, not velar) both potential changes occur (6.8b); if the final consonant is not coronal or velar there is no palatalisation (6.8c). (If the final consonant is velar, it labialises rather than palatalises, but I cannot address this here.)

(6.8)   Combined labialisation and palatalisation

	Personal	Impersonal	Gloss
a.	nätär	nätär	'separate'
	g^{y}äk^{y}är	g^{y}äk^{y}är	'straighten out'
b.	käfät	käf^{w}äč	'open'
c.	bänär	b^{w}änär	'demolish'
	sänäb	sänäb^w	'spin'

Finally note that in forms with discontinuous geminates, *both slots are affected* (6.9). This is unusual, since only one target is normally allowed: *käf^w äč* 'open IMPERSONAL', not * *k^w äf^w äč*.

(6.9)   Discontinuous geminates are double targets

Personal	Impersonal	Gloss
säkäk	säk^{w}äk^w	'plant in the ground'
gerädäd	geräjäj	'cut in big pieces'
meräqäq	meräq^{w}äq^w	'scratch in a straight line'

Masculine	Feminine	Gloss
bätet	bäčeč	'be wide'
äses	äšeš	'sweep'

The data then is fairly simple, except for (6.9). Here a non-final stop is palatalised, and a non-rightmost stop is velarised. McCarthy argues that this indicates the affected melody must form part of a discontinuous geminate. (For discussion on whether this is a side-effect, see § 6.3.3.) Let me turn now to the problem of voicing and gemination.

Long Distance Dependencies   205

6.3.2 Nonlocal inalterability in geminate devoicing

Corresponding to the 'intensive' stem of other Ethiopic languages (and see also Arabic Form 2), which is the form with gemination of the second radical, Chaha has 'Type B' displaying *voicelessness* of the second radical. The historical process was one of allophonic devoicing of geminates, followed by a switch of contrast from length to voice as gemination was lost.[7] Modern intensives with a medial voiceless obstruent formerly had a medial voiced geminate:

(6.10) Geminate devoicing plus degemination

Reconstructed	Synchronic	Gloss
dabbara	dapara	'race'
gaddara	gatara	'put to sleep'
maggara	makara	'suppurate'
magg^{y}ara	mak^{y}ara	'burn'
jagg^{w}ara	jak^{w}ara	'become flexible'
gajja	gača	'rope an animal'
azzara	asara	'carry child'
gažža	gaša	'raid'

A rule that McCarthy proposes to devoice geminates is the primary concern of this section. We can determine what the rule must contain quite easily. It must mention two segmental slots and it must show that they share a melody token which is characterised as [−son]. [−voice] must be added to the token.

(6.11)
$$[-son] \rightarrow [-voice] \; / \; \underline{\quad} \quad \overset{\text{C} \;\; \text{C}}{\underset{}{\vee}}$$

There is an interesting subregularity to this pattern of devoicing and degemination. Leslau (1948) points out that devoicing did not apply in a certain context. Though Leslau treats the phenomenon as involving a voicing harmony, McCarthy takes a much more radical approach.

There are 17 forms in McCarthy's exhaustive list which still show voicing in a second radical which was historically a geminate.

They *all* involve a situation where the second and third radical are of the same type:

(6.12) Systematic exceptions to geminate devoicing

Reconstructed	Synchronic	Gloss
addada	adada	'pick peas'
faggaga	fagaga	'die (of cattle)'
azzaza	azaza	'command'

McCarthy approach is to suggest that the rule of geminate devoicing applies *prior* to plane conflation, but *after* the consonantism is mapped to the skeleton. This, he claims, accounts for (6.12) since nonlocal inalterability prevents the rule matching to the input. The repeated consonant in these biliteral forms must arise, in his framework, from a single token associated to nonadjacent slots. The rule, which specifies *two* (adjacent) slots, is not strongly satisfied by a form with three slots (6.13).[8]

(6.13)

This analysis provides support for a multiplanar representation with discontinuous tokens which phonological rules can apply to. Moreover, because the rule is subject to nonlocal inalterability, it follows that structure sharing in the multiplanar representation has at least some of the *same* properties that local multiple association shows.

6.3.3 A problem: the case of /b/

There are two problems for McCarthy, one of which he addresses at length. This involves certain form which do *not* show nonlocal inalterability — they devoice even though their melody is attached to three slots in all. This is clearly troublesome since the whole analysis is based on the discontinuous geminate linkage serving to block the rule. The forms in (6.14) and (6.12) are structurally identical.

(6.14) Exceptions to the exceptions to geminate devoicing

Reconstructed	Synchronic	Gloss
...bb...b	qapaba	'shave'
...bb...b	čapaba	'close halfway'
...bb...b	xrapaba	'cover'

Although we would expect forms like *qababa*, in fact we find *qapaba*. These forms seem to indicate (like Tigrinya spirantisation) that the rule must apply *after* plane conflation. McCarthy's solution to this problem is to apply the devoicing rule to all obstruents bar /b/ before plane conflation, and to apply it to /b/ after plane conflation. Consequently nonlocal inalterability does not affect the devoicing of medial /b/ in those cases where the final consonant is also /b/.

(6.15) Chaha derivations

gaddada	gaddara	qabbaba	dabbara	*reconstructed form*
dd...d	dd	bb...b	bb	*structure type*
		tt	pp	*devoicing*
dd d		bb b		*conflation/mitosis*
		pp b		*devoicing*
d d	t	p b	p	*degemination*
gadada	gatara	qapaba	dapara	*current form*

(6.15) as it stands is *ad hoc*, and McCarthy intends to derive this behaviour from the fact that there was no voicing contrast between /p/ and /b/ at the time of these changes, whereas all the other consonants involved *did* contrast in voice (though not when geminates, of course). McCarthy suggests that the devoicing rule applies before *and* after plane conflation. It affects all geminates when it applies before conflation, other than those excluded by nonlocal inalterability — this includes the /bb...b/ forms. *After* plane conflation, the /CC...C/ forms are now able to be affected, but the rule ignores every form but /bb/. The reason given is that [p] and [b] do not contrast phonemically. McCarthy suggests that plane conflation does not produce a 'derived environment' (Kiparsky 1973). Adding [–*voice*] to /d/ is taken to be a feature-*changing* rule because /d/ and /t/ contrast. In the framework of Kiparsky (1973) feature changing rules only operate in a derived environment, so after conflation /dd/ is ignored. With /bb/ there is no such requirement for a derived environment because devoicing is a feature-filling rule when it applies to /b/.

I agree that the key to the behaviour of /b/ is that [p] and [b] are noncontrastive allophones whereas other obstruents contrast for voice. But the mechanics of the derivation are far too complex. It crucially depends on certain assumptions from Lexical Phonology, such as 'derived environment' and 'the alternation condition', Kiparsky (1973). If these assumptions are altered in it unclear how the analysis can stand up. Particularly relevant is McCarthy's admission (1986b:216) that

> recent work [of Kiparsky] has reconstructed the notion of derived environment ... as a consequence of the Elsewhere Condition ... this account is not consistent, so far as I can judge, with the analysis I give for Chaha.

Furthermore, voicing simply is *not* contrastive for geminates in the intensive. Why a geminate devoicing rule should require a derived environment is therefore unclear.

Another flaw in McCarthy's analysis is that nonlocal inalterability is required for devoicing, but the rules of palatalisation and velarisation discussed above must not be subject to nonlocal inalterability. McCarthy assumes that these latter rules must apply before plane conflation but *after* association to the skeleton. It is this second assumption which must be rejected if the analysis of devoicing is not to be undermined. In one case the *rightmost* consonant is affected, but if it is part of a discontinuous geminate a non-rightmost slot is affected (6.9). In the other case it is the *word-final* segment which is affected, but if it is part of a discontinuous geminate a non-final consonant is *also* affected (6.9). Instead of these non-matching slots causing the rule to fail (as happens in devoicing), the rule applies anyway — a SIDE-EFFECT. The importance of this is that McCarthy uses the rules to motivate multiplanar phonology, yet they are clearly incompatible with his conception of multiplanar phonology when it comes to devoicing.

As it happens, in the case of palatalisation and velarisation there is no need for a multiplanar analysis — such rules can affect the consonant melody only and do not require reference to the skeleton. In other words, the data in (6.9) is not evidence for

multiplanar phonology if the data in (6.12) *is*, and *vice versa*. It is
clear that, whichever decision is taken, AP does not *predict* it.

6.3.4 An alternative analysis of devoicing

At the time of the changes under discussion, Chaha, as far as I am
aware, did not permit a consonantism to have adjacent homorganic
segments, a standard OCP effect in Semitic languages (Greenberg
1950) and one which still holds. The synchronic situation is that
there is no productive relationship between the intensive and other
forms of the verb (Leslau 1950), and the system is heavily lexicalised.

I interpret geminate 'devoicing' as a phonotactic statement
to the effect that the contrastive voicing of obstruents in geminates
is neutralised.[9] In a reconstructed form like *gaddara* 'put to sleep',
the geminate [tt] ambiguously indicated either *gdr* or *gtr* as its root.
Through time the gemination was lost, to be replaced by voiceless
[t]. This, I suggest, was phonemicised as /t/ since elsewhere /d/
and /t/ contrast. Consequently the root became fixed as *gtr* for
Type B. There is no reason to telescope the rules of devoicing and
degemination together.

In a form such as reconstructed *gaddada* 'tear', geminate
devoicing meant *gattada* was a permissible form. There was no
ambiguity about the root, since the final [d] can only come from
/d/. The medial [tt] is a neutralised form and can come from either
/dd/ or /tt/. When the gemination of neutralised [tt] was lost, the
medial consonant, if it were to be still pronounced [t], could now
only be an allophone of /t/. This would mean the form was interpreted as being derived from the consonantism *gtd*. As this is
independently impermissible, due to the ban on adjacent homorganic consonants, [d] had to be the choice of medial consonant. [d]
is the realisation of /d/, so the consonantism can remain *gd*.[10]

In the case of reconstructed *qabbaba* 'shave' geminate 'devoicing' produced *qappaba* which again was only interpretable as having
a consonantism *qb*. After degemination there was no need to pronounce the medial form [b], because [p] and [b] did not contrast.
The choice of [p] is entirely regular given that voiceless segments
appears in the second radical in the intensive if possible. Chaha
has moved phonologically further and further from the rest of the

Semitic group, and these alternations have become fossilised.

Although McCarthy's analysis is based on the differences between the contrastive and noncontrastive status of voicing in certain segments, it fails to recognise the noncontrastive status of voicing in geminates. It is difficult to accept the idea that when devoicing applies after conflation in (6.15) /dd/ is immune because it can only be devoiced in a derived environment, simply because the devoicing of a geminate is not feature-changing: in geminates the distinction is neutralised. Moreover, ordering 'devoicing' and 'degemination' as rules of Lexical Phonology does not relate the behaviour to the part played by the restrictions Semitic places on roots. The disappearance of the geminate position in Type B resulted in the lexical restructuring of the second radical in triliteral consonantisms. In biliteral consonantisms, however, such restructuring would result in a root like *gtd*, which is impossible. As a result the devoicing had to be either lost, or extended to nongeminate /d/. The former option was chosen.[11] This does not apply in the case of /b/, since [p] and [b] do not contrast. The *phonotactic constraint* banning /t/ and /d/ from the same root is the source of the 'nonlocal inalterability'.

6.4 Side-effects

If AP posits a phonological level of multiplanar structures then we surely require of it that phonological rules of a familiar kind apply in a familiar way. Otherwise we must doubt that they are 'phonological' in any meaningful sense. McCarthy's analysis of Chaha devoicing attempts to show that multiplanar structures *are* phonological in this sense. In this section I discuss a second class of analyses (two analyses in fact) which have been argued to require multiplanar representations. Unlike Chaha, the multiplanar structures are exploited in a manner impossible in monoplanar phonology.

Pitted against the single case of Chaha are two analyses (Archangeli 1983; Kenstowicz 1986) which hinge on the use of side-effects, and so are the exact opposite to the case of Chaha. Archangeli and Kenstowicz claim that a multiplanar phonology is required to account for certain apparent vowel harmony processes;

namely lowering in the Gashowu dialect of Yokuts, and two processes in Javanese (laxing and rounding). I will concentrate on Javanese, mentioning Yokuts briefly at the end.

6.4.1 Javanese

C/V planes in Javanese

Kenstowicz, reporting work by Uhlenbeck (1950), notes Javanese has strong phonotactic constraints operating between nonadjacent items, similar to those established by Greenberg (1960) for Semitic. The most common root has a CVCVC shape; 6,354 instances. Over a third of these have identical vowels, though since six vowels contrast, by chance alone only a sixth would have identical vowels. Furthermore, the consonants patterns in that there is a very strong tendency to avoid two homorganic consonants in the first and second position, unless they are identical. Thus when C_1 is /g/ and C_2 is velar, 43 times out of 44 it the velar is /g/. These facts help motivate C/V planes in Javanese, planes which Kenstowicz then uses to analyse a vowel harmony.

Low vowel rounding

Certain root-final vowels appear as [ɔ] when word-final and [a] elsewhere, *i.e.* when the root is suffixed (6.16a). These alternations suggest a rule like (6.17)

(6.16) Javanese a∼ɔ **alternation**
    a. mejɔ 'table'   mejaku   'my table'
        təkɔ   'to come' nəka-ʔake 'make come'
    b. bɔsɔ 'language' basamu   'your language'
        wɔsɔ 'to read'   macaʔake 'read for someone'

(6.17)   a → ɔ / _____]$_{word}$

The difficulty in description arises because if final [ɔ] alternates with [a], previous nonfinal [ɔ] also alternate, *although they cannot satisfy the structural description of the rule.* Kenstowicz discusses alternative phonological treatments but concludes that the optimal solution demands the vowel in question, call it /A/, be linked autosegmentally both to the word-final slot and to the nonfinal slots which alternate. The rule clearly must apply *before* plane conflation, but unlike the Chaha palatalisation rule it must apply to a multiplanar structure, because rounding needs access both to a vocalism and a skeleton. This is apparent from forms like *maŋan* 'eat', which does not undergo rounding (∗ *mɔŋɔn*) because the vowel, though final in the vocalism, is not word-final.

Midvowel laxing

Similar arguments are advanced by Kenstowicz to describe midvowel distribution, couched in terms of a rule laxing underlying tense vowels in final syllables (not shown). In Javanese, final midvowels /E, O/ are lax [ɛ, ɔ] in a closed syllable (6.18a) but tense [e, o] in an open syllable (6.18b). A penultimate midvowel is harmonically lax (6.18c) *regardless of whether it is in a closed syllable*, and *only if the midvowels are identical*. If they differ in backness, the harmony does not apply (6.18d) suggesting an interpretation of the harmony as a side-effect of the final syllable laxing.

(6.18) Javanese e~ɛ, o~ɔ alternations

    a.   katɔn   'alone'
           aŋɛl   'difficult'
    b.   suwe   'bowl'
           cuwo   'long time'
    c.   gɔdɔg   'to boil'
           ɔmɔn   'to talk'
           lɛrɛn   'to rest'
           ɛlɛʔ   'ugly'
    d.   ketɔʔ   'to appear as a spirit'
           olɛh   'to get'
           doŋɛŋ   'story'

The rule acts on the final vowel in the vocalism, but this vowel must be attached to the skeleton since the distribution is based on the distinction open/closed. The rule must therefore apply to multiplanar representation. This analysis explains why the vowels must be identical (6.19b) more neatly than the regressive harmony rules in (6.20) because the rules could equally easily lax

/E/ before [ɔ]. Such an alternation is not possible when the mid-vowels differ in backness given the side-effect analysis because in (6.19a) there is no discontinuous geminate.

(6.19) a.
```
     o   e
     |   |
  C  V C V C
     (doŋɛŋ)
```
b.
```
        e
       /|
  C  V C V C
     (lɛrɛn)
```

(6.20)   e ⟶ ɛ/ _____ Cɛ
         o ⟶ ɔ/ _____ Cɔ

What is of interest here is that the success of the rules Kenstowicz proposes depends entirely on the use of a doubly linked melody and the existence of a side-effect. One of the slots the melody is linked to is word-final and meets the structural description of the rule, while the other does not, in either the rounding or laxing case. Under the assumptions of Hayes's Linking Constraint and Schein & Steriade's UAC, such a configuration would display nonlocal inalterability, because the input does not strongly satisfy the rule.

In Kenstowicz's analysis of Javanese it is essential that the extra linkage does *not* interrupt the application of the rule, contrary to the Chaha devoicing analysis in the previous section. Thus for Kenstowicz the only point in assuming that the pre-conflation structure is *phonological* is to allow the side-effect causing rules to apply to it. This only serves to highlight the *non*-phonological nature of the analysis.

6.4.2 Against Javanese side-effects

Suppose for a minute we accept Kenstowicz's hypothesis that side-effect rules behave as they do because they precede plane conflation, and that at such a level of grammar different phonological principles apply. Whether rules preceding plane conflation show inalterability or side-effects could be a matter of language-specific choice.[12]

Recall in the case of Semitic spirantisations it was possible to imagine a rule applying to *mäsäkakärä* giving *mäsäxaxärä* by means of altering the shared melody /k/ (6.2). This application broke inalterability, but it was not a side-effect rule, since each slot fulfilled the structural description independently. Since it has no side-effects, it can be treated by ordering it *after* plane conflation and mitosis. In addition recall there were forms with local geminates such as *räqqiq* (*räqqiχ*). That the geminates do not spirantise while the short segments do shows conclusively that the rule follows conflation. So we have no evidence about whether inalterability holds prior to conflation or not from such examples.

This all suggests that in AP those rules without side-effects *must* follow mitosis. But that means rules which must apply to a multiplanar representation are extremely rare, even relative to the number of languages which can support multiplanar analyses. Consequently it is not sufficient to assume, as Kenstowicz does (1986:247), that a side-effect is the result of a simple parametric difference:

> if our analysis is correct then the mid-vowel laxing process with its reference to a closed syllable is a serious violation of the inalterability condition [of Hayes 1986b and Schein & Steriade 1986]. It is possible that 'true' geminates and 'long-distance' geminates respect partially different principles.

Normally the 'principles' that long-distance geminates respect are those of separate, individual, phonologically unconnected segments.

Given the almost total lack of side-effects cases the only reasonable assumption must be that, if possible, the facts should be dealt with in another way. The handful of side-effects cases are a puzzle to be accounted for, not evidence for a new type of phonology. That two languages (to my knowledge) have been argued to show side-effects is not what would be expected if rules are free to precede or follow conflation by parametric variation. It is exactly what would be expected when a powerful formalism is created to deal with a few problematic cases.

Suppose now that multiplanar phonological structure does not exist at all — that the appearance of melodies on various slots is not to be achieved with multiple association. In these circumstances we have 'planes' (phonological representations just consisting of vowels or consonants) a 'skeleton' (a highly underspecified prosodic representation) and their combination, where the combination is merely the monoplanar post-conflation structure. There would be no need to suppose any intermediate phonological stage. Its only use as a level of representation is to provide discontinuous geminates suitable for analysing side-effects. A great deal more is to be lost than gained in our understanding of phonological systems if we permit such nonlocal sharing to be part of the phonological canon.

6.4.3 The status of the Javanese data

Rounding

If discontinuous geminates do *not* exist as phonological entities, then how can the side-effect cases be handled? Looking at the Javanese case, we become aware that there is little to explain, and that the formal mechanism of a multiplanar representation is of no use in any case. Such criticism is possible thanks in large part to Kenstowicz himself, who is assiduous in pointing drawbacks to his analysis. Such problems are typical of a highly lexicalised, non-phonological paradigm, giving another reason for rejecting his use of association and structure-sharing. Midvowel laxing, for instance, occurs in closed syllables, but this is not the phonetic syllable: see ŋaŋɛli 'make difficult', where the mid front vowel [ɛ] is lax. A rule of high vowel laxing, which *does* depend on phonetic syllable structure, has no side-effects. Kenstowicz writes (1986:237):[13]

> [The problems] are mentioned here in the hope that further study of Javanese will clarify their ultimate bearing (either positive or negative) on the major thesis of this paper ... One problem concerns cases where we do not observe ATB effects where we might otherwise expect them. The other problem is the inverse: a case where ATB effects appear to obtain in a situation where we do not expect them.

In addition to these problems of the lexeme-specific arbitrariness of the rules, Kenstowicz discusses a formal problem. A suffix

-A 'imperative' is round [ɔ] if it is final: maŋan-ɔ 'eat!'. It does not cause the previous /A/ vowels in maŋan to round, so the suffixual /A/ cannot have merged with the /A/ vocalism to form a single token. This can be handled in AP if the suffixation follows conflation. The consonant /n/ in maŋan prevents any merger of vowel melodies in this monoplanar representation. A vowel-final form *does* undergo rounding — nəkɔ-ɔ 'come!'. This is possible after conflation since the vowels are string adjacent and therefore able to merge.

However, if conflation precedes imperative suffixation, then though the final vowel slot merges its melody with the suffix, there cannot possibly be any side-effects with any previous root vowel. *But this is exactly what does happen* — when mAcA 'to read' is suffixed (mAcA-A), following plane conflation, all three vowels are rounded: mɔcɔ-ɔ 'read!'. Some solution other than using multiplanar representations is required here, harmony for instance, and so this solution could be used in all the simpler cases.[14]

The motivation for planes in Javanese

I noted above that consonantal homorganicity constraints indicate C/V separation for Javanese, but I gave the most favourable example. There are, in fact, many exceptions, from which I infer that these constraints are remnants of a generalisation that is not synchronically valid. The generalisations are just throwbacks to a former C/V system, and are best explained in these concrete terms. For an example of the restricted import of the generalisation that homorganic $C_1 C_2$ must be identical, take the case where C_1 is /t/ and C_2 is also dental. 46 times out of 68 C_2 will also be /t/, but *22 times* it will be /d/ or /n/ (Kenstowicz 1986:244). It is difficult to classify these as synchronic OCP exceptions — if such a classification were accepted many grammars could churn out similar 'generalisations'. Javanese C/V planes are fossilised, and this is my explanation for the apparent side-effects, which are merely rather idiosyncratic harmony rules. If this seems less than satisfactory, remember that the use of side-effects raises more questions than it answers, and that the onus of proof lies on the other side.

6.4.4 Secondary lowering in Yokuts

I turn now to a brief consideration of the second case of side-effects of which I am aware. Archangeli (1983) discusses a pattern of 'lowering' in two dialects of Yokuts; Gashowu and Yawelmani (Newman 1944). Lowering in Yokuts ensures that long [oː] appears instead of [uː]. In the Gashowu dialect there is a 'side-effect' in that preceding [u] is also ruled out, with the result that [o...oː] appears instead. That short [o] appears is called 'secondary lowering'. In the Yawelmani dialect there is no such side-effect and [u...oː] is the analogous pattern. A standard derivation of *suduuk'-t* 'remove' in each dialect is shown in (6.21).

(6.21) Yokuts secondary lowering

Gashowu	Yawelmani	
suduuk'-t	suduuk'-t	(*underlying*)
sodook'ut	sudook'ut	(*surface*)

If a multiplanar analysis is used to analyse these patterns, as Archangeli suggests, then a rule lowering a final long /uː/ would *follow* plane conflation in Yawelmani but *precede* plane conflation in Gashowu. The side-effect lowers the discontinuous geminate association of the melody:

(6.22) Goshowu lowering

Archangeli & Pulleyblank (1986) reanalyse the data discussed here and reject a multiplanar analysis in favour of a long distance harmonic sharing of the secondary place node (*PoA2*).[15] Consonants do not possess this node so form no barrier to it being shared between nonadjacent vowels. This is interesting since it shows that a multiplanar phonology is rendered obsolete given sufficiently powerful feature geometry (see Steriade 1987ab).

Given the excessive power of multiplanar representations, we should be wary that this is merely a notational shift. If the nature of the phenomenon itself is recast then such problems do not arise.

Consequently I agre with A&P's general sentiment that Yokuts exhibits a harmony phenomenon. I will not propose a specific analysis here of the workings of this harmony, however. For two recent analyses of Yokuts see Steriade (1986) and Prince (1987). It is to the general problem of harmony in AVP to which I now turn, in order to further investigate the evidence in favour of nonlocal multiple association.

6.5 Harmony

The use of multiple association in harmony systems, due mainly to Clements (1976) and Goldsmith (1976), can account for two major characteristics of the phenomenon (see Chapter 3). These are the use of opacity to define the harmonic domain (Clements & Sezer 1982) and harmonic simplicity. Of course the actual theory of 'possible harmony systems' is quite another matter. The point at issue here is that, when employed in harmony, the multiple associationfamiliar from gemination is problematic and inelegant for a number of reasons.

- It undermines AP's account of local multiple association.
- It does *not* in fact capture opacity.
- It demands a complex phonetics/phonology interface.
- Once banned, the distinction between local and nonlocal association reappears in other ways.

I discuss an alternative approach to harmonic phenomena below but my purpose here is to defend the distinction which the Sharing Constraint demands between local and long distance phenomena.

AP adopts the configuration in (6.23); the multiple association of a single token of structure to nonadjacent slots. This is the *same* association relation that is used between adjacent slots. What are the consequences of the universal availability of association?

(6.23)

Long Distance Dependencies 219

In AP association behaves in quite different ways depending on whether the slots that are bearing the association are adjacent or not. This is accepted both explicitly in discussions of the properties of one or other dependency (Goldsmith 1990:47,334; Schein & Steriade 1986:appendix; Hayes 1986b:328; Kenstowicz 1986:247) — see Chapters 3, 4, 5 — but also implicitly. The implicit acceptance of a local/long distance dichotomy results in a *conspiracy* in the ways in which other aspects of phonology — rules, phonetic interpretation, principles — interact with configurations using multiple association.

The conspiracy treats (6.23) just as if it were a sequence of two tokens rather than a single token shared by two slots. It treats such long distance association as being different in kind from local association.

Harmonic spread. When AP spreads a token across the skeleton, and the spread is halted, this does not cause the harmony rule itself to fail. Harmonic spreading acts as if it created a collection of individual structures, where the failure to create one of these structures (as a result of crossing lines, feature co-occurrence and so on) did not affect the others. Local assimilations are *never* partly successful, but harmony 'does the best it can'.

The NCC. Crossed associations are ill-formed, but the action taken to deal with this ill-formedness is different when local and nonlocal associations are involved. As noted in §3.2.3, the NCC-as-filter effectively bans the creation of crossing lines in cases of unbounded spread given the definition of the Association Convention (Goldsmith 1990:14) but the NCC-as-repair-strategy deals with the consequence of single association line addition by permitting 'the line that formerly existed [to be] ... automatically erased' (ibid, p47). These two *modi operandi* act as if local and nonlocal crossing association were different configurations.[16]

The phonetics/phonology interface. I assume that phonetic gestures are convex. In a simple AP conception of the interface with such a phonetics, different tokens of phonological structure would describe different phonetic gestures, but structures would not map to different gestures unless nonconvexity would result. In sum, each structure would correspond to the lowest whole number of gestures possible. Although plausible, this picture of the phonetic/phonology mapping treats the nonlocal multiple associations as if they did not exist. The relationship between these levels would be simplified even further if phonological entities were convex too. A one-to-one mapping would suffice.

If the differences between local and long distance dependencies were dependent solely on the string adjacency of the slots involved, then one type of association *would* suffice for both types of dependency. Local dependencies could be characterised as the conjunction of the properties in (6.24a). Long distance dependencies could be described as (6.24b).

(6.24) Definitions
a. **Local** = *multiple association* ∧ *adjacent*
b. **Long distance** = *multiple association* ∧ *not adjacent*

But this is impossible. The problem is that the transition from (6.24a) to (6.24b) cannot be prevented,[17] because 'adjacency' is perfectly able to become 'nonadjacency', by epenthesis for instance. If (6.24) were correct, then local dependencies could become local distance dependencies. *But perhaps the most important property of local dependencies is that they cannot.*

If 'adjacency' can become 'nonadjacency', then the way to prevent the pair of properties in (6.24a) becoming the pair in (6.24b) is to use two types of 'association'. In AVP, thanks to the Sharing Constraint, structure sharing is the local association, some other means ('spreading') being used to capture long distance dependencies.

In Autosegmental Phonology multiple associations are differentiated as local or long distance, rule by rule, situation by situation. This conspiracy clearly demands that a fundamental distinction be made. If we try to use simple adjacency to make this distinction, then we would expect that those local geminates which are made nonlocal will automatically adopt nonlocal characteristics. The point cannot be laboured too much: one of the most important characteristics of geminates is that they *cannot* become nonlocal. Only if the geminate and the harmonic feature utilise fundamentally different types of association can this be described.

6.6 Long distance dependencies in AVP

Having concentrated on local dependencies almost to the exclusion of long distance dependencies, I feel I should offer some speculative remarks on the treatment of such dependencies in a framework that does not employ structure sharing nonlocally.

6.6.1 Phonetic factors

My point of departure is a consideration of intonational features. The main phonetic correlate of tone/intonation is pitch, characterised as F_0. A value of F_0 can be detected phonetically throughout an utterance, but this does not mean that every vowel or syllable bears a phonological tone feature, let alone *single shared feature*. Pierrehumbert & Beckman (1988) argue convincingly that unaccented phrases in Tokyo Japanese bear no tonal specification, despite the fact that their value for F_0 is higher following a *H* accented phrase than elsewhere. For example, in the phrase *moriyano mawari-no oma'warisan* ('the policeman of the Forrests' neighbourhood'), they assign an initial accent *L%H* on *mori* and a *L%* boundary tone on the second *-no*. The traditional approach relies on the multiple association of the *H* feature to all following syllables up to the *-no* and assumes that phonetic interpretation gradually lowers F_0. This is rejected, despite the fact that a variety of different approaches are suggested, because the simplest way to predict F_0 is from a phonological representation which employs only a sparse distribution of tones.

I believe that such argumentation could prove equally forceful in other areas of autosegmental representation, were the appropriate research done. All that I can do at present is to point out the elegance of a system like Pierrehumbert & Beckman's, which specifies a phonetic TARGET for each piece of phonological structure, and computes interpolation in the phonetics only.

Such elegance is lacking elsewhere in the phonology/phonetics interface in AP. In a phonological harmony system it is highly unlikely that anyone would support the claim that the harmonic feature(s) condition a single oral tract configuration.[18] Instead each vowel/syllable most likely triggers its own set of phonetic realisations. Each vowel acts as if it bore an independent copy of the harmonic specification.

Note that in intonation, the appearance of a tonal specification dependent on another in the same sentence is best handled by the copying of the tone in question. Consider the sentence *where are you going?* with *L* on *where* and *HL* on *going* (main stress). It can be usefully compared to the sentence *where the hell are you going?* with the same patterning of *L* on *where* and *HL* on *going*, and a copied *L* on *hell* (Bob Ladd, p.c.) (6.25b). Any analysis which posited the multiple association of this *L* (6.25a) would have the same problems in predicting F_0 that Pierrehumbert & Beckman discuss. Yet such sharing of structure is exactly what AP posits in other cases of long distance dependency, such as harmony.

(6.25)

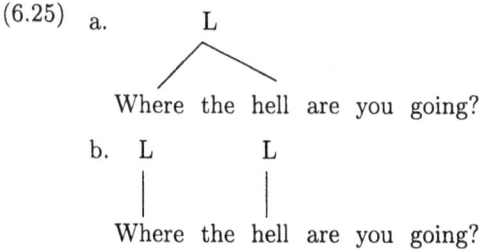

Each vowel in a harmony system is like the accented vowels in Japanese, surrounding consonants being like unaccented syllables. The question is not really whether the harmonic vowels trigger a single phonetic gesture or not — although I have no evidence one way or the other, I think it is reasonable to assume that each harmonic vowel is an instigator of a unique phonetic mapping. The question is about the relationship between phonological structures and phonetic gestures.

Autosegmental Phonology makes use of nonlocal multiple association. Consequently it requires either that a single phonetic gesture results from every autosegment regardless of how many skeletal slots share the autosegment, or it allows an autosegment to be realised by any number of independent gestures. I have suggested the latter approach as the more likely, so a one-many relationship is permitted in the phonetic/phonology interface in AP. In AVP I have suggested a one-to-one mapping at this interface, in which each token of phonological structure is related to a single phonetic target. This means different phonological tokens (of the same type) must be involved in nonlocal dependencies, as the Sharing Constraint demands. The one-many mapping to phonetics is replaced by a type/token relationship within the phonology.

Further research is required to investigate the impact of this claim on phonetics, but I will briefly consider a means to express the long distance dependencies in the phonology.

6.6.2 Structure spreading in harmony

I reject the characterisation of harmonic behaviour as being long distance assimilation or alternately that of assimilation as a local harmony. I do not deny that the two are related in that they reduce potential contrasts by increasing redundancy, and that they both license apparent violations of the OCP. We have seen, however, that there are differences in the way the hypothesised nonlocal associations used in AP to analyse harmony behave, both internal to the phonology and perhaps in the interface to phonetics.

Harmony in AP is the association of a token to a number of slots. Harmonic simplicity is accounted for by there being a single token, the harmonic domain is defined (mainly) by the NCC. Informally, harmony in AVP could consist of the SPREADING of a type, rather than the sharing of a token. Harmonic simplicity is accounted for by there being a single type. Spreading consists of defining the DOMAIN of the harmony. Within the domain every slot which can bear a token of the harmonic type does so. Blocking sets the boundaries of the domain, and results from the clashing of types. Consequently a token compatible with the harmonic type can be INCORPORATED into the domain of harmony, as in Coeur d'Alène or the [+ATR] analysis of Khalkha Mongolian (see Chapter 3). Within the domain each root matrix must (if the sort assignment permits it) unify with a copy of the harmonic structure.

I do not intend to speculate further on a type-based conception of long distance dependencies, and leave this issue for future research. What is clear, however, is that creating the distinction between spreading and sharing prevents unwanted interaction between them. The enormous body of research into harmonies can, given an appropriate characterisation of spreading, be cast as a relationship of types rather than tokens. Given that harmony in AP uses a different rule-type to local assimilations already (Archangeli & Pulleyblank 1986), this promises to be less of an upheaval than it first appears.

6.6.3 Spreading in nonconcatenative morphology

Long distance geminates have all the characteristics of fake geminates, other than the morphophonemic predictability of their appearance. Fake geminates are usually accidental juxtapositions of heteromorphemic segments. Long distance geminates are interdependent distributionally, while (and this is the crucial point) they are nevertheless independent phonologically. The use of *phonological* association (going back to McCarthy 1979) may capture this nonphonological relationship, but it is at the cost of a predictive phonological theory.

'Phonological' associations have been used to obtain more or less the correct patterning of segments in nonconcatenative systems, but such patterns must be destroyed before any phonological operation has access to them. This is in tune with the one-one interface with phonetics discussed above. It is essential to realise that the only reason for discontinuous geminates at all is because of the familiar, available operation of autosegmental association being used as the mechanism which realises consonantal tokens on different slots.

That Semitic languages have vowel-only morphemes is uncontestable. This fact does *not* entail C/V planes, merely a monoplanar representation of a string consisting exclusively of a weak ordering of vowels. Of course some mechanism is required to shuffle the tokens of this morpheme together with the tokens from similarly monoplanar representations which are exclusively consonantal. The problems arise when this shuffling is assumed to be a phonological operation, rather than morphological.

Long Distance Dependencies 225

I have pointed out above that in AVP (and AP) roots must not be ordered by immediate precedence, otherwise epenthesis would always be impossible. (6.26) is the root *ktb* (where $i\prec^* j\prec^* k$):

(6.26) $\{\langle i,\mathrm{k}\rangle, \langle j,\mathrm{t}\rangle, \langle k,\mathrm{b}\rangle\}$

If (6.26) is to be morphologically combined with another morpheme consisting only of vowels, the result must be phonologically well-formed.[19] Unsurprisingly, the option of all the vowels preceding the consonants is not available, so prefixation and suffixation are not the central morphological relationships in a language which has vowel-only and consonant-only morphemes.[20] Consequently nonconcatenative methods are used.

For example the weak orderings

$\{\langle i,\mathrm{k}\rangle, \langle j,\mathrm{t}\rangle, \langle k,\mathrm{b}\rangle\}$, where $i\prec^* j\prec^* k$,

$\{\langle m,\mathrm{i}\rangle, \langle n,\mathrm{a}\rangle\}$ where $m\prec^* n$ and

$\{\langle p, light\text{-}\sigma\rangle, \langle q, heavy\text{-}\sigma\rangle\}$ where $p\prec^* q$

together will define *kitab*. Such a combination would have to respect the assumptions that no element precedes *light-σ*, that none follows *heavy-σ*, and that each structure is 'maximal' (Itô 1989).[21] The index p is equated to the sequence i, which gives rise (following syllabification) to a sequence of two structures at i and j where the value of SYLL is shared.

(6.27) $\left\langle \begin{bmatrix} \text{MELODY} & \boxed{1}\text{'k'} \\ \text{SYLLABLE}\boxed{2} & \begin{bmatrix} \text{ONSET} & \boxed{1} \\ \text{NUCLEUS}\boxed{3} \end{bmatrix} \end{bmatrix}, \begin{bmatrix} \text{MELODY} & \boxed{3}\text{'i'} \\ \text{SYLLABLE}\boxed{2} & \end{bmatrix} \right\rangle$

This combination of orderings does not address one problem, that of biliteral roots and other instances of multiple discontinuous association. There are two means to deal with this requirement that an element of the consonantism must somehow appear in two places after catenation. Either the element (generally the rightmost) can be marked in some way to condition the appearance of extra tokens as part of the combination of partial orders (see Bird 1990a), or the slot provided by the template can remain blank. In the second case a later process of default feature filling or harmonic spread then fills the value in.

I prefer the latter characterisation of the problem because this same need to fill an empty slot arises elsewhere. As a result of epenthesis, for example, an empty slot (one required by prosody but given no melodic content by the available morphemes) is filled in some cases by language-wide defaults, and in some cases by spreading rules.[22] On this approach the /m/ of *samam* spreads to an empty final slot in the same way that an epenthetic vowel will be /u/ when the following vowel is /u/. I think it is a mistake to treat the former case of melody copy as a discontinuous geminate in a multiplanar structure if the latter is not to be similarly analysed. However, this again raises questions of the proper analysis of consonant and vowel harmony which I am unable to tackle properly here.

Notes

[1] A phonological representation can be said to consist of a number of planes, where each plane consists of no more than one instance of every tier.

[2] McCarthy & Prince (1989) argue that skeletal units (C/V slots) are not part of nonconcatenative morphology, prosodic units such as the mora being employed instead as a kind of skeleton. Since consonant and vowel morphemes are still nonlocally associated to these morae, and since multiplanar analyses are still employed, this issue does not bear on the arguments here.

[3] I am ignoring the vowel quality here.

[4] And hence evidence against plane conflation.

[5] The north Ethiopian Semitic group includes Tigre and Tigrinya, the south group includes Gurage, Amharic, Harari, Gafat.

[6] Some forms I take from McCarthy, and these are uninflected, some I take from Leslau and these are surface representations from which I have removed affixes in order to match McCarthy's forms.

[7] Leslau (1950) notes that a handful of geminate forms do still occur: *əmmat* 'alone' *ənnəm* 'all'. He offers also *attəm* 'none' *əkkəm* 'thus', but is less confident of these forms.

[8] As it happens, he adopts the Linking Constraint account of inalterability, but it is plain the UAC could prevent a rule with a

geminate target from applying to a trigeminate.

[9] Compare English with its neutralised voicing contrast for stops after onset /s/; *stop*, * *sdop*. Would we wish a rule of 'post-/s/ devoicing?'

[10] A consonantism *gt* would imply a voicing rule for which there is no evidence.

[11] I would expect that either option is equally likely, all things being equal.

[12] This is all very well, but only one language has been found which chooses nonlocal inalterability and two which choose side-effects. No other languages appear to allow rules before plane conflation at all.

[13] Kenstowicz uses the term 'across-the-board' (ATB) effects.

[14] Kenstowicz advances a lexical phonology solution.

[15] They treat Javanese in a similar way.

[16] That I do not countenance the use of non-monotonic 'repair strategies' such as deletion rules or disassociation is irrelevant here. The point is that AP repeatedly requires a distinction between local and nonlocal dependency.

[17] This is discussed at length in Chapter 4.

[18] Such 'resonances' are *very* common over quite long distances and are dialect-specific (John Local, p.c.), but are *local*, and are to be contrasted with harmony systems in which a harmonising vowel is *categorially distinct* from other vowels of the contrastive system.

[19] Consonant-only roots are not ill-formed since the rest of the phonology provides a way to pronounce them, *i.e.* if they are combined with the appropriate prosodic and vocalic structures.

[20] Note the reversal of the standard implication that a nonconcatenative system results in morphemes composed solely of vowels and consonants.

[21] This approach is similar to the combination of partial orderings discussed by McCarthy (1989). See also Reape (1991) for a similar approach to word-order within a unification-based framework.

[22] See Goldsmith (1990:77) on Pero for example. An interesting example is Scottish Gaelic, which has a historic epenthetic vowel, the 'svarabhakti vowel'. In some dialects this vowel always has the same quality regardless of context, in others its value is determined by the closest vowel (Meg Bateman, p.c.).

Chapter 7

Conclusion

I have attempted to draw together two concerns in this work. First, I have determined the basic requirements of an autosegmental-style phonology: the type of structures required and the relations between them. Second, I have been concerned to present a declarative approach to phonology which fulfills these requirements, drawing on the techniques of the developing unification grammars. The result, Attribute Value Phonology, shows that it is possible to balance these demands to the mutual benefit of each area of enquiry.

The picture of phonological representations I have presented is that of a single sequence of complex feature structures, similar to the sequence of feature bundles in SPE (7.1a) but internally hierarchical.

(7.1) a. (SPE) $[+A]_i[+A]_j$ 	b. (AP) $\underset{+}{\overset{i \quad j}{\vee}}$ root tier
$\phantom{(7.1) a. (SPE) [+A]_i[+A]_j \quad b. (AP) \underset{+}{\overset{i \quad j}{\vee}}}$ A tier

c. (AVP)

$$\left[A\boxed{1}+\right]_i \left[A\boxed{1}+\right]_j$$

Using attribute-value structures as the formal means to encode feature structures means that nonlinear aspects of phonology (*eg* features which 'belong' to no particular segmental unit more than to any other) can be analysed as cases of re-entrancy (7.1c). Such sharing of information replaces the temporal coordination of Autosegmental Phonology (7.1b). [1]

Since re-entrancy is a very powerful tool, I sought to constrain its use. The No Crossing Constraint, which performs a similar function in AP, was shown to be unsuitable, and the Sharing Constraint was proposed instead. This constraint limits re-entrancy to a contiguous stretch of the skeleton, with the consequence that structure sharing is available as a re-interpretation of multiple association in only some cases. Chapters 4, 5 and 6 examined the consequences of this dichotomy of sharing *vs* spreading.

In AVP, the sharing of a value between two paths is not in any important way different from the simple domination of a value by a single path. When it comes to the operation of the constraints on well-formed structure, (7.2a) is identical to (7.2b). They differ only when it comes to the extra sensitivity of (7.2b) to its immediate context — the shared value $\boxed{3}$ must be a compatible component of *two* structures, which naturally narrows down its variability. $\boxed{1}$ and $\boxed{2}$ can be completely incompatible.

(7.2)   a. $\left\langle \begin{bmatrix} \text{ATTR}\,\boxed{1} \end{bmatrix}, \begin{bmatrix} \text{ATTR}\,\boxed{2} \end{bmatrix} \right\rangle$

         b. $\left\langle \begin{bmatrix} \text{ATTR}\,\boxed{3} \end{bmatrix}, \begin{bmatrix} \text{ATTR}\,\boxed{3} \end{bmatrix} \right\rangle$

The Sharing Constraint prevents (7.2b) becoming discontinuous, so helps account neatly for geminate integrity. The autosegmental approach is dogged by the availability of nonlocal association.

In AP true geminates and fake geminates are quite different objects, not in the AVP sense that in one case there is shared information which cannot become unshared, but in the sense that only the former makes use of multiple associations. Thanks to the Linking Constraint or the Uniform Applicability Condition, rules then apply to multiply-linked structures and singly-linked structures in different ways. This is the basis of the phenomenon of inalterability. I proposed a constraint-based approach to data discussed under

Conclusion

the titles of 'inalterability' and 'coda weakening' which promises to provide a single account of geminate (and simple segment) distribution. Although Goldsmith (1990) is similarly optimistic and offers Autosegmental Licensing as a unified account, he relies on the use of a novel 'licensing' relation rather using standard phonotactic statements.

Since AP permits nonlocal association, it predicts that inalterability data should be observable nonlocally. In fact only a single case has been proposed, that of Chaha, and after evaluating the data I concluded that the prediction is unfounded. Javanese and Yokuts, which are claimed to involve exactly the opposite phenomenon of nonlocal side-effects, were also surveyed briefly and found to be unconvincing evidence in favour of the single/multiple association dichotomy.

While much important work remains to be done, from the development of a theory of nonlocal structure spreading to an extensive constraint-based analysis of a given language, I hope to have demonstrated the benefits of drawing on cross-disciplinary knowledge in the study of phonology. Attribute Value Phonology represents a step in the pursuit of a theory of declarative phonology, and it is to be hoped that its positive proposals and evident shortcomings alike act only as incentives for the formal characterisation of phonological competence.

Notes

[1] Lass (1984: 113–117) is of historical interest in this regard since he argues for the hierarchical segment (*cf* Lass & Anderson 1975) and mentions in passing the possibility of extending the use of the α-variable to cover "a whole submatrix" and supplies a "general formula for a homorganic stop+nasal cluster" which looks strikingly familiar to a constraint expressed in the AVS matrix notation, though it is firmly rooted in the SPE perspective.

References

Aagesen, H. (1987) Some remarks on the system of West Greenlandic phonology. *Acta Linguistica Hafniensia* **20**, 1–28.

Abu-Salim, I. (1980) Epenthesis and geminate consonants in Palestinian Arabic. *Studies in the Linguistic Sciences* **10**, 1–11.

Anderson, S.R. (1985) *Phonology in the twentieth century: theories of rules and theories of representations.* Chicago: University of Chichago Press.

Archangeli, D. (1983) The root CV template as a property of the affix: evidence from Yawelmani. *Natural Language and Linguistic Theory* **1**, 347–384.

Archangeli, D. (1984) *Underspecification in Yawelmani phonology and morphology.* PhD Thesis, MIT. Published 1988 New York: Garland.

Archangeli, D. (1988) Aspects of underspecification theory. *Phonology* **5**, 183–208.

Archangeli, D. and Pulleyblank, D. (1986) *The content and structure of phonological representations.* ms. Tucson: University of Arizona.

Archangeli, D. and Pulleyblank, D. (1987) Maximal and minimal rules: effects of tier scansion. In Bosch, A., Need, B. and Schiller, E. (eds.) *NELS* **17**, 16–35.

Archangeli, D. and Pulleyblank, D. (1989) Yoruba vowel harmony. *Linguistic Inquiry* **20**, 173–219.

Avery, P. and Rice, K. (1989) Segment structure and coronal underspecification. *Phonology* **6**, 179–201.

Bach, E. (1976) An extension of classical transformational grammar. In the *Proceedings of the Michigan State University Conference on Problems in Linguistic Metatheory*, 183–224.

van Benthem, J. (1983) *The logic of time: a model theoretical investigation into the varieties of temporal ontology and temporal discourse*. Dordrecht: Reidel.

Bazell, C., Catford, J.C., Halliday, M.A.K. and Robins, R.H. (eds) (1966) *In memory of J.R. Firth*. London: Longman.

Bird, S. (1990a) Prosodic morphology and constraint-based phonology. *Edinburgh Research Papers in Cognitive Science* **RP-38**, Edinburgh: Centre for Cognitive Science.

Bird, S. (1990b) *Constraint-based phonology*. PhD Thesis, Edinburgh.

Bird, S. and Klein, E.H. (1990) Phonological events. *Journal of Linguistics* **26**, 33–56.

Borowsky, T. (1989) Structure preservation and the syllable coda in English. *Natural Language and Linguistic Theory* **7**, 145–167.

Bresnan, J. (ed) (1982) *The mental representation of grammatical relations*. Cambridge, Mass: MIT Press.

Broe, M. (1988) A unification-based approach to prosodic analysis. *Edinburgh University Department of Linguistics Work in Progress* **21**, 63–82.

Broe, M. (*in preparation*) *Unification-based prosodic analysis*. PhD Thesis, Edinburgh.

Browman, C. and Goldstein, L. (1986) Towards an articulatory phonology. *Phonology Yearbook* **3**, 219–252.

Browman, C. and Goldstein, L. (1989) Articulatory gestures as phonological units. *Phonology* **6**, 201–251.

Cairns, C.E. (1988) Phonotactics, markedness and lexical representations. *Phonology* **5**, 209–237.

Calabrese, A. (1987) The interaction of phonological rules and filters in Salentino. In McDonough, J. and Plunkett, B. (eds) *NELS* **17**, 79–98.

Calder, J. Klein, E. and Zeevat, H. (1988) Unification categorial grammar: a concise, extendable grammar for natural language processing. In *24th Annual Meeting of the Association for Computational Linguistics: COLING 88*, 83–86. Budapest.

Chomsky, N. and Halle, M. (1968) *The sound pattern of English*. New York: Harper & Row.

Clements, G.N. (1976) The autosegmental treatment of vowel harmony. In Dressler, W. and Pfeiffer, O.E. (eds) *Phonologica 1976*, 111–119.

Clements, G.N. (1985) The geometry of phonological features. *Phonology Yearbook* 2, 225–252.

Clements, G.N. (1987) Phonological feature representation and the description of intrusive stops. In Bosch, A., Need, B. and Schiller, E. (eds.) *CLS* 23, 29–51.

Clements, G.N. (1990) The role of the sonority cycle in core syllabification. In Kingston, J. and Beckman, M.E. (eds) *Between the grammar and physics of speech: Papers in laboratory phonology* 1, 283–334. Cambridge: CUP

Clements, G.N. and Sezer, E. (1982) Vowel and consonant disharmony in Turkish. In van der Hulst, H. and Smith, N. (eds) *The structure of phonological representations Part 2*, 213–255. Dordrecht: Foris.

Clements, G.N. and Keyser, S.J. (1983) *CV Phonology: a generative theory of the syllable*. Cambridge, Mass: MIT Press.

Cole, J. (1987) *Planar Phonology and Morphology*. PhD Thesis, MIT.

Coleman, J. and Local, J. (1989) The 'No Crossing Constraint' in autosegmental phonology. *York Papers in Linguistics*, 14, 169–219. (To appear in *Linguistics and Philosophy*.)

Evans, R. and Gazdar, G. (eds) (1990) *The DATR papers*. Cognitive Science Research Reports,University of Sussex.

Firth, J.R. (1948) Sounds and Prosodies. *Transactions of the Philological Society*, 92–132. Also published in Jones, W. and Laver, J. (eds) (1973) *Phonetics in linguistics: a book of readings*, 47–66. London: Longman.

Fujimura, O. (1976) Syllables as concatenated demisyllables and affixes. Presented to the 91st meeting of the Acousti-

cal Society of America, April 1976, Washington DC.
Fujimura, O. (1990) Demisyllables as sets of features: comments on Clements's paper. In Kingston, J. and Beckman, M.E. (eds) *Between the grammar and physics of speech. Papers in laboratory phonology* 1, 334–341. Cambridge: CUP
Gazdar, G. (1981) Unbounded dependencies and coordinate structure. *Linguistic Inquiry* 12, 155–184.
Gazdar, G. (1982) Phrase Structure Grammar. In Jabobsen, P. and Pullum, G. (eds) *The nature of syntactic representation*, 131–186. Dordrecht: Reidel.
Gazdar, G., Klein, E., Pullum, G., and Sag I. (1985) *Generalised phrase structure grammar.* London: Blackwell.
Goldsmith, J. (1976) *Autosegmental phonology.* PhD Thesis, MIT. Distributed 1979 by Indiana University Linguistics Club.
Goldsmith, J. (1979) The aims of autosegmental phonology. In Dinnsen, D. A. (ed.) *Current approaches to phonological theory*, 202–222. Bloomington: Indiana University Press.
Goldsmith, J. (1985) Vowel harmony in Khalkha Mongolian, Yaka, Finnish and Hungarian. *Phonology Yearbook* 2, 251–274.
Goldsmith, J. (1990) *Autosegmental and metrical phonology.* Oxford: Blackwell.
Greenberg, J.H. (1950) The patterning of root morphemes in Semitic. *Word* 6, 162–181.
Guerssel, M. (1977) Constraints on phonological rules. *Linguistic Analysis* 3, 267–305.
Guerssel, M. (1978) A condition on assimilation rules. *Linguistic Analysis* 4, 225–254.
Gussman, E. (1980) *Studies in abstract phonology. Linguistic Inquiry Monograph* 4. Cambridge, Mass: MIT Press.
Halle, M. and Vergnaud, J.R. (1980) Three-dimensional phonology. *Journal of Linguistic Research* 1, 83–105.
Halle, M. and Vergnaud, J.R. (1982) On the framework of autosegmental phonology. In van der Hulst, H. and Smith, N. (eds) *The structure of phonological representations Part 1*, 65–82. Dordrecht: Foris.
Hammond, M. (1988) On deriving the Well-Formedness Condition. *Linguistic Inquiry* 19, 319–325.

Harms, R.T. (1968) *Introduction to phonological theory.* Englewood Cliffs: Prentice-Hall.
Hayes, B. (1986a) Assimilation as Spreading in Toba Batak. *Linguistic Inquiry* **17**, 467–499.
Hayes, B. (1986b) Inalterability in CV phonology. *Language* **62**, 321–351.
Hayes, B. (1988) Diphthongisation and co-indexing. In M. Crowhurst (ed) *Proceedings of the Arizona Phonology Conference 1*, 1–35. *Coyote Papers* **9**, Tucson: University of Arizona. Revised as Hayes (1990).
Hayes, B. (1989) Compensatory lengthening in moraic phonology. *Linguistic Inquiry* **20**, 253–306.
Hayes, B. (1990) Diphthongisation and co-indexing. *Phonology* **7**, 31–73.
Hirst, D. (1985) Linearisation and the single segment hypothesis. In Guéron, J., Obenauer, H. and Pollock, J-F. (eds) *Grammatical Representation.* Dordrecht: Foris.
Hooper, J. (1976) *An introduction to natural generative phonology.* New York: Academic Press.
Huffman, M.K. (1990) Implementation of Nasal: timing and articulatory landmarks. *UCLA Working Papers in Phonetics* **75**.
Hyman, L. (1975) *Phonology: theory and analysis.* New York: Holt, Reinhart and Winston.
Hyman, L. (1985) *A theory of phonological weight.* Dordrecht: Foris.
Itô, J. (1986) *Syllable theory in prosodic phonology.* PhD Thesis, University of Mass., Amherst. Distributed by Graduate Linguistics Student Association, Amherst.
Itô, J. (1989) A prosodic theory of epenthesis. *Natural Language and Linguistic Theory* **333**, 123–123.
Iverson, G.K. (1989) On the category supralaryngeal. *Phonology* **6**, 285–305.
Johnson, M. (1988) *Attribute-value logic and the theory of grammar.* Centre for the study of language and information, Lecture notes **16**.
Kasper, R. and Rounds, W. (1986) A logical semantics for feature structures. In *24th annual meeting of the association for computational linguistics: COLING 88*, 257–266.

Budapest.
Kay, M. (1979) Functional Grammar. *Proceedings of the Berkeley Linguistics Society* **5**.
Kaye, J., Lowenstamm, J. and Vergnaud, J-R. (1985) The internal structure of phonological segments: a theory of charm and government. *Phonology Yearbook* **2**, 305–328.
Kenstowicz, M. (1970) On the notation of vowel length in Lithuanian. *Papers in Linguistics* **1**, 73–113.
Kenstowicz, M. (1982) Gemination and spirantisation in Tigrinya. *Studies in the Linguistic Sciences* **12**.
Kenstowicz, M. (1986) Multiple linking in Javanese. *NELS* **16**, 230–248.
Kenstowicz, M., Bader, Y. and Benkeddache, R. (1982) The phonology of state in Kabyle Berber. ms. University of Illinois, Urbana-Champaign.
Kenstowicz, M. and Kidda, M. (1985) The obligatory contour principle in Tangale phonology. Paper presented at MIT, March 1985.
Kenstowicz, M. and Pyle, C. (1973) On the phonological integrity of geminate clusters. In Kenstowicz, M. and Kisseberth, C. (eds.) (1973), 27–43.
Kingston, J. (1990) Articulatory binding. In Kingston, J. and Beckman, M.E. (eds) *Between the grammar and physics of speech: Papers in laboratory phonology* **1**, 406–435. Cambridge: CUP
Kiparsky, P. (1973) Elsewhere in phonology. In Anderson, S. and Kiparsky, P. (eds) *A festschrift for Morris Halle*. New York: Holt Rinehart and Winston.
Kiparsky, P. (1982) Lexical morphology and phonology. In Yang (ed) *Linguistics in the morning calm*, 3–91. Seoul: Hanshin.
Kiparsky, P. (1985) Some consequences of lexical phonology. *Phonology Yearbook* **2**, 83–187.
Kiparsky, P. (1989) Phonological change. In Newmeyer, F. (ed) *Linguistics: the Cambridge survey. Volume 1, Linguistic theory: foundations*, 363–416. Cambridge: CUP.
Kisseberth, C. (1970) On the functional unity of phonological rules. *Linguistic Inquiry* **1**, 291–306.

Kitagawa, Y. (1988) Redoing reduplication. In Huck, G.J. and Ojeda, A.E. (eds) *Syntax and semantics. Volume 20, Discontinuous constituency*, 71–106. Orlando: Academic Press Inc.

Klein, E. and Calder, J. (1987) Unification in Phonology. ms. University of Edinburgh.

Klingenheben, A. (1928) Die Silbenauslautsgesetze des Hausa. *Zeitschrift für Eingeborenen Sprachen* 18, 272–297.

Koskenniemi, K. (1983) Two-level morphology: a general computational model for word-form recognition and production. University of Helsinki.

Koutsoudas, A., Sanders, G. and Noll, C. (1974) The application of phonological rules. *Language* 50, 1–28.

Lass, R. (1976) *English phonology and phonological theory: synchronic and diachronic studies*. Cambridge: CUP.

Lass, R. and Anderson, J. (1975) *Old English Phonology*. Cambridge: CUP.

Leben, W. (1973) *Suprasegmental phonology*. PhD Thesis, MIT. Published 1979, New York: Garland.

Leben, W.R. (1977) Length and syllable structure in Hausa. *Studies in African Linguistics* X, Supplement 7, 137–143.

Leben, W. (1980) A metrical analysis of length. *Linguistic Inquiry* 11, 497–509.

Lehiste, I. (1970) *Suprasegmentals*. Cambridge, Mass: MIT Press.

Leslau, W. (1941) *Documents Tigrinya (Éthiopien septentrional): grammaire et textes*. Collection linguistique publiée par la société de linguistique de Paris 48. Paris: C. Klincksieck.

Leslau, W. (1948) Le problèm de la gémination du verbe Tchaha (Gouragué). *Word*, 4, 42–47.

Leslau, W. (1950) *Ethiopic documents: Gurage*. Viking Fund Publications in Anthropology 14, New York:Viking Fund.

Lombardi, L. (1990) The nonlinear organisation of the affricate. *Natural Language and Linguistic Theory* 8, 375–427.

McCarthy, J.J. (1979) *Formal problems in Semitic phonology and morphology*. PhD Thesis, MIT.

McCarthy, J.J. (1981) A prosodic theory of nonconcatenative morphology. *Linguistic Inquiry* 12, 373–418.

McCarthy, J.J. (1983) Consonantal morphology in the Chaha verb. In Barlow, M., Flickinger, D. and Wescoat, M. (eds) *Proceedings of the West Coast conference in formal linguistics* **2**, 176–188.
McCarthy, J.J. (1986a) OCP effects: gemination and antigemination. *Linguistic Inquiry* **17**, 207–265.
McCarthy, J.J. (1986b) Lexical phonology and nonconcatenative morphology in the history of Chaha. *Revue Québécoise de Linguistique* **16**, 209–228.
McCarthy, J.J. (1989) Linear order in phonological representation. *Linguistic Inquiry* **20**, 71–101.
McCarthy, J.J. and Prince, A. (1989) Prosodic morphology and templatic morphology. In Eid and McCarthy, J.J. (eds) *Proceedings of the second annual synposium on Arabic Linguistics*. Amsterdam: John Benjamins.
Mascaró, J. (1984) Continuant spreading in Basque, Catalan and Spanish. In Aronoff M. and Oehrle, R. (eds), *Language sound structure: studies in phonology presented to Morris Halle by his teacher and students*, 287–298. Cambridge, Mass: MIT Press.
Mohanan, K.P. (1983) The structure of the melody. Unpublished ms. MIT.
Nespor, M. and Vogel, I. (1986) *Prosodic phonology.* Dordrecht: Foris.
Newman, S. (1944) *Yokuts Language of California.* Viking Fund Publications in Anthropology **2**. New York:Viking Fund.
Ohala, J.J. (1990) The generality of articulatory binding: some comments on Kingston's paper. In Kingston, J. and Beckman, M.E. (eds) *Between the grammar and physics of speech: Papers in laboratory phonology* **1**, 435–445. Cambridge: CUP
Odden, D. (1988) Anti-antigemination and the OCP. *Linguistic Inquiry* **19**, 451–475.
Palmer, F. (1957) Gemination in Tigrinya. *Studies in Linguistic Analysis* 139–149. Special Volume of the Philological Society.
Palmer, F. (1970) *Prosodic Analysis.* London: OUP.
Paradis, C. and Prunet, J-F. (1990) On explaining some OCP violations. *Linguistic Inquiry* **21**, 456–467.

Payne, D.L. (1981) *The phonology and morphology of Axininca Campa*. Dallas: Summer Institute of Linguistics.

Pierrehumbert, J. and Beckman, M. (1988) *Japanese tone structure*. Cambridge, Mass: MIT Press.

Pinkel, M. and Gregor, B. (eds) (1989) *Unification in linguistic analysis*.

Pollard, C. (1989) Sorts in Unification-based grammar and what they mean. In M. Pinkel and B. Gregor (eds) (1989).

Pollard, C. and Sag, I. (1987) *Information-based syntax and phonology*. Volume 1. Centre for the Study of Language and Information, Lecture notes 13.

Postal, P. (1968) *Aspects of phonological theory*. New York: Harper & Row.

Prince, A. (1984) Phonology with tiers. In Aronoff M. and Oehrle, R. (eds), *Language sound structure: studies in phonology presented to Morris Halle by his teacher and students*, Cambridge, Mass: MIT Press.

Prince, A. (1987) Planes and Copying. *Linguistic Inquiry*, 18, 491–511.

Pulleyblank, D. (1983) *Tone in lexical phonology*. PhD Thesis, MIT. Published as Pulleyblank (1986).

Pulleyblank, D. (1986) *Tone in lexical phonology*. Dordrecht: Reidel.

Pyle, C. (1970) West Greenlandic Eskimo and the representation of vowel length. *Papers in Linguistics* 1, 101–126.

Reape, M. (1991) *A formal theory of word order: a case study in Germanic*. PhD Thesis, University of Edinburgh.

Rialland, A. and Djamouri R. (1984) Harmonie vocalique, consonantique et structures de dépendance dans le mot en Mongol Khalkha. In *Bulletin de la Societé de Linguistique de Paris* 79.

Robins, R.H. (1957) Aspects of prosodic analysis. In Jones, W. and Laver, J. (eds) (1973) *Phonetics in linguistics: a book of readings*, 262–278. London: Longman.

Rounds, K. (1990) Set values for unification-based grammar formalisms and logic programming. ms, Stanford: CLSI.

Sag, I., Kaplan, R., Karttunen, L., Kay, M., Pollard, C., Shieber, S. and Zaenen, A. (1986) Unification and Grammatical Theory. *West Coast Conference in Formal Lin-*

guistics **5**, 238–254.

Sagey, E. (**1986**) *The representation of features and relations in non-linear phonology.* PhD Thesis, MIT.

Sagey, E. (**1988**) On the ill-formedness of crossing association lines. *Linguistic Inquiry* **19**, 109–118.

Sampson, G. (**1973**) Duration in Hebrew Consonants. *Linguistic Inquiry* **4**, 101–104.

Saussure, F. (**1915**) *Cours de linguistique générale.* Translated 1959 as *Course in general linguistics*, New York: The Philosophical Library.

Schein, B. (**1981**) Spirantisation in Tigrinya. In Borer, H. and Aoun, J. (eds.) *Theoretical issues in the grammars of Semitic languages*, MIT Working Papers in Linguistics **3**, 32–43.

Schein, B. and Steriade, D. (**1986**) On geminates. *Linguistic Inquiry* **17**, 691–744.

Scobbie, J.M. (**1988**) Minimal redundancy in the sequencing of autosegments. *Edinburgh University Department of Linguistics Work in Progress* **21**, 51–63.

Scobbie, J.M. (**1990**) Association as dominance in a constraint-based phonology. *Edinburgh Research Papers in Cognitive Science* **RP-43**. Edinburgh: Centre for Cognitive Science.

Selkirk, E. (**1982**) The syllable. In van der Hulst, H. and Smith, N. (eds) *The structure of phonological representations Part 2*, 337–383. Dordrecht: Foris.

Shaw, P. (**1987**) Non-conservation of melodic structure in reduplication. In Bosch, A., Need, B. and Schiller, E. (eds.) *CLS* **23**, 291–307.

Shibatani, M. (**1973**) The role of surface phonetic constraints in generative phonology. *Language* **49**, 117–127.

Singh, R. (**1987**) Well-formedness conditions and phonological theory. In Dressler *et al* (eds) *Phonologica 1984*, 273–285. Cambridge: CUP.

Shieber, S. (**1986**) *An introduction to unification-based approaches to grammar.* Centre for the Study of Language and Information, Lecture notes **4**. Stanford.

Shieber, S., Uszkoreit, H., Pereira, F.C.N., Robinson, J.J. and Tyson, M. (**1983**) The formalism and implementation of PATR-II. In Grosz and Stickel (eds) *Research on interactive acquisition and use of knowledge*, 39–79. Menlo Park, Cal:

SRI International.
Sommerstein, A.H. (1977) *Modern phonology*. London: Arnold.
Stanley, R. (1967) Redundancy rules in phonology. *Language* **43**, 393–436.
Steriade, D. (1982) *Greek prosodies and the nature of syllabification*. PhD Thesis, MIT.
Steriade, D. (1986) Yokuts and the vowel plane. *Linguistic Inquiry* **17**, 129–147.
Steriade, D. (1987a) Locality conditions and feature geometry. In McDonough, J. and Plunkett, B. (eds) *NELS* **17**, 595–617.
Steriade, D. (1987b) Redundant values. In Bosch, A., Need, B. and Schiller, E. (eds.), *CLS* **23**, 339–362.
Street (1963) *Khalkha Structure*. Indiana University Research and Studies in Uralic and Altaic Languages, Volume **24**. The Hague: Mouton.
Sturtevant, E. (1940) *The pronunciation of Latin and Greek*. Chicago: Ares Publishers.
Svantesson, J-0. (1985) Vowel harmony shift in Mongolian. *Lingua* **67**, 283–327.
Uhlenbeck, E. (1950) The structure of the Javanese morpheme. *Lingua* **2**, 239–270.
Venneman, T. (1972a) On the theory of syllabic phonology. *Linguistische berichte* **18**, 1–18.
Venneman, T. (1972b) Phonological concreteness in natural generative grammar. *Glossa* **6**, 105–116.
Venneman, T. (1974a) Phonological concreteness in natural generative grammar. In Shuy, R. and Bailey, C.J. (eds) *Toward tomorrow's linguistics*. Washington: Georgetown University Press.
Venneman, T. (1974b) Words and syllables in natural generative grammar. it CLS: natural phonology parasession, 346–374.
Waksler, R. (1990) *A formal account of glide/vowel alternations in prosodic theory*. PhD Thesis: Harvard University.
Wedekind, J. (ed) (1990) *A survey of linguistically motivated extensions to unification-based formalisms*. DYANA: Dynamic Interpretation of Natural Language, Deliverable R3.1.A. Centre for Cognitive Science, Edinburgh.

Wells, J.C. (1982) *Accents of English: Volume 1, an introduction.* Cambridge: CUP.

Wheeler, D. (1988) Consequences of some categorially motivated phonological assumptions. In Oehrle, D. Bach, E. and Wheeler, D. (eds) *Categorial grammars and natural language structures.* Dordrecht: Reidel.

Wheeler, D. and Touretzky D. (1989) A connectionist implementation of cognitive phonology. *CMU-CS* 89-144. Carnegie-Mellon University.

Yip, M. (1989) Feature geometry and cooccurrence restrictions. *Phonology* 6, 349–374.

Yip, M. (1988) The obligatory contour principle and phonological rules: a loss of identity. *Linguistic Inquiry* 19, 65–100.

Younes, M. (1983) The representation of geminate consonants. ms: University of Texas, Austin.

Zec, D. (1988) *Sonority constraints on prosodic structure.* PhD Thesis: Stanford University.

Index

⊥ 26, 175
→ 16, 31
⊓ 28, 29
⊔ 29
⊤ 26, 33
∨ 33
≺ 48, 121
≺* 48, 121
α-variables 101, 102
⪰ 28, 29

Absolute Slicing Hypothesis 21
Abstract representations 201
Abstractness controversy 14, 20
Across the board effects 227
Adjacency 113, 121, 123, 125, 126, 131, 136, 220
Adjacency Identity Constraint 127
Affricates 49, 50
Alignment 91, 225
Alterability 182–184
Alternations
    glide-vowel 41, 184
    with rewrite rules 7
Ambisyllabicity 106
Anchoring 55–65, 107
    definition 57, 65
Anderson, J. 14, 15
Apparent movement of information 75
Appendix 46, 48
Arabic 98

morphology 103, 197ff
Archangeli, D. 54, 81, 95, 96, 130, 133, 217
Arcs 27, 53, 108
Articulatory Phonology 19, 20
Articulatory scores 17–20, 37
Aspiration 50
Assimilation 27, 73–75, 101ff, 105, 144
    vs. harmony 223
    partial 106
Assocation (see also Multiple association)
    Association Convention 55, 87, 95
    asymmetric 64ff
    definition 65
    deletion 96, 129, 134, 201
    different types 60ff, 220
    dominance 5, 63–66, 69
    harmonic 130
    Hayes 60–63
    index equation 90
    intransitive 69, 71
    lines 43, 44, 55–58, 62, 64ff, 67, 79, 129
        crossing 16ff, 66ff, 85–89, 93ff, 129, 197
        diacritic use 159
        in rules 152
        many-one and one-many 34, 49
        multiple vs. single or lo-

cal vs. nonlocal 196, 218–220, 227
non-harmonic 130
and crossing lines 127-134
phonetic interpretation 77, 222
association relation 5, 88
definitions 57ff, 90
spreading vs. sharing 196ff, 220ff
subsumption 152, 153
transitive 63
Atomic sorts 25, 31
Atomic structures 26, 38
Attribute 25
Attribute Value Phonology 5, 24, 39–78, 89–93, 104–110, 163, 173, 190, 193
Attribute-value structures 23–35, 39ff, 43, 44, 67, 123, 144
as graphs 27
definition 25
in long distance dependencies 221
sequence 51, 42, 43, 48ff, 69
Attribute path 26, 27, 79, 89–91
Autosegmental association 5, 55–57, 66
Autosegmental licensing 185
Autosegmental Phonology 4, 5, 11–13, 20–22, 43, 51, 55, 72, 93–98, 99–104, 109, 110, 139, 170, 192
and phonetics 20–23
basic configurations 66ff, 218
differences with AVP 5, 34, 43, 44, 49–55, 65, 67, 68, 72, 75, 84, 85, 88, 89, 93, 104, 124–129, 136, 172, 174, 180, 188–193, 196
Autosegmental tiers 22, 55ff, 202
Axininca Campa 148

Bead curtain analogy 53, 54, 68
Beckman, M. 196, 221
Berber 159
Biliteral Arabic roots 210
Binary features 30, 31
Bird, S. 59, 60, 86, 93
Blocking 119, 128, 129, 130, 133, 134, 136, 223
Bottom — see ⊥
Bracket erasure 202
Broe, M. 15, 37
Browman, C. 19, 20, 77

Calabrese, A. 35, 36
Chaha 203ff
Chart 111
Clements, G. 39, 50, 57, 102
Cluster simplification 114, 117, 120, 168
Coda Filter 118, 119, 121, 137, 161, 163, 185
definition 161
Coda place 118
Coda weakening 141, 148, 150, 160, 163, 176, 184–190
and inalterability 188
Goldsmith's 185
hierarchy 189, 190
in AVP 188
Coeur d'Alène 97, 98, 223
Cole, J. 97
Coleman, J. 98
Computational phonology 36

Index

Concreteness Problem 19–23
Conflation 132, 207
Conjunctivity Condition 164, 192, 193
 definition 164
Consonant clusters 46, 122
Conspiracies of rules 9, 135, 141, 165, 168, 169, 175, 219, 220
Constituent structure 44, 106
Constraint based approach 143
Constraint interaction 15, 16, 29, 32, 35, 72, 105, 122, 143, 151, 162, 165, 169, 170, 179, 204, 223
Constraint satisfaction 74, 75, 105, 106, 161, 168, 180, 191
Constraints 16, 35, 118, 139, 141, 150, 165, 166, 177
 blocking 161
 conditional 16, 31–33, 45, 73, 106, 172ff, 191
 conflict 8, 9, 24, 26, 36, 170
 context-sensitive 73
 default 82, 122, 137, 166, 172, 180
 deletion of 5, 24
 disjunctive 31, 33, 136, 172, 174, 180
 domain of application 71
 FCR 12, 32, 33
 feature filling 124
 filters 9, 36, 161, 167, 219
 inalterability 172
 lexical entry 15, 16, 24, 35, 72, 74, 105
 logical equivalence 16, 32, 33, 72, 175, 176
 negative 31–33, 37, 70, 72, 124
 partial descriptions 15, 16, 30, 31, 35, 38
 phonotactic 141, 169
 pool of 13, 16, 24, 32, 35, 78
 repair strategies 9, 36, 82, 88, 130, 219
 strong satisfaction 161
 syllabification 453–48, 117, 184ff
 templates 12, 30–32, 169
  conditional 36
Contour segments 49, 50, 67
Contrastiveness in singletons and geminates 210
Convexity 5, 104, 106, 136
 phonetic 93, 219
 syllables 106
 phonological 220
Copying 222
Crossing association lines 66, 68, 83–110, 197

DAG 27
Declarative phonology, precursors 13
Declarative phonology 4, 7–10, 73, 173
Declarative syntax 10
Declarativeness 7–16, 24, 29, 75, 106, 110, 112, 113
 in generative phonology 3, 11
 in Natural Generative Phonology 14
 phonotactics 8
Defaults 82, 132ff, 137, 170, 172, 173, 177, 181, 226
Defaults vs. constraints 175
Deficiencies of this account 196

Degemination 117, 120, 123ff, 137
Deletion 5, 10, 14, 24, 88, 124, 129, 136
Derived environment 207, 208
Derived structure 106
Description language 31, 37
Diagrams 27, 34, 38
Differences between AVP and AP 5, 34, 43, 44, 49–55, 65, 67, 68, 72, 75, 84, 85, 88, 89, 93, 104, 124–129, 136, 172, 174, 180, 188–193, 196
Diphthongisation 60, 61, 81
Directed acyclic graph 27
Directional assimilation 75
Disjunction 31, 33
Dissimilation 125, 126
Distinctness 123
Domain of rule application 71, 76, 97, 102
Dominance 44, 63-66, 69, 144, 188
    definition 65
    Hayes 61
    phonetic interpretation 77
    relation 5, 27

Edge-effects 50
Elsewhere Condition 208
English 22, 81, 100, 136, 227
Epenthesis 113–120, 122, 126, 128–132, 136, 137, 160, 168
    of empty slots 122ff, 132ff, 226
    prosodic causes 116ff
    same-plane stipulation 131
Erosion of support for procedural phonology 11, 13
Events 59

Extension 122
External sandhi 91, 117
Extrasyllabicity 117
Extrinsic rule ordering 4, 7, 10, 11, 13, 14, 214
Extrinsic rule ordering paradox 207, 216

FCR (feature co-occurrence restrictions) 12, 32, 33, 70–72, 95, 175, 181
Feature changing rules 10, 14, 36, 207
Feature checking 72
Feature filling rules 36, 72, 75–77, 165, 208
Features
    geometry 11, 39, 50, 54, 56, 70–72, 217
    class node 41
    within AVP 25, 40, 41, 44
  in AVP
    as paths 52, 54, 89
    as underspecified segments 52
  percolation 11, 49
Filters 9, 36, 161, 163, 171, 185
Firthian Prosodic Analysis 13, 15, 192
Fission 130
Floating features 56, 111
Fossilised phonology 210, 216
Free word order 91
Function words 47

Gaelic 227
Gashowu 217
Gazdar, G. 14
Geminates 99, 105, 135, 139, 140, 146, 170, 173, 180, 184, 187, 196, 197, 202

Index

alterability 182ff
contrastiveness 162
discontinuous 104, 114–116, 131–135, 197–200, 204, 214, 215, 224
discontinuous vs. fake 201, 202, 214
integrity 201
distribution 141
fake 100, 105, 113, 114, 115, 116, 118, 121, 126, 127, 128, 129, 147, 200, 224
inalterability 5, 85, 109, 140-184
integrity 5, 85, 109, 113, 114-136
licensing 121
long distance 104, 214, 224
no special principles in AVP 139
partial 106, 113, 122, 148, 161
tri-geminates 124
true 100, 104, 105, 113, 114, 115, 116, 121, 122, 126, 128, 129, 130, 132, 136, 153, 161, 201, 214
underlying 106
vowels in AVP 124
Generative paradigm 7
Generative phonology 10, 16, 140
Gestures
convex 93, 219
overlap 19, 37, 77
root matrices 77
score 19, 20, 77, 193
Glide-vowel alternations 41, 149, 150, 184

Goldsmith, J. 11, 12, 20–22, 37, 43, 44, 51, 55, 57, 58, 66, 85, 87, 96, 111, 117, 121, 129, 132, 134, 137, 142–144, 164, 165, 168, 185, 189, 192, 219
Goldstein, L. 19, 20, 77
Graph diagrams 27, 52
Guerssel, M. 127

Hammond, M. 66, 81, 86
Ordering Principle 86
Harmony 97, 102ff, 105, 109, 165, 196, 208ff, 223
harmonic domain 102, 218, 223
harmonic simplicity 102, 218
incorporation 223
multiple association 218
opacity 218
vs. assimilation 223
Hausa 148, 187
Hayes, B. 38, 49, 60–63, 79, 109, 119, 149, 150, 151, 213, 219
Heavy syllables 44–49
Hiatus vs. length 100
Hooper, J. 14, 191
HPSG 10, 35, 106
Huffman, M. 20

Identical structures 33, 51, 68, 124
Ill-formed structures 68, 137, 173, 227
Immediate precedence 48, 225
Inalterability 5, 85, 109, 137, 139, 140–188, 195, 202
in AP (summary) 154
alterability 182-184

and coda weakening 188–190
AVP analyses 177ff
blocking vs. AVP 180, 181
blocking 140–143, 146, 151–166, 170, 173, 185, 190
characteristics 151
constraint-based approach 166–184, 187, 188
definition 140, 143
expectations 143, 148, 149, 150, 159, 160, 179
in AVP 177–183
in plane conflation 201
licensing 142, 190
nonlocal 198–206, 213
phonotactic 148
reinterpretation 172
unified account 149, 150
Inconsistent feature structures 32, 49, 50, 67, 90, 129, 161
Index
  for structure sharing 33, 38, 45, 51, 63, 76
  of sequence 42, 45, 48, 51, 52, 63, 68, 76, 79, 90, 123, 225
  morphosyntactic 91
  variable over 111
  weak order 79
Inheritance between sorts 44
Integrity 5, 85, 109, 114–135, 146, 161, 195, 201, 202, 220
  crossing lines approach 127–135
  default rules 132ff
  formal account 121ff
  formal account in AP 129ff
  formal vs. prosodic 119

Interaction question 185
Intermediate levels of representation 4, 133, 201, 202, 215
Intonation 196, 221
Intrusive stops 22
Itô, J. 12, 38, 61, 118, 119, 121, 126, 128, 137, 142, 160, 161, 163, 169

Japanese 160, 221, 222
Javanese 211–216, 227
Join 26

Kasper, R. 38
Kenstowicz, M. 101, 211, 214, 215, 219
Khalkha 96, 97, 134, 223
Kingston, J. 50
Kiparsky, P. 94, 193
Kisseberth, C. 9, 15
Kitagawa, Y. 112
Klein, E. 59, 86, 93
Klingenheben's Law 148

Laboratory Phonology 221
Labouring the point 220
Ladd, D.R. 222
Language change 37, 78
Latin 70, 126, 144, 150, 152, 161, 162, 166, 181, 182
Leben, W. 55
Leslau, W. 205, 209, 226
Levels, intermediate 4, 202, 215
Lexical entry 15, 16, 24, 35, 72, 74, 105
Lexical Phonology 208, 210
Lexical stress 47
Lexicalised generalisations 209
Licensing (also see anchoring) 48, 117, 121, 139–144
  domain 70

licensing relation 187
autosegmental 57, 65, 185, 188
  definition 186
  by onset 179, 181, 184, 187
    definition 187
  general and specific cases 187
  hypothetical approach 188
  prosodic 56, 65, 119, 185, 188
    definition 187
  syllabic 107, 137
Light syllables 44
Linear phonology 99, 127, 128, 192
Linear/non-linear balance 70
Linking Constraint 119, 121, 141, 151, 153, 155, 164, 165, 198, 213
  applied to filters 185
  definition 152
  false prediction 198-200
  vs. the UAC 156-158
Lithuanian 101, 115, 144, 151, 183
Local vs. long distance dependencies 5, 84, 87, 105, 109, 114, 126, 129-131, 192-196, 199, 219, 220
Local, J. 98, 227
Locality 68, 70, 88, 92-97, 125
  Sharing Constraint 91-93
Logical connectives 31, 32
Logical equivalence of constraints 16
Lombardi, L. 50, 80
Long distance dependencies 98, 102, 104, 109, 113, 114, 125, 126, 221
  using type identity 224

Long vowels as segments in AVP 124
Long vs. short segments 162
Luganda 183

Many-one associations 34, 49
Matching constraints to input 70-77, 161, 162, 180
Matching of rules to input 70, 141, 151, 153, 155, 163, 164, 173
Matrix diagrams 25, 27, 30, 31, 38, 52, 54
  Hayes 38
McCarthy, J. 98, 103, 147, 202, 205ff, 224, 227
Meet 26, 28
Melody attribute 44
Melody sort 30
Menomini 156-158
Metathesis 111
Metrical weight 186
Mitosis 114-116, 127, 129-136, 201, 202, 214
  as repair 130
  caused by defult rule 134
  only applicable nonlocally 130
  restrictions on 130
Model theoretic approach 17
Monostratal syntactic theories 10
Monostratal 24, 105, 191
Monosyllabic words 47
Monotonicity 4, 24, 127, 129, 165
Moras 44
Morpheme Structure Rules 8ff
Morphotactics 9
Multiplanar input to phonological rules 198-217, 227

Multiplanar phonology 5, 97, 98, 103, 130, 197, 199ff
Multiple association 5, 34, 49, 66ff, 84, 92, 94–97, 101, 102, 106, 129, 192, 196
  harmonic 130, 219
  non-harmonic 130
  nonlocal 222
  problems when used in harmony 218
  redundancy 119

Nasalisation 78
Natural Generative Phonology 13, 14, 191
Navajo 14
Negative constraints 31, 32, 37
No Crossing Constraint (NCC) 5, 12, 55, 66, 68, 84ff, 93, 95, 97, 127–134
  as filter 219
  as repair strategy 219
Node Activation Convention 54
Non-rhoticity 136
Non-transformational syntax 14
Nonconcatenative morphology 98, 103ff, 130, 196ff, 224ff
  skeletal weak ordering 225
Nonlinear phonology 192
Nonlocal association 68, 222
Nonlocal inalterability 199–208, 213
  Chaha 203ff
Nonlocal integrity 201
Nonlocal side effect 198–208, 213, 214, 217
  Javanese 210ff
Nonphonological alternations 37, 60

Notation 16, 70, 124, 154, 159, 174, 186, 191, 217
  matrices 38, 40
Notational conventions 26, 38, 42–45, 51–54, 76, 79, 82, 108, 125

Obligatory Contour Principle (OCP) 12, 100, 123ff, 192, 197, 209
  and set theory 123
  blocking 147
  effects in Javanese roots 211
  Index OCP 123
  nonlocal 125
  Sharing Principle 125
  syllable structure 124
Ohala, J. 50
One-many associations 49
Onset/coda asymmetry 188
Opacity 95–97, 103, 218
Ordering Principle 86
Overlap 5, 19, 58ff, 71, 86

Paddle-wheel analogy 56
Palestinian Arabic epenthesis 114, 115, 128
Palmer, F. 192
Partial description 15, 16, 21, 24, 31, 35, 37, 52, 105
Partial specification 42
Partition 26, 41
Path 26, 27, 51ff, 89
  indexed 52ff
Percolation 11, 49
  Hayes 61
Phonetics
  assimilation 19, 78
  detail 16–23
  gestures 223
  implementation 17, 50, 56, 87, 93, 193

interpolation 104, 196, 221
sequence 18, 19, 50
segments 21
Phonetics-phonology interface 16–23, 54, 60, 77, 78, 93, 193, 219, 223
in AP 222
Phonological
rules 27, 45, 73, 75, 91, 96, 185
detail 17, 19–23
frameworks 4
length 99ff, 109
sequence 17–19, 42, 43, 48ff, 88
segments 21, 37, 52
of vowels 42
multiple tiers 49, 88, 89
syllable 168
word 47
Phonology attribute 17
Phonotactics 7, 12, 15, 118, 141, 143, 167, 168
and declarativeness 8
using MSRs 8
vs. morphotactics 9
Phrase structure grammars 14
Pierrehumbert, J. 196, 221
Plane conflation 130, 132, 201ff, 207
inalterability 201
mitosis 132, 202
Planes 98, 103, 197
definition 215
Pollard, C. 7, 10, 23, 25, 34, 48, 106
Pool of constraints 13, 16, 24, 32, 35, 105, 136, 169, 172, 193, 196
Postal, P. 9
Precedence 48, 108, 121, 202

Predictions about...
discontinuous inalterability 198
geminates 109ff
inalterability and long distance dependencies 193
integrity 122, 127, 136
local vs. long distance phenomena 195
locality 96
phonological sequence 50
phonological structure 85
Primitive phonological unit 43
Prince, A. 137, 191
Procedural phonology 7ff, 166
Prosodic Analysis 15
Prosodic Licensing 119, 169, 185, 188
definition 187
Prosodic morphology 226
Prosodic structure 106
Pulleyblank, D. 54, 81, 95, 96, 130, 133, 217

Québec French, 81

/r/-sandhi 136
Railway track analogy 55, 56
Re-entrancy 27, 33, 34, 50, 53, 78, 84, 124, 144, 196
Reape, M. 227
Recursiveness of structure 25
Redundancy 72, 119
Repair strategies 9, 36, 96, 97, 129, 130, 227
Resonance 227
Rewrite rules 16, 141, 150, 167, 168, 185
Root matrix 42–44, 48, 51, 54, 70, 121
and the segment 43, 124
unique status 43

Rounds, W. 38
Rules
  application 11, 70–72, 74, 105, 140, 151
  in multiplanar representations 200
  blocking 219
  context sensitive 101
  extrinsic ordering 7, 10, 11, 13, 14, 127
  feature changing 10, 14, 36
  feature filling 36, 106, 122
  generalisations over output 141
  interaction 8, 9, 15, 36, 169, 170
  multiplanar 198
  ordering 137, 201, 208
  rewrite 7
  telescoping 209
  transformations 14
  vs. representations 15, 16, 31, 35
Rule-to-rule hypothesis 34

Sag, I. 7, 10, 23, 34, 48, 106
Sagey, E. 22, 50, 57–59, 63, 66–69, 86
Salentino 35
Sanskrit 149
Satisfaction of structural description 199
Schein, B. 70, 110, 132–134, 150, 154–159, 213, 219
Scobbie, J. 52, 86
Segment 21, 43, 52, 124
Semitic 211, 224
  roots 125
Sequence
  in AVP 5, 42, 43, 48ff
  in morphology and syntax 91
  in phonetics and phonology 17–19
  index — see Index of sequence
Shared structure 51, 70, 144
  vs. spreading 196ff, 220ff
Sharing Constraint 5, 6, 68, 84, 91–93, 104, 113, 121ff, 193, 195, 218, 220
  definition 93
Sharing Principle 125
Side-effects 118, 198–203, 208, 210–218, 227
  Javanese 211–217
Sign-based grammar 17, 34, 91
Simultaneity 5, 57, 86
Singh, R. 36
Skeleton 5, 48–56, 89, 104, 108, 122, 153, 202, 215
  weak ordering 224
Sommerstein, A. 9, 167, 168
Sorts 23, 25, 27, 40
  assignment 40, 45, 46
  preventing impossible associations 41
  conjunction 26
  disjunction 26
  heavy-σ 44
  inheritance 44
  lattice 25, 26, 41, 47
  melody 30
  partial ordering 26, 41
  partition 26, 41
  root 42
  syllabic 45
    subsorts 48
    word-edge effects 46
  variable 26
SPE 8, 43, 51, 69, 101, 143, 150, 151, 167, 191
Spirantisation 146, 147, 150,

Index

152, 159, 166, 171, 172, 197, 198
Spreading 102, 165, 196, 220, 226
  harmony 223ff
  vs. sharing 196ff, 220–224
Steriade, D. 70, 110, 126, 132–134, 150, 154–159, 213, 219
Straight lines in diagrams 38
Stray erasure 117
Strong satisfaction 141, 142, 151–153, 158, 161–165, 169, 198, 206, 213
  definition 141
  in phonotactics 160
Structural description 74, 140, 141, 151–153, 158, 163, 168, 199, 211
Structure building rules 12, 36, 72
Structure changing rules 14, 36, 75
Structure Preservation 163, 193
Structure sharing 22, 27, 34, 38, 43, 45, 49, 50, 73, 77, 82, 85, 104, 106, 121, 123, 128, 146, 184, 187, 192, 195
  discontinuous or nonlocal 92, 113, 125, 136, 215
  in feature geometry 45
  in syllabification 45
Submodules of a phonological theory 8
Subsumption 25–29, 113, 127, 141
  lattice 26, 29
  of associations 152, 153
Surface representation 7, 106, 137, 165, 166, 172

Syllabic licensing 48
Syllabification 30, 79, 107, 142, 160, 168
Syllable in AVP 43–48, 106
Syntax 91, 106

Tangale 120, 137
Templates 12, 13, 30–32, 36, 169
Temporal overlap 19
Three dimensional phonology 112
Tiberian Hebrew 146–148, 181, 197, 198, 200, 201, 214
Tiers 49, 51–55, 58, 69, 88
  association 55
  class tiers 54, 56, 89
  conflation 130, 201
  multiple tiers 97
  structural dependency 89
  subtiers 43
  subtier ordering 48, 49, 51, 63, 67, 68, 86, 88, 126
Tigrinya 131, 146, 152, 163, 166, 171, 172, 177–182, 188, 197, 198, 200, 201, 207, 214, 226
Token identity 33, 34, 38, 100, 125, 219, 223
Tone 104, 105, 109, 196, 221
Top — see T
Transparency 98
Tree structures 27
True Generalisation Condition 14, 172, 191
Turkish 120, 137
Type identity 34, 100, 125, 136, 196, 219, 222, 223
Type spreading 223
Typed feature structures 25

UAC (Uniform Applicability Condition) 141, 154–159, 163–165, 199, 213
  context 163, 165
  definition 155
  focus 163
  vs. Linking Constraint 156—159
Uhlenbeck, E. 211
Underlying representation 72, 102, 137, 173, 198, 201
Underspecification 11, 34, 42, 43, 52, 73–75, 119, 132, 133, 171, 178, 180
  using general sorts 26, 33, 41
Unification 28ff, 75, 105
  declarative interpretation 28, 29
  of conditionals 32
  of incompatible values 26
  of sets 91
  of co-indexed paths 42
Unification-based grammar 4, 10, 13, 24, 127
Uniform Applicability Condition — see UAC
Unspecified structures 25
Unspecified value 25, 41

Valid case of crossing lines 68
Value of an attribute 25
Variables 26
Vertical vs. horizontal bias 69, 78
Vertices 27, 108
Vowel harmony 134ff
  transparency 134

Waksler, R. 194

Weak ordering of sequence indices 42, 48, 79
Weak satisfaction 141, 151–153
  definition 141
Well-formedness condition 55, 87
West Greenlandic 183
Word-edge syllable types 46

Yawelmani 9, 217
Yokuts 211, 217, 218
Yoruba 95
Younes, M. 202

For Product Safety Concerns and Information please contact our EU representative GPSR@taylorandfrancis.com
Taylor & Francis Verlag GmbH, Kaufingerstraße 24, 80331 München, Germany

www.ingramcontent.com/pod-product-compliance
Lightning Source LLC
Chambersburg PA
CBHW071348290426
44108CB00014B/1475